Youth and Sport for Development

Holly Collison

Youth and Sport for Development

The Seduction of Football in Liberia

palgrave
macmillan

Holly Collison
School of Sport, Exercise and Health Sciences
Loughborough University
Leicestershire, United Kingdom

ISBN 978-1-137-52468-3   ISBN 978-1-137-52470-6   (eBook)
DOI 10.1057/978-1-137-52470-6

Library of Congress Control Number: 2016944990

Cover illustration: © Westend61 GmbH / Alamy Stock Photo

Printed on acid-free paper

This Palgrave Macmillan imprint is published by Springer Nature
The registered company is Macmillan Publishers Ltd. London

Map of Matadi

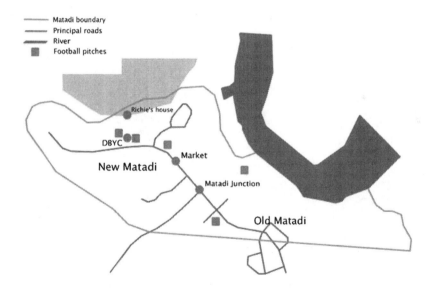

Source: The map was created by Dr Holly Collison and Dr Will Rollason.

Preface

This book considers the concept of Sport for Development and Peace (SDP) in post-conflict Liberia. The topic of reconciliation, rehabilitation and peace-building has become a central theme for global organisations tasked with intervening in broken and divided societies after violent conflicts. The question for some time has been this: What can reunite populations divided by war and violence whilst attempting to build a peaceful civil society? Youth in particular have been consistently identified by development agencies as being either potentially volatile or, in contrast, vulnerable during and after conflict (World Youth Report 2005). SDP has become fashionable within development agendas, in what Kidd (2008) termed as a 'new social movement', yet it remains an aspirational image, rather than a tested method of reintegration and youth development in post-conflict environments. My intention in this book is to question the assumptions of SDP rhetoric and programmes, and to trace the effects of football—the favoured vehicle of SDP—for youth in post-conflict Liberia.

This is important as it will lead to a better understanding of the developmental impact and social effect of sport—specifically football—on a post-conflict youth population. I will argue that this strategy can be highly counterproductive for the purpose of youth development and the rebuilding of a post-war society in Liberia because *football constitutes and reinforces the marginal status of* youth. The SDP genre may—in its stated aim—contribute to building 'civil society', and integrating youth into it, but it also confirms their youth status in an ever-competitive and exclusionary age-based hierarchy. Despite the Liberia focus many of the issues and themes under consideration are primary topics researched by those examining the SDP sector in multiple global contexts. Therefore the intention of this work is to highlight the challenges, assumptions, methodological approach and anthropological perspectives that have facilitated such commentary as they can be applied to other cultural systems.

For clarity it is important to define and comment on a number of primary themes that are deconstructed and conceptualised within this work. SDP has evolved into what Kidd (2008) describes as a 'movement', a development strategy now endorsed and implemented by individuals, civil society, non-governmental organisations (NGOs), national governments, international organisations, faith-based groups and philanthropic agencies. Fieldwork conducted in Liberia over a 4-year period highlights the multiple and diverse SDP stakeholders and their various motivations and objectives. Crucial to this commentary is a commitment to unpacking and conceptualising the ambiguous terminology, complex social effects and the lived experience of SDP. Whilst many of my academic peers have significantly contributed to greater understandings of SDP in different global contexts, this book endeavours to deepen our knowledge by looking within and beyond the intervention. Central to this is the reflective and interpretative process that draws upon participant voices and my own lived experience within SDP to gain symbolic understandings of culture, identity and the formal and informal social structures in which participants and interventions operate.

This book considers three primary themes: post-conflict development, youth and community. These are considered through an ethnography and narratives of young football players in Liberia. It is the position of this work in participatory fieldwork and the deconstruction and conceptualisation of the complex cultural systems surrounding post-conflict development and sport that can unpack important effects and impacts of SDP. The anthropological perspectives gained are framed within the notion of seduction.

Seduction

Paramount to any sense of moral obligation within the development discourse is the requirement to engage and access local populations, sustain resourceful partnerships and produce evidence of worth and success. This is inherently a seductive process. Local populations need to be attracted to the programmes being offered and charmed into cooperating, sponsors need to be lured into financing projects and be confident they will be rewarded with the recognition via emotive success stories and images. Caught in this cycle of seduction are specific terms that construct the language of development practices: youth, community and, increasingly, football. I will propose that such concepts are also individually inherently seductive. Throughout this book I aim to initially highlight the problems associated with such terms in post-conflict Liberia, specifically in relation to development discourse; latter chapters will demonstrate the role and practice of football in relation to Liberian communities, youth and institutions. Seduction frames this book and is the key theoretical concept drawn upon throughout the analysis. Despite the attention given to other relevant concepts, it is seduction that pulls the analysis together and directs the conclusion.

In Liberia many have looked to *seduce* youth to engage them, potentially exploiting youths for their strength in number. The concept of seduction can be applied to a multitude of settings and scenarios: 'Seduction is central to political life' (Minogue 2006, p. 17). Definitions of the notion vary; Baudrillard suggested that 'seduction is merely an immoral, frivolous, superficial, and superfluous process; one within the realm of signs and appearances; one that is devoted to pleasure and to the usufruct of useless bodies' (1988, p. 162); he adds that 'seduction is that which extracts meaning from discourse and detracts it from the truth' (1988, p. 149). Synonyms include attraction, lure, draw, charm, corruptive, dishonour or take away someone's innocence. By contrast, in the words of Robben, 'Persuasion seems to be the counterpole of seduction' (1995, p. 180). Seduction thus marks the opposite of rational discursive activity designed to cause compliances: 'To seduce is to weaken' (Novellino 2003, p. 287).

Seduction takes various forms and has multiple functions. A certain amount of cooperation by the local population is needed for any aid agency or development organisation to conduct projects in unfamiliar communities and environments. In some cases seduction has been identified by ethnographers as valuable tools for access and for gaining results. Novellino (2003) conducted ethnographic research within an indigenous community in the Philippines. This particular community had dealings with conservation development organisations. Novellino observed the interaction and negotiations between community members and project workers. He was primarily interested with identifying the types of knowledge that were used to *seduce* the other into confessing details of local or project information and which were used to protect against discursive forms of deception (in Bicker et al. 2003, pp. 273–274). Novellino observed that 'seduction was the desired ingredient which steered the required outcome' for NGOs (ibid, p. 288) and concluded that 'perhaps the most effective form of people's counter-strategy to "seduction" is to refuse to reply or take part in the conversation, but ultimately remaining silent' (ibid, p. 291).

This may be why football, in the form of SDP, is such an important element of development practice in Liberia and elsewhere. Through its seductive properties, it fundamentally guarantees access to youth. Youth football teams in Liberia never asked why they had been invited—by adults—to tournaments: they merely enjoyed the acknowledgement given to them and looked forward to the game. Minogue claimed that the two essentials of seduction are 'drama' (in this case, the game) and 'flattery' (in this case, acknowledgement from adults and 'Big Men') (2006, p. 21). Football seduces—even in the absence of obvious outcomes or purpose—and even if the purpose is made clear by adults the will to play is stronger than the need or reason to ask why. Arguably then, football is a way of getting people to do things without their rational engagement. As Althusser (2008) claimed, people practise ideology without being consciously aware of it. The initial 'flattery' for access, 'distraction' through drama, competition and performance recruit youths for the projects of others, who may well not share their interests.

Holly Collison
School of Sport, Exercise and Health Sciences
Loughborough University
Leicestershire, UK

Acknowledgements

The last 4 years have been truly humbling and it is difficult to put into words the depth of gratitude I have towards so many amazing individuals. This project began because of the faith one person had in me, Dr Gary Armstrong. Thank you does not quite say it, but for your encouragements, support, belief and friendship, I am so grateful. Thank you for the opportunity and all the time you have invested in me.

This project would be meaningless without all of the truly incredible people I spent time with in Liberia. A very scared and inexperienced girl found a home, family and friends through the openness and hospitality of many Liberians. My time with all of you has given me confidence, direction and has seen me grow into a much different and, hopefully, better person. There are so many of you to mention, but in particular, I would like to thank all the Don Bosco staff and the Fathers in the Youth Centre for allowing me into their place of work. To the Zatti football team, who quickly became my energetic, supportive and loyal extended family; to all the players thank you. Thank you to Dorbor who has always given words of encouragement and was one of the first to accept me in Matadi; your continued friendship over the years is truly special. Coach Tamba and Coach Cooper, you two are a credit to Liberian football and because of you I was always welcomed at the LFA and given many opportunities.

To Richie, my Liberian brother, this work is dedicated to you—for teaching me the Liberian way, keeping me safe and being my friend. You

xii   **Acknowledgements**

are an incredible example of all that is good and should be recognised in Liberia. Thank you.

To my parents, thank you for trusting and supporting my decision to research in Liberia. For the months of worry and stress I apologise! For all your words of encouragement and patience I thank, love and appreciate you. This message can also be extended to the rest of my family who are very special to me and just as appreciated. I also need to take this opportunity to thank a group of very special ladies who have seen me go through the roller coaster of emotions throughout this process: Antonia, Natalie, Gemma, Claire, Katie, Catherine and Lisa, sorry and thank you.

To Dr Alison Maitland, our conversations throughout this journey have provided so much clarity; thank you for your friendship. To Dr Eric Hirsh, your feedback and support during difficult times have been invaluable and motivating throughout.

To Dr William Rollason, for supporting me in completing this work as I envisioned, thank you. My development as an anthropologist is credited to you, your time, patience, foresight, perception and ability to encourage and challenge me. For having confidence and belief in me when I questioned myself, thank you. I cannot express how grateful I am for your friendship, commitment to this project and making this process one I look back upon with happy memories and a smile.

Contents

1   Sport, Anthropology and Research Methodology   1

2   Land of the Free? The Origin of Conflict and Peace   25

3   Richie   45

4   In Pursuit of the Winners: SDP and Football Interventions   55

5   Matadi: Structure and Power in a Post-Conflict Urban Community   95

6   Becoming Somebody: Escaping from Youthhood   127

7   Creating a New Community   167

8   The Seduction of Football   199

Epilogue   227

Bibliography   237

Index   239

1

Sport, Anthropology and Research Methodology

Sport and Anthropology: Late to the Game

Play, games and sport are culturally constructed behaviours. The performance of such activities highlights traditions, customs and ways of acting and provides insights into the cultures of a group, how they relate, share boundaries and rules, deviate, punish and indeed draw attention to a whole host of social interactions. The point of studying sport and play here is not only to observe culturally constructed behaviours but to distinguish participants and the subcultural groups that they form. Anthropology has long considered the study of religion, kinship, economics and political and social institutions but, the consideration of sport and games remained peripheral until recently. As Sands argues, 'Primitive play and games were rarely considered by anthropologists, it is only in the last 50 years that the study of sport and culture has emerged and this has been accomplished in academic fields other than anthropology' (2002, p. 1).

One of the first social scientists to make the connection between the significance of games and anthropology was Sir Edward Burnett Tylor, who in 1879 published an article titled 'The History of Games'. Not only was he able to justify the importance of games and their significance to

© The Editor(s) (if applicable) and The Author(s) 2016
H. Collison, *Youth and Sport for Development*,
DOI 10.1057/978-1-137-52470-6_1

linguistics, culture, evolution and civilisations but he also pointed out the weakness of ethnographies which did not pursue further investigation into unique styles of play. He used the example of Cook's 'Third Voyage':

> It is mentioned that the Sandwich Islanders played a game like draughts with black and white pebbles on a board of fourteen by seventeen squares. Had the explorer spent an hour in learning it, we should perhaps have known whether it was the Chinese or the Malay game, or what it was; and this might have been the very clue, lost to native memory, to the connection of the Polynesians with a higher Asiatic culture in ages before a European ship had come within their coral reefs. (Tylor 1879)

His consideration of sport and games within ethnographic fieldwork identified possible links between cultural groupings and their contact with others. Few anthropologists took his advice over the next century.

The study of sport and culture has been rigorously explored by sociologists; many consider such activities as an ideal method to study social systems. Yet, arguably, anthropology and its methods allow for greater insights and reflection into the practice of sport, games and play as an indicator of culture, social organisations and practices. This was eventually recognised during the 1970s. Play theorist Brian Sutton-Smith stated: 'When it comes to explaining play, including games and sports, anthropology has a distinct advantage over most other disciplines because it must deal with strange play materials which simply do not fit our own twentieth-century preconceptions' (cited in Blanchard 1995, p. xi). Anthropology could follow sociology's lead when identifying a subject area.

It was Edward Norbeck who advocated as follows:

> In view of the objectives of anthropology of learning the nature of man as a living organism and the nature of his culture, the learned and socially transmitted ways of human life, the anthropological neglect of the study of play seems astonishing. (1974, p. 267)

Instead of considering play as a disconnected superfluous behaviour to social reality Norbeck believed that 'modern anthropologists now view play as universal and strikingly conspicuous human behaviour that must be studied to reach the goal of understanding man and his culture' (ibid).

This enthusiasm received what might be considered official recognition in 1974 with the creation of The Anthropological Association for the Study of Play (TAASP). This collection of scholars drawn from multiple disciplines held annual meetings in conjunction with Popular Culture Associations throughout the 1980s; yearly edited volumes were produced as a result. As a consequence, sport was acknowledged by anthropologists and as Blanchard stated in the mid 1980s: 'No longer is sport simply a topic of idle conversation and pastime activity among anthropologists; it has become a legitimate subject of serious study' (1985, p. 293).

TAASP was an important forum for academics to share their views and ideas on the concept of play and use this opportunity to promote its significance to multiple disciplines, including anthropology. For some 'play' had been ignored due to, in the eyes of one academic, 'a protestant ethic' which devalued games as somehow 'sinful' and trivial in favour of 'virtuous', serious work (Norbeck 1974, p. 267). Others believed that the very label 'play' was too broad and not specific enough to engage serious academics. The theories of play and its function were however under much scrutiny, most notably via the question 'what made an activity play or "not play"?' (Bateson 1955). By way of reply many gave their individual theories: Huizinga placed play at the forefront of human endeavours (1950). Norbeck (1974)) reduced the scope of play. Carlton (1975)) considered sports as art forms and highlighted the role of the spectator. There was much to debate.

As one can tell from the question, play and sport was and remains a contested area for research. This contest, however, has allowed much flexibility in ethnographic fieldwork. Play by definition is not particularly structured, predictable or rehearsed. Agreed ritual, rules and hierarchy are all important aspects of play but play itself, due to its very nature, is not a theme to be rigidly defined. Research on play and sport amongst specific populations will inevitably produce numerous conflicting observations and entail many variations of the above elements. This above all is what separates play, games and sports from other research focuses and facilitates culturally specific observations.

Yet, the evolution of anthropological thought represented by the formation of TAASP seemed to be short-lived and remained a superficial inclusion in ethnographies. Although some noted anthropologists have been adamant supporters of the study of sport, games and play, with some tangible success, the teaching of anthropology and ethnographic research continues to follow the more traditional anthropological methods and focuses on conventional topics, to the detriment of the study of sport. As Sands argues, 'For anthropology to survive and prosper, the student must be able to connect this very traditional discipline, with contemporary and extensive research on the modern human condition' (1999, p. 9). That sentiment informs this inquiry.

One cannot deny the global phenomenon that is sport. Its presence in culture is ever visible, accessible and reflective of society and its people. The justification of sport and its inclusion in this ethnography is clear: sport, play and games are participated in regularly by huge numbers of Liberians—both formally and informally. Excluding an activity of such importance and with such high levels of participation would be naive and unrepresentative of Liberian social life. It is true in this case that the research is centred within the area of sport yet more is considered than just the game itself and its practice, delivery and effects. Football, whilst the focus of this book, is also a medium for accessing other pressing social concerns (Rollason 2011), namely the status and prospects of youth in relation to Sport for Development and Peace (SDP). What emerge are groups of youths who create a separate subculture and arrangement based on the game of football that reflects and rejects the social structures around them (Davies 2008; Hebdige 1979). Here playing football is a lens through which to understand the construction and place of youths in social life.

My Journey

In this section I offer an account of my research methodology in the form of a personal narrative of the work completed in Liberia. This book is supported throughout by personal stories that Liberian colleagues and friends volunteered to share. Upon reflection I thought it only fair to reveal my journey in the same manner.

My undergraduate degree in Sports Science satisfied a number of my interests as a developing academic, sportswoman and multi-sports coach. In the first 2 years I found success in the areas I enjoyed, namely sociology, history, philosophy and coaching. I found the scientific aspects of my programme far less engaging and much more challenging. In my final year I pursued my dissertation subject with real vigour and discovered my real passion for the notion of SDP. In many ways this book represents my transition from final year advocate to post-doctoral sceptic. SDP in international contexts combined my interests in history, politics, sociology and philosophy. I was rightly told by my dissertation supervisor that I was taking the wrong degree! Whilst studying I pursued my interests with work experience; I gained employment as a youth worker and member of the sports development team for my local authority. Although not an exact match it confirmed my key interests: development, youth and sport. Upon completing my undergraduate degree I was keen to develop my academic interests in post-conflict development—within the appropriate academic department—and incorporate my coaching and youth work skill set. Fortunately, my supervisor shared and supported my interest; he had experience of Liberia and suggested a short trip there to see if I could find research potential. I returned determined to pursue the topic and sought supervision and learning support from the anthropology department. My initial ideas were welcomed and for the next 3 years I kept going back to Liberia and developing my academic knowledge.

Liberia ticked all the SDP boxes: post-conflict, a majority youth population central to Liberia's violent past and present challenges, a strong football heritage and a hub for international and national development agencies. I planned to have a three-pronged enquiry: governing body, local non-governmental organisation (NGO) and grassroots. My supervisor had given me contact details for a first division Coach—Coach Cooper—and a Liberian-managed NGO called Don Bosco Homes (DBH). I contacted both over phone and they agreed to help in any way they could. Coach Cooper was a well-respected man in the game and an invaluable employee of the Liberia Football Association (LFA); he facilitated all manner of access to meetings, matches and ministries. I learnt a great deal about the Liberian game, its structures, football's place in Liberian society and the status that comes with the game. However, despite the doors this opened, the LFA operated in the relative absence of youth, development and community programmes. The LFA's programming limitations were my research limitations. I stayed close to the LFA and in particular to Coach Cooper and Head of Liberia Football Coaches Association (LIFOCA), Coach Tamba, who continued to include me in their work with the Coaches' Association, but this area ceased to be a key contributor to the research focus.

Before arriving in Liberia I spent time researching DBH, and the work they promoted on their web site. They endorsed the game as part of their development and youth strategy. This NGO appeared to suit the research topic; they were a youth-focused Liberian-run organisation who had a well-known and widely promoted history with SDP. I observed their work in peace-building projects, reconciliation and reintegration, and vocational training but there was a distinct lack of football or any sporting intervention. SDP was a factor in their development image but was not evident in its delivery and practice strategy. Many of the staff were active youth workers throughout the years of civil conflict and were heavily involved in the Disarmament, Demobilisation, Rehabilitation and Reintegration (DDRR) programmes after the conflict. They had a wealth of knowledge, skill sets and had gained the trust of difficult populations. Through them I learnt about youth and children during the conflict, post-conflict challenges for the young, adult–youth relationships and community social structures. I remained a loyal intern with them for 3 years. They enabled me to travel and experience Liberia outside of Monrovia and gave me insight into areas that would otherwise have been off-limits to an outsider. Despite the knowledge and experience I was gaining I was still unable to pursue the key theme under consideration— what SDP did and how it worked in practice.

Initially I lived in the capital city of Monrovia, firstly for my safety as I had been advised and secondly because I had no idea where else to start. I would sit on the pavement watching young boys fix cars, carry water and generally loiter about without purpose. I would also observe the many large, bright white United Nations (UN) and other aid agency vehicles filled with white men and women travelling from expensive hotels to their sites of work. Their separation from the Liberian people—especially the youth—was obvious. I did not want to be one of these outsiders, a white person who does not engage and seems forever distant and unreachable. I needed to remove myself from the city centre where such outsiders gathered and where I could not escape association with them. The guest house was ideal but proved too restrictive as strict curfews were in place; visitors to the hostel were not allowed and washing and cooking had to be done by young boys employed there. These same employees were not allowed to communicate with guests. It would have been impossible to conduct the research from such a setting.

A chance visit to a community called Matadi inspired a move outside of the city centre that combined rural and urban living. Initially a suburb of the capital, Matadi grew throughout the conflict as people migrated from their rural homes seeking the safety of the capital. This was an example of the post-conflict living structure and condition in and around Monrovia; families from all corners of Liberia cohabited in limited space creating a multi-ethnic population. Matadi is split into two sections divided by a crossroad: Old Matadi and New Matadi. I chose to place myself in the New Matadi area, which was more recently developed and had a more diverse population as a consequence of the conflict. This was ideal and I instantly felt at home as I was welcomed by my neighbours and encouraged to attend and pursue community events and traditions. I felt a sense of openness and familiarity that was absent in the city.

The main attraction in Matadi, both for its residents and me, was the Don Bosco Youth Centre. As a visiting intern with DBH I was welcomed by the youth centre staff and I immediately recognised the potential for research there. I had finally found a place where people of all ages gathered daily and played sport. Moreover, the youth centre used this to achieve its various aims of reconciliation, rehabilitation and education, a clear reflection of SDP goals and practices.

Building an Identity

My principal gatekeeper and key informant was Richie, the captain of the Matadi youth football team (see Chap. 3). His role in my research is well captured by O'Reilly's description of gatekeepers as 'sponsors or individuals who smooth access to the group. They are key people who let us in, give us permission, or grant access' (2009, p. 132). He worked in the compound where I first resided. Unable to afford schooling he sought work to save money for tuition fees. He also worked for an American man, washing clothes, cooking meals, cleaning his home, fetching water and buying him supplies from the market. I would regularly talk to Richie and we would wash clothes together. He advised me on how to cook on charcoal and what ingredients I should buy; in turn, I would invite him to eat with me if he was still working in the evening. As our friendship formed he began calling me 'sister'. Richie could be considered, according to what James Spradley (1979) described, as an 'encultured informant'. Such people 'are consciously reflexive about their culture, and enjoy sharing local knowledge' (O'Reilly 2009, p. 133). Richie asked questions and immediately saw a role for himself in the research, often suggesting, 'You should talk to…' and 'I'll take you to…'. He enjoyed passing on his knowledge and finding himself a role within my research experience.

Richie introduced me to the youth centre Fatherhood, players on the team and his family, of which I was to become a member. When I returned to Liberia in 2010, 2011 and 2012, Richie lived with me in Matadi. He wanted to make sure I was looked after, alth ough I still insisted on doing my own chores; he made sure the place was always secured and accompanied me regularly to interviews to help me understand the Liberian colloquia.

Diary entry 20 April 2009

Richie took me to his football practice at the youth centre. We arrived 10 minutes before the practice began but the security staff let us in before the other queuing children—I presumed because he's captain and I was with him we were given special treatment. He told me to sit on the concrete steps while he went to team bench and changed. The players arrived late and casually, acknowledging me with side glances, sly smiles and polite handshakes from bolder players. I over-heard them refer to me as 'white woman'. Some think I'm a talent scout and start doing tricks in my eye line (I don't want them to perform to me). Others think I'm a journalist reporting on the youth centre and regard me with suspicion and possible contempt (I don't want to be another white authority figure they don't trust). I notice Richie looking at me from the pitch, he's surrounded by the players who are talking in strong colloquia and laughing whilst playfully nudging him and mockingly punching his arm. …
He seemed embarrassed. They were asking him about our living arrangement and relationship, I don't want them to see me like that and I don't want to

make Richie feel uncomfortable. I'm on the outside, literally. The Fathers came to speak to me, they didn't say much but wanted to make sure I was welcomed and I think they wanted the other spectators to notice that they knew me—I don't want to be one of them—the players distance themselves and become submissive around them. The girls and women glare at me, they don't want to be friends—are the players their boyfriends? At the end of training the players sit on the floor whilst their Coach and the Fathers talk to them about their behaviour and their expectations, they finish with a prayer, the Fathers look in my direction which directs the players to copy. I don't join them, it doesn't feel right, I'm an outsider. The walk home is a quiet one, people on Matadi's main road still stare at me not sure whether they can stop me and talk or if I am to be feared. Maybe my hesitation and uncertainty is being perceived as distancing myself—I can see people's curiosity. Richie doesn't talk until we plan dinner when we arrived by our fence. Need to ask him what the players said to him and if he's ok with me going to the youth centre with him. Frustrated by being a silent observer—this isn't my style, I need a role, something people can warm to and something where I can be some use to people as a community member. The players need to trust and respect me, they need to know my name otherwise I'm always going to be the 'white woman'.

After speaking with Richie later that night he assured me that the players were being foolish and he did not want me to be ashamed or embarrassed.

One of my favourite times in Liberia was in the evenings; Richie and I would sit outside in our yard, surrounded by a concrete fence separating us from the outside world and we would talk for hours. Football was always the initial conversation as I would give him feedback on his training session, we would comment on the players, the coach and how the team was performing. The next day I would observe him subtly passing on my comments, guiding the players on how they could improve and he would try new exercises and drills that I had taught him at home. After a few more team observations Richie's coach came to speak to me—Richie had told him about me—and without much warning he introduced me to the players and I was invited to assist with coaching the team. My role was formed and almost immediately I was Coach Holly and had inherited a large squad of players eager to learn, keen to talk to me and willing to present me to the rest of Matadi as their coach. I was now in a unique position as an anthropologist; I was centrally positioned in an organisation that identified with SDP and became a legitimate and valuable member of the team. Most importantly I was using my skill set to its best effect; I understood football, training and coaching. I had personal experience and theoretical knowledge of the parameters and workings of a coach–player relationship and understood the ethical, professional and personal obligations this role demanded. Significantly, in Liberia this role and the status it brought provided opportunities for acceptance amongst other community citizens. I was now able to consider grassroots community football, SDP and youth as a whole without being disjointed and disconnected from each other. I had negotiated a framework for a lived experience through SDP; in part this aligns with Atkinson's theorisation of 'Realist Ethnography' and the need to become a member of a culture in order to experience substantive and theoretical understandings (Michael Atkinson 2012, p. 25). Within my own fieldwork methodology, I pursue membership not only through a sustained long-term presence but also through community and sports participation.

The role of coach gave me confidence to tackle and narrow the divide between me and my neighbours. I understood the preconceived ideas many Liberians had about white people who were occupying their country. It became my goal to prove myself to Matadi's adult population in the hope that they would accept me, not as their own but as a valid member of their immediate society. The success of my ethnography depended on my ability to integrate and break down the stereotypes associated with my gender and race. I set about going to Matadi's market to learn about food where the majority of women shopped daily. Richie taught me how to prepare the fire and cook food. I travelled by motorbike and local taxi if I travelled outside of Matadi and competed with the others for my space in cars. I attempted carrying water on my head from the community well but this caused much embarrassment and laughter. My laughter in return and obvious disappointment incited many to reassure me. It worked; people became familiar with me and the news of my work as coach spread. Residents began to greet me and were much more open and at ease with my presence; most importantly, they knew my name.

With many potential obstacles to gaining data and authentic everyday experiences within and beyond SDP I wanted to begin with an open approach to my purpose. Richie knew from the day I met him that I was a student conducting research on sport. I had email communication with DBH prior to my arrival and they were fully aware of my intentions for research; the fact that I had experience of youth work, sports coaching and was seeking an active voluntary role was secondary to my intent. When the coach of Zatti FC asked me to assist with coaching the team I sat with the players after training and explained that I was a student who was interested in football in Liberia and wanted to learn through them. They reciprocated by clapping and encouraged me to ask them questions and spend time with them off the field. Arguably, this research project was flattering, and it brought some validation and prestige to their activities. This provoked an initial higher level of exchange as many footballers were themselves aspiring students but their consent was openly discussed and granted. As time progressed and my involvement with the team became a full-time pursuit my relationship with the players became more and more normal and informal off the football field. As I became immersed in the field and within the everyday, it potentially diluted their awareness and acknowledgement of me as a researcher but there was no masking of my objective. Adopting a participatory approach aided my ability to ethically study youth in Liberia as there was an exchange of knowledge and learning and I tried to empower them through the research process. Liberia had a reputation of operating through corruption and secrecy amongst local people and elsewhere, but I actively ensured that the people who became part my experience and research never felt deceived.

Gender

There are many issues that need to be considered in any ethnography, and Brewer, an anthropologist, claims that 'negotiating access, trust, recording data unobtrusively, ethical practice in the field, the question of gender and other identities' are some of them (2000, p. 82). My identity as a woman in a multitude of male-dominated environments was an initial concern to gaining access and building an identity in the hope of obtaining some form of membership. My concerns were perhaps not that pressing, as women in Liberia had taken on powerful positions after the war.

President Ellen Johnson Sirleaf was now the first female African leader, the head of the Liberian police was a woman and even the position of President of the LFA had been filled by a female by democratic election. In this post-conflict phase women had been given an opportunity to lead.

Being a woman in Liberia had its advantages and disadvantages, especially when negotiating contact and setting boundaries. My gender and race were not a barrier but created a number of issues and challenges. Initially my presence was seen as unique and as many of the players were confident on the football field they tested my interest in them. Some players desired a romantic encounter, an attractive possibility which would give them great status in their community and amongst their peers, and the potential of a new life in Europe was a chance some were not willing to let pass by. It was not uncommon to receive phone calls late at night or in the early hours of the morning for no apparent reason.[1] People who called never spoke boldly of their intentions but claimed they wanted to talk about my day or just enjoy directionless conversations. This proved challenging. I needed to create boundaries but boundaries that did not push them too far away. This was important not only for my sanity and safety but also for the reliability and validity of my data; I did not want colleagues or players to tell me what they thought I wanted to hear to impress me. I had to make clear my purpose, intentions and expectations of them away from football.

Richie was fundamental in this process alongside Dorbor, a senior member of the team, who had become an important informant within the youth centre and away from the football field. They explained to the players in an informal way that I was not interested in having that kind of relationship and that I was there to learn and coach them. This allowed me to retain my place as coach without embarrassing them or becoming a formal authoritative figure, which would have been detrimental to the relationships formed between us. As time passed I was accepted and my presence became normal and less significant. I became 'Sister Holly' to many of them off the field and 'Coach Holly' on it; some even gave me indigenous names off the field to accept me into their families, so I was known as Carebir by my Kpelle friends.

---

[1] A popular phone network company provided free calls from midnight until 5 am; this was known as the 'lovers' hours' because young people were able to make unlimited calls to potential lovers.

I recognise a limitation to this study is the lack of scope and consideration given to women. It was not a conscious decision and neither a methodological one, but an organic evolution of the research process. What became obvious was that youths in Liberia are predominantly male, which is supported by Comaroff and Comaroff (2005), who claim that 'youths are almost exclusively male' (Honwana and De Boeck, 2005, p. 24). The institutions observed and the modes of SDP examined targeted males and were predominantly staffed by males. This gave little opportunity to interact with women in specific environments, and in less formal settings younger girls seemed shy and in many cases unhappy with the attention I was giving to their male counterparts. What was considered were the relationships young men and women pursued as this seemed to be their most significant pastime away from the football field. The absence of women in this book is also a reflection and consequence of their differing roles in society; young women were expected to help with domestic chores in the family home, assist parents with money-making and care for younger siblings—the fortunate ones were also expected to perform well in school. That is not to say they were removed from male-dominated environments like the football field but they were always on the periphery looking in, in the hope of catching the eye of a potential lover. For young girls and women men were a source of financial gain and livelihood opportunities. Although kick ball presented a sporting activity for the girls it was predominantly at school level that participatory opportunities were provided. SDP was overwhelmingly focused on football and males. In relation to this it was intriguing that my race—specifically 'whiteness'—was more significant and advantageous to me than my gender. Gaining access, being accepted and spending time with youths and footballers were far more dependent on my status as a white person than being a woman.

The participatory approach that I endorsed throughout my time in Liberia enabled the methodological process to be organic, fluid and one that reacted to the unpredictable environment I found myself in. My identity as a European, white female in her mid-twenties was one which posed a degree of uncertainty and challenges when trying to immerse into and interact with a complex post-conflict culture and society. In many ways the most obvious contrasting identity traits—from that of the local population and research demographic—were race and gender.

Although these are separated in this discussion there is of course space for intersectionality within this methodological analysis. Intersectionality is how one locates oneself and individuals in the context of their identity, commonly pertaining to race, class and gender (Berger and Guidroz 2010). Intersectionality can be a complex process of strategically engaging with identity characteristics, negotiating, gaining access and building rapport, according to Mazzei and O'Brien:

> We see the field researcher as decidedly more active in determining how alignment between her field-relevant status group memberships and informants' influence access and rapport. Our view is that this is an *interactive, negotiative* process whereby ethical researchers can read which of their attributes matter in a particular field setting (and field interaction), come to understand the scripts operating about these attributes, and then, usually strategically negotiate their gender and/or host of identities to build access and rapport. Ethical researchers do not challenge the overall scripts operating in the culture, then. Rather, they adopt, strategically deploy, and challenge the applicability of these scripts to them by marshaling their intersectional self in light of what the field setting has determined particular attributes mean. (Mazzei and O'Brien 2009, p. 363)

In this regard such identity characteristics can intersect, align and become important functions of research strategy and a tool to be used when/if necessary. Despite the separation in analysis it is appreciated how both gender and race combine and are indicators and tools used for access, engagement and building a form of membership.

Race

I quickly learnt that being a lone foreign woman made me a slightly odd commodity in Liberia, especially as a football coach. Being white, however, was the key factor in my ability to access and engage with senior people and organisations; it provided me with unquestioned status and protected me from the normal patriarchal structures. My colour was a constant reminder of my European (although usually mistaken for American) heritage. This also presented a challenge as white people are generally seen as special, superior, powerful and, above all, holding a possible connection to wealth, opportunity and the potential for migration.

Working at the LFA and DBH provided different challenges. In both places I was in the company of established adults who had high status in their professions amongst their colleagues and likewise in society. I inadvertently became a pawn that possessed power and reinforced their status; they were very protective of me and at times reluctant to share me with other colleagues or allow me to network and socially navigate by myself. It felt like they competed for ownership or the rights to me. For example, during a Premiership League game at the ATS in Monrovia, a coach of another premiership club came and sat with me. We were talking for a short time when Coach Tamba arrived and tapped him on the shoulder. He immediately said 'goodbye' and sat elsewhere. Coach Tamba sat with me for the rest of the game. While it was obvious that others wanted to come over and talk, in the presence of such an authority within the LFA they felt they were unable to. This potential limitation had to be addressed but I could not do it upfront. Instead, I asked for their assistance to network and introductions to others. This reflected their status and gave them power and control. Although overall this limited some chance meetings and what might be termed the natural flow of ethnography, I had to work within the evident hierarchies of Liberian life. At the same time this very process highlighted many cultural idiosyncrasies and demonstrated the expectations and complexities of relationships. The relationship I formed with certain elders and authorities enabled far more access than it denied and as long as these gatekeepers felt empowered and in control I was able to seek many potential research avenues.

The football players in Matadi took great pride in having a white coach; this gave their team and the individual players higher status than the other teams. Forming a coach–player relationship with the Matadi youth centre team required trust and loyalty (as is the case with any effective and functional player–coach relationship). I made a conscious effort throughout to separate myself from adults when in the youth centre. In this environment I wanted to be their coach, not an adult with authority based upon some notion of inherent European superiority. The youth–adult relationship was a contentious area and one that could potentially isolate me from the team and prevent them from trusting me. I had worked hard to transition from outsider to insider and passive to active, and maintaining this was crucial. When I needed to converse with the youth centre staff and Fathers I would schedule meetings before training so that my contact with the adults would not keep me away from the pitch or from the players.

The overall advantage of being a white female football coach in Liberia was exhausting and at times overwhelming. I had inherited a squad of football players, I was becoming a community member and that required constant efforts to sustain my acceptance. I was working with youth workers for child protection and peace-building and was in regular contact with the LFA, which asked for my help running coaching workshops and observing coaching sessions. There were times when the only way I could gain clarity and perspective was to travel into central Monrovia and join the NGO expats in the city's nicest hotels. It was part of the reflection process that became my guilty pleasure. I would venture into central Monrovia and in the comfort of an air-conditioned room type out further descriptive passages or conversations in the comfort of invisibility. The separation from the primary research site allowed initial reflective interpretation and facilitated planning for the next stages of inquiry.

There was no great plan. As Van Maanen claims: 'Fieldworkers may present themselves as delicately lurking, working, and getting results, but the results they achieve are always experimentally contingent and highly variable by setting and by person' (1988, p. 4). As already discussed my method of fieldwork began experimentally but on reflection is believed to have been an important element in finding my setting, population and theoretical framework. I had concerns of entering a society that was recovering from conflict, in what seemed to be a male-dominant environment, with Liberia recording some of the highest rates of rape and domestic violence in Africa. However, the post-conflict setting had seen the role of woman evolve and steps were in place, supported by the newly elected first female president and a plethora of aid agencies, to facilitate empowerment for women. My initial concerns regarding access quickly diminished. Actually, the fact that I am white gave more access, opportunity and status than the question of gender even within a male-dominated sport like football. My main challenge was to try to gain access without fostering expectations of financial support or social mobility. Another limitation was that my commitment to spending time with the Matadi footballers, DBH and the LFA meant that the majority of my contact was with males and this at times alienated me from building relationships with women. With so many young single males living in Matadi, competition between the girls to find love interests was rife and I was generally seen as a threat as I was occupying their time. There was never any hostility shown to me by the girls and women but they would watch their men intently during practices and would never sit nearby or acknowledge me.

Judging the Observations

Consequences of My Race and Gender: Staging and Performances

As previously stated my presence was special to many. As a white female European sports coach I was in a potentially powerful position, but to gain valid and accurate data my main challenge was to integrate, gain respect and be accepted. The problem I faced was that informants tried to stage performances of their work and activities which they thought were appropriate for a white audience.

DBH in particular had clear ideas of best practice and the results they were seeking. I had witnessed a visit by UK funders and saw first-hand the discrepancy between everyday realities and practices versus the standards enforced and content delivered during a monitoring and evaluation exercise (see Chap. 4). Once the visitors had left with their image of Don Bosco I wanted to be part of the real everyday practices and observe their challenges, techniques and styles of work. I actively avoided being the recipient of any special treatment. I travelled to the head office the same way all employees did, by means of Liberian transport. I refused to sit in the front of the car preferring the back of the pick-up truck with the other employees. When transport was not available (which happened regularly) I would walk for hours with the child protection social workers doing follow-ups on youths who had been reunited with their families. As with most of the issues I faced, time proved invaluable in rectifying perceptions, gaining an identity and unmasking realities. Soon my presence was less significant and they would joke, calling me a 'Liberian girl'.

Another example of staging to show good practice was at the youth centre; initially the football coach would shout at the boys to begin the session on time, he would pace up and down the football pitch shouting instructions. As the weeks went on his performance could not be maintained, the coach was regularly late or did not attend and the proceedings of training would run on typical 'Liberian time', usually 20 minutes after schedule, and would begin in a very casual manner without focus. He was trying to present himself to me as an able, knowledgeable and dedicated coach. This was his idea of best practice but it was short-lived as I never intervened or questioned him. My mimicry of the players' laid-back behaviour and not presenting myself as an authority figure removed the fear of the players and the coach to perform and aided the reinstatement of normal proceedings. The players' initial apprehension around me and their early performances could not be sustained; they were most open to my presence as a friend or 'sister' and were least inclined to put up any pretence or provide an unrealistic portrayal of themselves.

The LFA and its members also enjoyed staging best practices and acting as they thought befitting around me. Yet in this setting I believe it was for rather different reasons. Working for the LFA in any capacity gave status and authority, and this allowed me to see challenges, deviant practices and everyday realities of the organisations that were somehow detracted from what the members perceived as workings of a flawless powerful entity, which in turn reduced the status they were so keen to maintain. Piles of paperwork on desks, working laptops, employees hustling and bustling around each other and attending games at the stadiums during the afternoon to watch league matches, all gave the impression of a well-run productive organisation. Yet, with time, as its members grew to trust me and have less formal relationships with me they would confide the realities, the most memorable being 'we haven't been paid for two months,' and the actual implementation of projects, or lack thereof, was explained to me. As my presence in the offices became a day-to-day occurrence the pretence of busy working was reduced, arguments became commonplace, corruption and suspensions were openly discussed in my presence and I was able to discover the realities of running a football association in Liberia.

Adaptive Methods for Data Collection

Ethnography is created through what Atkinson (1992, p. 5) characterises as 'a double process of textual production and reproduction'. Although culminating in an integrated, coherent ethnographic account, this process begins with the day-to-day writing of field notes, 'observations and reflections concerning "the field"' (Atkinson 1992, Cited in Emerson et al. 2001, p. 353). The day-to-day was the initial focus of my data collection and becoming familiar with the routines and cultural norms of youth. I would prepare myself with a researcher's kit of notebook, pens and Dictaphone ready for the day ahead. Proximity required that field notes were written more or less 'contemporaneously' with the events, experiences and interactions described and recounted (Ibid., p. 353).

Here lay the problem: it took a few weeks to integrate within Matadi; as people learnt my name or gave me an affectionate title this was my cue that I could begin delving further into their culture and participate more freely. This I was able to do, yet when they saw a notebook or Dictaphone in my hand, they would withdraw or change their behaviour. The idiosyncrasies I was drawn to diminished, the banter stopped and the playfulness reduced, and they tried to adapt the language they spoke to English with an American accent or 'standard English' as they called it. Their colloquia and pigeon slang stopped as they thought they had to satisfy my needs. I realised early on in the research process that the use of research aids only reinforced my position as an outsider and proved intrusive to them. If I was to retain my position as an integrated community member and gain valid and authentic data I had to change my methods and drop the visible tools of research.

I began adapting my schedule so I could spend time with DBH, the LFA or the Matadi youth during the day and go to the youth centre in the afternoons. In between I would visit homes or find a quiet place to write down the events of the morning and prepare for the next research session. Of course it should be remembered that every minute of the day and night presented potential areas of interest and incidents. I did not visit the fieldwork site; I was living in it so the process never left me, but I kept to this loose framework as often as possible to give myself an opportunity to write up short notes or important points. Emerson et al. suggest that fieldnotes are produced incrementally on a day-to-day basis, without any sustained logic or underlying principle and on the assumption that not every observation will be ultimately useful... a fieldnote corpus need have little or no overall coherence or consistency; it typically contains bits and pieces of incidents, beginnings and ends of narratives, accounts of chance meetings and rare occurrences, and details of a wide range of unconnected matters. (Emerson et al. 2001, p. 353)

Acting on this premise my field notes did not need to be overly detailed or richly descriptive but enough to trigger a potential focus and recall if necessary. Throughout the day field notes were taken on an opportunistic basis and were later made more coherent and complete, often by candlelight.

The methods I eventually adopted meant that formal interviews were restricted to senior members of organisations to whom I had very little regular access and who were not part of my everyday fieldwork in Matadi. I mainly relied on day-to-day observations and conversations that were informal and unstructured. I had to present myself as a community member or colleague, not as an outsider with ulterior motives or desires to create change.

Working with Youth and Marginal People

The concept of youthhood was central to this enquiry (see Chap. 6). After considering definitions provided by Liberia's government and development agencies I endeavoured to construct a specific definition and understanding of the notion in the context of Liberia. I identified that footballers were youths and youths were divided between adults and elders according to a set of locally constructed benchmarks. From the beginning I wanted to consider youths who had experienced conflict and for this reason I studied a very specific generation of Liberians. In accordance with this I was able to dissect their culture in two specific ways: firstly within the youth centre as football players and recipients of SDP tutelage and secondly outside the youth centre in their daily lives. Many researchers have focused on youths and their transitions from 'being' to 'becoming' or as 'having problems' to 'being a problem' (Jones et al. 2003,

p. 61). Much of my theoretical framing was conceived post-fieldwork as I wanted to ensure that the ethnography directed the theory and not the other way around. In hindsight I can appreciate how easy it would have been to allow the ethnography to be influenced by previous theorisation and assumption-based ideology. By going into the field and participating without prejudice or a fixed mindset I considered the players as players and allowed local perceptions of youths to construct a definition.

For the purpose of methodology, it is important to recognise that youths in Liberia were marginal beings in society. My main gatekeepers and informants were youths; on a practical level this was ideal as generally they had a lot of local knowledge and in the absence of a sense of loyalty to adults they were open to conversing about potentially sensitive topics. They also tended to have plenty of free time. Youths were outside adult social conventions whilst on the inside of community structures; in a similar vein Rabinow commented on one of his informants that 'Ali was an insider's outsider,' a great vantage point for any researcher (2007, p. 157).

Limitations and Reflections

Any ethnographer will face limitations and struggles in the quest for effective research, whether with regard to access, acceptance, strategy, interpretation, politics or personal interruptions. The practices of ethnography and anthropology were new to me as I clumsily made my way to Liberia without focus or plan. I learnt my craft as I made mistakes and gained experience. My ability to relate, participate and integrate allowed for acceptance and research possibilities. In this respect my initial fieldwork was extremely unstructured and fortuitous, and no theory or hypothesis was formulated until I had spent substantial time within Matadi working with various development actors. I initially viewed this as a limitation as I spent the initial weeks feeling overwhelmed, unprepared and lost, but on the other hand I was never closed to opportunities that presented themselves. I established theoretical ideas without bias or prejudice as they were constructed at the time within the research setting. A constant theme throughout this process has been learning on the job with continuous efforts to gain knowledge and understanding of the academic field I had entered whilst trying to justify and support my findings and theory through ethnography.

Devoting oneself to ethnography and the pursuit of academia is a full-time job, yet whereas many workers are able to switch off after work, research never leaves you and the reflection and thought processes never end. My experience of conducting fieldwork and writing ethnography was one of enlightenment and frustration. I was unable to dedicate myself full-time in Liberia, as financial constraints led me to conduct my fieldwork in 4- to 6-month segments with time in between devoted to writing up notes and seeking employment to cover the costs of tuition fees and fieldtrips. This was never an ideal scenario and my concerns were that the ethnography would be disjointed and the writing inconsistent. Despite this I feel I have made this strategy work. Fortunately little changed in Matadi during my absences; the same people lived there and the routine did not deviate. The time spent writing in between fieldwork allowed for in-depth reflection, interpretation and identification of potential gaps in the theoretical context and to focus on the subsequent trip.

As a researcher in a post-conflict setting where the experiences of people I met were still so fresh I could not help but feel a sense of responsibility towards my participants. Their voices were powerful and instrumental in my findings and I was obligated to handle their words with sensitivity, caution and appropriate detail and confidentiality. I would never be able to fully relate to their circumstances; although I could see the pain and trauma caused by conflict, violence and poverty, I had no frame for comparison. And although I sought to live as they did, I always knew I would be returning to a settled, secure and, in comparison, luxurious form of living in the UK. In essence this is the strength of the participatory methodology I endorsed, and by immersing myself in the everyday lived experiences within and beyond SDP I was able to navigate and interpret their experiences and the impact of football with increased accuracy and beyond superficial outsider observations. This led to vivid descriptions (Geertz 1973) and allowed youths to direct the fieldwork, a far more empowering process for the researched population than standing on the sidelines under the guise of formal investigation.

References

Atkinson, P. (1992). *Understanding ethnographic texts*. Newbury Park: Sage Publications.

Atkinson, M. (2012). Chapter 2 The Empirical Strikes Back: Doing Realist Ethnography, in Kevin Young, Michael Atkinson (ed.) *Qualitative Research on Sport and Physical Culture (Research in the Sociology of Sport, Volume 6)* Emerald Group Publishing Limited, pp. 23–49

Bateson, G. (1955). A theory of play and fantasy. *Psychiatric Research Report, 2,* 39–51.

Berger, M. T., & Guidroz, K. (Eds.). (2010). *The intersectional approach: Transforming the academy through race, class, and gender.* Chapel Hill: University of North Carolina Press.

Blanchard, K. (1985). Sports studies and the anthropology of sport. In W. Umphlett (Ed.), *American sport culture: The humanistic dimensions*. Lewisburg: Bucknell University Press.

Blanchard, K. (1995). *The anthropology of sport: An introduction*. Westport/London: Bergin & Garvey.

Brewer, J. D. (2000). *Ethnography: Understanding social research*. Buckingham/Philadelphia: Open University Press.

Carlton, R. (1975). Sport as art: Some reflections on definitional problems in the sociology of sport. Address to the first annual meeting of The Association for the Anthropological Study of Play, Detroit, Michigan.

Comaroff, J., & Comaroff, J. (2005). Reflections on youth: From the past to the postcolony. In A. Honwana & F. De Boeck (Eds.), *Makers and breakers: Children & youth in postcolonial Africa*. Oxford: James Currey.

Davies, M. (2008). A childish culture? Shared understanding, agency and intervention: An anthropological study of street children in Northwest Kenya. *Childhood, 15*(3), 309–330.

Emerson, R. M., Fretz, R. I., & Shaw, L. L. (2001). Participant observation and fieldnotes. In P. Atkinson, A. Coffey, S. Delamont, J. Lofland, & L. Lofland (Eds.), *Handbook of ethnography* (pp. 352–368). London: Sage Publications.

Geertz, C. (1973). *The interpretation of cultures: Selected essays*. New York: Basic Books.

Hebdige, D. (1979). *Subculture: The meaning of style*. London: Routledge.

Honwana, A., & De Boeck, F. (2005). *Makers and breakers: Children & youth in postcolonial Africa*. Oxford: James Currey.

Huizinga, J. (1950). *Homo Ludens: A study of the play element in culture*. Boston: Beacon.

Jones, M., Starkey, F., Orme, J. (2003). *Framing youth: Reviewing locally commissioned research on young people, drug use and drug education* (pp. 55–65). Palgrave Macmillan.

Maanen, J. V. (1988). *Tales of the field: On writing ethnography*. Chicago: The University of Chicago Press.

Mazzei, J., & O'Brien, E. E. (2009). You got it, so when do you flaunt it? Building rapport, intersectionality, and the strategic deployment of gender in the field. *Journal of Contemporary Ethnography, 38*(3), 358–383.

Norbeck, E. (1974). Anthropological views of play. *American Zoologist, 14*(1), 267–273.

O'Reilly, K. (2009). *Key concepts in ethnography*. Los Angeles: Sage Publications.

Rabinow, P. (2007). *Reflections on fieldwork in Morocco*. Berkeley/Los Angeles/London: University of California Press.

Rollason, W. (2011). *We are playing football: Sport and postcolonial subjectivity, Panapompom, Papua New Guinea*. Newcastle upon Tyne: Cambridge Scholars.

Sands, R. R. (1999). *Anthropology, sport and culture*. Westport: Bergin & Garvey.

Sands, R. R. (2002). *Sport ethnography*. Champaign: Human Kinetics.

Spradley, J. P. (1979). *The ethnographic interview*. Belmont: Wadsworth Group, Thomson Learning.

Tylor, E. B. (1879). The history of games. D. Appleton.

2

Land of the Free? The Origin of Conflict and Peace

The frame for any study of contemporary Liberia must be the 14-year civil conflict (1989–2003). This not only devastated millions and killed hundreds of thousands of men, women and children but left Liberia and its infrastructure in turmoil. Thousands of people were displaced without their loved ones and family and an entire generation who had experienced trauma were left without education, skills and guidance. Here I scrutinise the substantial presence of the UN peacekeeping forces and reconstruction, reconciliation and rehabilitation programmes put into place after the conflict to draw the reader to the realities of the position of youth in the present day.

The Foundation of Liberia

Liberia, Africa's first republic, was founded in the mid-nineteenth century by recently freed American and Caribbean slaves originally from Central and West Africa. This West African country came to be appropriately known as Liberia or 'Land of the Free' and was initially imagined to be a haven for 'free people of colour' (Moran 2006, p. 2). The

© The Editor(s) (if applicable) and The Author(s) 2016
H. Collison, *Youth and Sport for Development*,
DOI 10.1057/978-1-137-52470-6_2

first immigrants to arrive in Liberia in 1820 settled in Chrisopolis, now known as Monrovia, named in honour of US President James Monroe. Thousands of freed slaves from the USA were to join them to form many settlements throughout the country; they came to be known to the indigenous people as both the *Americo-Liberians* and the *settlers*.

The American Colonization Society (ACS), founded in 1816, was the predominant force striving to resettle ex-slaves. The ACS was an organisation of white Clergymen, abolitionists and slave owners founded in 1816 by Robert Finley, a Presbyterian Minister. The ACS governed the 'commonwealth of Liberia' until its independence from the ACS in 1847. In 1821 the ACS purchased Cape Mesurado (now Monrovia) from the indigenous ruler King Peter. By 1835 five more colonies had been formed by other American Societies. In 1824 this group of colonies was named Liberia and in 1939 the country was renamed the Commonwealth of Liberia bringing the colonies together. Between 1821 and 1867 the ACS resettled some 10,000 Africans from interdicted ships. Approximately 4500 were born free; the others were emancipated from slavery on condition they emigrate to Africa (Liebenow 1987, Staudenraus 1961, West 1970, Beyan 1991). The dispersal of freed slaves to Liberia served many purposes; missionaries wanted to use them to bring Christianity to West Africa; American slave owners saw their repatriation as a means of removing independent, self-supporting blacks out of sight of their remaining slaves. Some white abolitionists who campaigned to end slavery on grounds of its immorality were, upon succeeding, uncomfortable with cohabiting with blacks as part of a multiracial society. White American merchants saw the prospect of securing an African Coastal base to their advantage in competition with their European counterparts for legitimate trade in palm oil and coffee.

Africans who were recaptured by the US Navy whilst aboard USA-bound slave ships and brought to Liberia were known as *Congos*.[1] The returning Americo-Liberians became the Liberian elite. Separation between the Congos and Americo-Liberians became less pronounced

---

[1] The term 'congos' was commonly used in Sierra Leone and Liberia to describe non-native black settlers as a large number originated from the Congo Basin. The Congo Basin is a sedimentary basin that is the drainage of the Congo River of West Equatorial Africa.

with time. The indigenous population of Liberia consisted of between two and three million people, divided into sixteen ethno-linguistic groups or 'tribes' (in Liberian usage), determined by region or religious affiliation. In this early era, periodic violence was reported between the settlers and the indigenous people. The Americo-Liberian settlers felt it their duty to represent superior Western culture and replace their indigenous customs, religion and political institutions. In response, indigenous Liberians deemed Americo-Liberians as liberated slaves who should occupy a lower status in society than themselves (Cassell 1970, see also Holsoe 1971).

The indigenous people were excluded from citizenship in the new Republic until 1904. A sense of nation only began to appear when representatives from different parts of the Commonwealth, including Montserrado, Grand Bassa and Sinoe signed *The Declaration of Independence of the Republic of Liberia* written by Baptist Minister Hilary Teage in 1847. The declaration echoed the Republican principles of centralism, popular sovereignty, limited government, separation of powers and the supremacy of the judiciary (Indiana University 2004). A Constitution based on the US model was drawn up by a Harvard professor in 1838 and professors from Cornell codified its laws in the 1950s (Dalton 1965, p. 572). Even today, American culture remains a vital influence in Liberian society, reflected especially in the common affectation of an American accent by ordinary Liberians. Liberia was formed as a nation state under unique circumstances: an African state with no prior history of colonisation. Yet, the intention of creating Liberia as a land for free peoples was a contradiction from the start and paved the way for a turbulent future.

The 'Tribal' People: True Liberians?

The term 'tribe' is not accepted as an appropriate description of people and groups by anthropologists, yet is used by Liberians in local vernacular to refer to the country's different ethno-linguistic groups. To its critics the word is considered 'as a term deeply embedded in a colonial lexicon of racism. … The use of the term obscures the complex nature of African identities and conflicts' (Ray 2008; see also Smock 1971, Schermerhorn 1970, Hlophe 1973). To Liberians the term does not simply reflect racism or colonial categories, despite its use in the organisation of violence in the civil conflict. This is partly, perhaps, because of Liberia's unusual colonial history. As Barth and Aronson have argued, tribal or ethnic identities are symbolic or ideological constructs (Barth 1969; Aronson 1976). It is thus important, in order to prevent misunderstandings on this issue, to consider specific Liberian indigenous and ethnic structures. Liberians are relaxed about such terminology and are indeed proud of their heritage. Colonial politics aside, the term 'tribe' remains extremely important in Liberian vernacular usage.

The indigenous people of Liberia have long lived in residential groupings known as communities in which chiefs, elders and priests are the most immediate authorities. Social structures, relationships and people's ideas of who exactly they are and to whom they have moral obligations are primarily based on notions of kinship (Bellman 1975). Paden believes 'ethnic groups emphasize *kinship*, a nation which may be transmuted in various ways in the concept of nationality' (Paden 1970, in Hlophe, 1973, p. 244). Only in the twentieth century did every area in Liberia come under the Republican rule of the state institutions based in Monrovia. It was in this process of interaction between national and local politics that the vaguely defined, kinship-based communities of the past, having no permanent political centre, became classified as distinct 'tribes', containing equally distinct subtribes called 'clans' (Ellis 1999, p. 31–32).

There were and remain sixteen distinguishable indigenous groups in Liberia.[2] Almost all of these groups—or at least their names—can be found in neighbouring African countries. These indigenous groups are distinct by language, culture, religion and/or region. According to Lowenkopf, 'The essential societal referents of the majority of tribal Liberians remain the kinship group of the sub-tribal political community, and the land which they work' (1976, p. 24). Shared myths, symbols and rituals perpetuate the expectations of ethnic roles through myths of origin, external symbols, dialect or body marks.[3] These are reinforced in

---

[2] These tribes are referred to as Bandi, Bassa, Dei, Gio, Gola, Grebo, Kisi, Kpelle, Krahn, Kru, Kwa, Loma, Mandingo, Mano, Mende and Vai.

[3] Such body marks are associated with graduation into the Poro and Sande societies. They are known as society markings and are usually scars across the back and the arms.

tribe-specific rituals during major feasts and celebrations or during rites of passage from childhood to being a member of the society (Hlophe 1973, p. 242).

Crucial to notions of belonging and, indeed, cosmology are the secret societies known as *Poro* for men and *Sande* for women—a common system of initiation rituals throughout northern Liberia and across different indigenous groups (Moran 2006, p. 30; see also Bellman 1984). These two entities incorporate fundamental principles of education: etiquette and training that defend tradition and act as frameworks for the formal and spiritual teaching of the young. Their bush schools teach vocational skills, social responsibilities and prepare youth to play specific roles in their communities, as well as reinforcing the hierarchical system of indigenous authority (Lowenkopf 1976, p. 28). Indigenous affiliation is still recognised in urban areas of Liberia where the Poro and Sande societies do not operate and ritual activities are dominated by Christian worship. Some Liberians hold indigenous beliefs whilst maintaining a belief in either Christianity or Islam. Here, indigenous groups act as behavioural and physiological stereotypes. I would be made aware of indigenous identity before meeting someone. During a visit to West Point in Monrovia in the company of employees of the LFA, I was told during the car journey that 'Kru live in West point, the same as George Weah. They will be curious but nice to you even though they can be aggressive … hot headed'. Ethnic groups were part of the construction of stereotypes and this was often referred to on the football field.

The topic of ethnic affiliation in Liberia is still relevant and has specific connotations in its post-conflict era due to the complex origins of violence and faction membership. This is not a focus of this work; however, such a reality provided me with clues when considering more complex social interactions and the conceptualisation of identity. The traditions and rituals—of indigenous communities—associated with rites of passage and ageing had significance when considering post-conflict youth who had migrated to Monrovia. This had consequences on their social position and status. It is nevertheless important to acknowledge indigenous identities in order to understand the roots of the civil conflict, to which I now turn.

Political Trends

The origins of the late twentieth-century conflict lie in the socio-political history of the nation of Liberia. For 130 years following Liberia's independence from the ACS, elections were held regularly for both national and local positions. Social tensions rose between the indigenous Liberians and Americo-Liberians as increasing government investment and revenue were embezzled by officials. Although Americo-Liberians held the majority of posts and monopolised positions of power, indigenous groups were fully enfranchised by the 1960s.

From its mid-nineteenth-century origins until 1980 Liberia's only legal political force was the True Whig Party. One-party rule throughout the twentieth century brought stability but came at a price. The election of President William Tubman in 1944 brought a new era into Liberian politics, specifically via the introduction of the Unification Policy: 'The primary objective of the "*Unification Policy*" as instituted by the Tubman administration was to encourage the alienation of indigenous Liberians by the settler class and the attendant xenophobic attitudes towards these groups in an effort to achieve national integration' (Oritsejafor, 2009, p. 105). In the first years of Tubman's presidency Liberia was at a crossroads. Indigenous people were administered by the settlers through a system of indirect rule while, 'most tribal people had acquiesced in their subordinate position in this broad and loosely regulated social system' (Lowenkopf, 1976, p. 44). In return for this acquiescence, traditional communities could preserve their social, religious and judicial customs. The dominant Monrovian elite were politically united in terms of its ruling-class role; the indigenous people had not acquired any great ambition for greater participation within the political system. However, economic growth dependent on the development of Liberia's natural resources—notably rubber and iron ore—would inevitably involve cooperation and required an increasing level of participation from a workforce drawn from the indigenous communities. This, it was feared, would encourage such groups to become more vocal and seek a share in Liberia's growing industries to the detriment of the ruling Americo-Liberian elite.

Tubman proved to be shrewd; intervention at a time of increased revenue from expanding industry saw financial rewards given to him for loyalty, thus strengthening his authority among the ruling classes. By his second term in office (1951–1955) Tubman had increased the ability of indigenous people to enter central government institutions, and encouraged the affiliation of indigenous leaders with the ruling-class structures. Tubman's presidency might best be divided into three significant phases: firstly 1944–1955, wherein he consolidated both elite support and centralised power in government institutions; secondly 1956–1966, which proved to be a period of modernisation as the economy grew rapidly; and finally 1966–1971, when Tubman was faced with an economic recession and a slowing down of political development. Liberia had a typically narrow African economy based on primary resource extraction, where profits were expatriated by multinational corporations and inward investment was very low (Indiana University 2015).

After Tubman's death in 1971 Vice-President William Tolbert assumed presidency of the True Whig Party. Tolbert was a member of one of the most affluent Americo-Liberian families and was accused of nepotism throughout his presidency. Tolbert was to continue to promote the hegemonic ideals dominant in the Tubman era and this was to the frustration of both the Americo-Liberians, who thought change was happening too quickly, and the indigenous populations, who believed the scope of change was not sufficient (Lowenkopf, 1976). In 1978 the first recognised opposition party, Progressive Alliance of Liberia, ended the unchallenged one-party system in Liberia. The following year, 1979, saw an exposed export-dependent economy cause public unrest and 'rice riots' that resulted in millions of dollars of damage (Harris, 1999, p. 432). In March 1980 Tolbert ordered the banning of the Progressive Alliance of Liberia, and 1 month later he was murdered.

Until the 1980s Liberia was considered a beacon of stability in Africa and was best known for its shipping flag of convenience.[4] Shortly thereafter Liberia was a global byword for atrocity, carnage and militias of child soldiers.

---

[4] The term has been used since the 1950s; the flagships fly to show their country of registration. The Liberian registry was formed in 1948, with the registration of a ship somewhat ironically named 'World Peace'. Over the next four decades, the easy registration system made Liberia the number one registry in the world.

Democracy was overthrown. On 12 April 1980 then President Tolbert was deposed in Monrovia by a military coup d'état, fronted by Sergeant Samuel Doe, an ethnic Krahn, and supported by the Peoples Redemption Council (PRC), which consisted of seventeen soldiers. Tolbert and his council were put on trial and sentenced to death with no right of defence.

The history of Liberia in the twentieth century is marked by two trends: struggles between indigenous people and settler Liberians for control of the state; and a cycle of boom and bust typical of Africa's narrow, primary resource-dependent economies. A combination of rising tension between the settler elite and indigenous Liberians—often expressed as an inter-tribal conflict—poor economic performance and increasing inequality had strained Liberia's social fabric to breaking point by the beginning of the 1990s (Wurbel 1971, in Hlophe, 1973).

Outbreak of Civil Conflict

The rebellion by the PRC represented the end of Americo-Liberian political dominance. The overthrow also marked the beginning of a decade of conflict and instability. By the late 1980s Liberia was characterised by arbitrary ethnically based rule, the suppression of political opposition, economic collapse and sporadic civil conflict, which at one time saw eight militia factions fighting and killing each other. Moran argues that whilst in recent years 'tribalism' has been invoked as an explanation for the violence in Liberia, local histories point to evidence of more conflict *within* than *between* ethnic categories (2006, p. 4). Years of politicians' false promises and attempts for unification had failed; powerless, they turned on each other. The youth became central to the conflict and violence that followed; huge numbers of young people were conscripted or displaced, causing mass disruption. The primary role that the youth played in the conflict—as perpetrators and victims—sets the basis for this enquiry.

The overthrow was quick and forced power by the new incumbents reflected ethnically motivated desire for change. The Doe government conducted public executions and became an essentially Krahn regime, and stability did not follow or become the pinnacle of future resistance. Doe's paranoia grew. Thomas Quiwonkpa, former Commanding

General of the Armed Forces of Liberia (AFL), whom Doe relieved of his position and who was therefore forced to flee to Sierra Leone, planned a coup which failed and ended the former commander's life. Ramifications followed in Nimba County, in northern Liberia, against the Gio and Mano ethnic groups where the majority of the coup plotters came from. Doe's AFL killed approximately 3000 Mano and Gio civilians in 1985 following the failed coup attempt (Howe, 1996–97, p. 148).

In 1989 Charles Taylor, a former ally of Doe, crossed into Liberia from neighbouring Cote d'Ivoire with a 150-strong militia to fight a guerrilla war against the PRC. Taylor's National Patriotic Front of Liberia (NPFL), supported by Libya and Burkina Faso, pushed government forces out of Nimba County, the region through which they entered the country. The NPFL gained a lot of support and were quick to recruit young men and women. The NPFL then split into two factions: the NPFL, led by Charles Taylor, and Prince Y. Johnson's breakaway Independent National Patriotic Front of Liberia (INPFL). Although these factions fought each other during specific stages of the war, they both succeeded in defeating the AFL and reached Monrovia by July 1990. The following month Prince Y. Johnson seemingly struck a strategic friendship with a West African Peacekeeping Force known as The Economic Community of West African States Monitoring Group (ECOMOG) and created under the leadership of the regional superpower Nigeria. The ECOMOG commanders had little intelligence or experience of the Liberian situation and were thrown into the fray without resources, having to borrow uniforms and boots from Johnson (Iweze 1960).

With Monrovia circled by militia, Doe's position became increasingly weak. On 5 September 1990 Doe and Johnson signed a 2-week ceasefire whereby Doe agreed not to enter into Johnson's territory without permission. However a visit by Doe to the ECOMOG headquarters on 9 September resulted in his capture, torture and murder by Prince Johnson and the INPFL. The ordeal was filmed by a Palestinian journalist. Doe's disfigured body was later paraded in a wheelbarrow through Monrovia to a medical clinic where he was pronounced dead and left on display to prove his death.

Upon Doe's death Johnson assumed the role of president. He was never elected or looked upon as president by the international community or by the majority of Liberians. This assuming of power proved an abysmal start for the newly arrived international peacekeeping mission. The INPFL continued to monopolise and be at the forefront of Monrovian politics until Prince Y. Johnson fled to Nigeria in 1992 to avoid capture by Taylor's rebels. During this time rebel groups continued to form. The United Liberation Movement of Liberia (ULIMO) was formed in Freetown, Sierra Leone, from the remnants of Doe's disintegrated army (Gberie 2005, p. 59). The Liberian army was joined and supported by the Liberian Peace Council (LPC) initially based in the southeast of the country. Many factions were formed as representatives of different counties, for example, the Lofa Defence Force (LDF). The United Nations Observer Mission in Liberia (UNOMIL) was established in 1993 to work with personnel from the monitoring group drawn from ECOMOG. In early 1994, 368 UN observers arrived in Monrovia, a number that was reduced to 60 in 1995 due to continued fighting. The sub-regional organisation named the Economic Community of West African States (ECOWAS) brokered a peace agreement in Cotonou, Benin, on 25 July 1993, supported by the Liberian factional leaders including the president of the Interim Government of Liberia (IGNU). All present agreed to end hostilities and hold democratic elections. The agreement, however, did not last even if democracy in Liberia had its plaudits.

Initial Intervention

ECOMOG's mission inside Liberia was to 'keep peace, restore law and order and ensure that a cease-fire agreed to by the warring factions in Liberia was respected' (Ero, np, 1995). ECOMOG was the first sub-regional military force that the UN agreed to work with as a secondary partner and Liberia was one of the first cases of conflict where both the UN and the major regional organisation, the Organisation of African Unity (OAU), intervened in a peacekeeping role (Howe, 1996–97, p. 146). Many saw in the creation of ECOMOG the ability of African states to act militarily in the region without the lead of former colonial powers. However, such an entity was faced with immediate problems of funding and political unity with clear divisions evident between the English- and French-speaking nations.

As Howe (1996–97) argues, whilst the efforts of ECOMOG to intervene while others watched were commendable it ultimately failed in its quest and potentially prolonged the conflict because

> it entered a contested situation with inadequate resources. It did not enjoy wide political support; it lacked detailed knowledge of Liberia and the conflict; its military capabilities and mandate were ineffective; and its commitment to remain had some destabilising effects, notably the aiding of surrogate forces. (p. 176)

In this milieu future peace was not hopeful, not least when the peace-keepers at times were looters and murderers, 'looting was so common among the troops—with stolen cars and household furniture and other goods being routinely shipped to Nigeria and elsewhere—that Liberians corrupted the acronym ECOMOG to stand for "Every Car or Moving Object Gone"' (Gberie 2005, p. 57).

The Strongman: Charles Taylor

The 1995 elections saw Charles Taylor, former leader of the NPFL, and his National Patriotic Party (NPP) elected to presidency in a strategy widely acknowledged by the electorate, who saw him as the only candidate capable of preventing a recurrence of war. His campaign had supporters chanting 'He killed my ma, he killed my pa, but I would vote for him.' Having brought about the conflict, only Taylor was thought to be able to end it but the peace was short-lived and Taylor's leadership was a failure. Anti-government insurgents resumed fighting on a nationwide scale in 1999.

Neighbours Ghana and Nigeria entered the dispute, accusing Taylor of supporting rebel movements in adjacent Sierra Leone. In 1999, a rebellion against Taylor began in Lofa County, northern Liberia, by a group called Liberians United for Reconciliation and Democracy (LURD) backed by Guinea. By 2001, 'the country imploded into destructive factional fighting, mainly as a result of Taylor's lack of commitment to reconciliation and state building' (Gberie 2005, p. 62). By 2003 LURD was in control of Bong, Bomi and Montserrado counties and the majority of northern Liberia. A second rebel group backed by the Ivory Coast named Movement for Democracy in Liberia (MODEL) secured control over southern Liberia. By the summer of 2003 Taylor's government controlled only one-third of Liberia. Fighting against the opposition force LURD continued until Taylor succumbed to international pressure from America,[5] Nigeria and neighbouring African states to resign. He then went into exile in Nigeria, courtesy of the Nigerian government. He was arrested by Nigerian Customs Officers during an escape attempt at a border crossing, he was transferred to Sierra Leone and once there arrested by UN peacekeepers and transported to The Hague where he was tried for 11 indictments for Crimes against Humanity. On 18 August 2003 the Comprehensive Peace Agreement was signed by the government of Charles Taylor, LURD and MODEL.

In The Hague in 2012 after a 4-year trial Taylor was convicted of eleven accounts of war crimes including terror, murder, rape and conscripting child soldiers. He was later sentenced to 50 years in prison to be served in the UK.

Post-War Relations and Structures

Following the Comprehensive Peace Accords in 2003, the United Nations Security Council established the United Nations Mission in Liberia (UNMIL). This consisted of some 15,000 UN personnel and included 250 military observers, 160 staff officers and 1115 civilian police officers. This force required an annual budget of $846 million (UNMIL 2012). The stated objectives of this mission were as follows:

> To support the implementation of a ceasefire agreement and the peace process: protect United Nations staff, facilities and civilians; support humanitarian and human rights activities; as well as assist in national security

---

[5] US President George W. Bush publicly stated that 'Taylor must leave Liberia,' and to implement this demand, Bush agreed to fund US peacekeeping resources if Taylor resigned and accepted his exile.

reform, including national police training and formation of a new, restructured military. (UN Resolution 1509)

One of UNMIL's primary concerns concentrated on the DDRR or DDR of former combatants. According to Jennings, 'DDR programmes have emerged as an essential element in the international community's toolbox for post-conflict reconstruction, to the extent that some donors see them as a substitute for wider recovery and development efforts' (2007, p. 204). The UN implementation of the DDRR process was to be supported by the National Commission for DDRR, whose main role was overall supervision and policy guidance; most of the implementation phases were undertaken by international humanitarian organisations, such as the United Nations Children's (originally International Children's Emergency) Fund (UNICEF) and the Norwegian Refugee Council (Paes 2005, p. 254).

The first stage of the DDRR process began on 7 December 2003 and was to consist of a 3-week disarmament and demobilisation period, although this was later reduced to 5 days: 'UNMIL was overwhelmed by the high turnout of ex-fighters for this first phase' (Jaye 2009, p. 12). Eligibility for DDRR benefits was based on the willingness of ex-combatants to hand in a weapon. As Paes comments, 'UNMIL was overwhelmed by a higher than anticipated response ... compounded by organisational and resource problems which led to riots that left several people dead, and led to rioting and looting in Monrovia' (2005, p. 254). The DDRR policy makers and implementers were poorly prepared; the dissatisfaction amongst an already disgruntled population was evident. According to the International Centre for Transitional Justice, initial failure can be accredited to a number of factors:

> Ex-fighters, stakeholders and community members were inadequately sensitized to the process... A second reason was the failure by the UN to reach out to and incorporate local perspectives and knowledge...The initial mistake by the UN team was its attempt to use the usual 'quick fix' and uncritical 'cut and paste,' 'one size fits all' approach...Implementing partners and service providers contracted by UNMIL were also poorly prepared for the start of the exercise. (Jaye 2009, pp. 12–13)

As part of DDRR, UNMIL peacekeepers processed 13,490 former fighters, collected 8679 weapons and more than 2.7 million rounds of ammunition. The lack of preparation from the UN was evident when the programme was suspended for 4 months until UNMIL could redesign the process. It was decided that the criteria for entry into the programme be extended to people who did not have a weapon but could hand in ammunition—'a change that may have been made to accommodate worries that "camp followers" (primarily considered to be women and children) would be excluded from the process' (Jennings 2008, p. 19). Four sites[6] were to be opened that covered a larger proportion of Liberia.

From the disarmament stage former fighters were then transported to a site where they were to receive medical attention and undergo human rights and peace training as well as trauma counselling. This was predominantly conducted by local and international NGOs.[7] According to the International Centre for Transitional Justice, 'ex-fighters should have undergone psychosocial evaluations … but this did not happen' (Jaye, 2009, p. 17). Originally the participants were expected to stay in the camp for 3 weeks to give them an opportunity to live separately from their former commanders and receive adequate training; however, this was reduced to 5 days as the UN could not accommodate such an influx of willing participants, both former fighters and those wanting to benefit from the programme. Fighters were not allowed to leave the camp during this process and upon completion of the programme were given food for a month, US$150 cash and free transport to a location of their choice within Liberia. Foreign ex-combatants were given the choice to return to their country of origin or advised to seek refugee status within Liberia. The final stage incorporated vocational training, education and job creation; such participants were given a second allowance of US$150. A fundamental flaw in the programme was that 'the number of reinte-

---

[6] Sites included, Montserrado County, Tubmanburg (Bomi County), Ganta (Nimba County) and Zwedru (Grand Gedeh County).

[7] A non-governmental organization (NGO, also often referred to as 'civil society organization' or CSO) is a not-for-profit group, principally independent from government, which is organized on a local, national or international level to address issues in support of the public good (United Nations Rule of Law: Non-Governmental Organisations: http://www.unrol.org/article. aspx?article_id=23).

gration slots did not grow in tandem with the number of demobilised fighters, forcing discharged ex-combatants to wait for months, often in destitute conditions in greater Monrovia' (Paes 2005, p. 255).

The programme ended in November 2004 with a total of 102,193 former fighters processed including over 11,000 children; some 27,000 guns and in excess of 6.15 million rounds of ammunition had been collected. The statistics proved that the young were central to the conflict and needed therefore to be positioned as a challenge for post-conflict rehabilitation and society building.[8]

Victims of the Liberian civil conflict received no UN-facilitated counselling for their trauma or development aid for their communities. Reintegration and rehabilitation are commendable goals for the future of ex-combatants but might be considered within a larger context wherein everyone and everything experienced change. In the post-conflict milieu women and youth played very different roles, around 80 % of the population was unemployed, large-scale displacement was evident and little infrastructure remained. The conflict may have ended but the socio-economic problems grew and in many cases were yet to be realised.

Since the 2003 ceasefire progress towards rebuilding state capacity and building a peaceful and functioning Liberia has been slow. Basic amenities like water, electricity and medical facilities are in short supply. Liberia still relies on petrol-fuelled generators for electricity—a luxury the majority cannot afford. The roads have never been fully repaired so travel between counties is hazardous and slow. Western medical facilities

---

[8] It has been suggested by Paes that another flaw in the DDRR process was in the $150 given upon surrendering a weapon. Some sources claimed that up to 60 % of the total participants on the DDR programme were not affiliated to fighting forces and more than a quarter of the people registered with the programme marked 'other' rather than stating their membership to one of the armed groups (Paes 2005, p. 257). By lowering the requirements for admission, offering $300 incentive for completion and accommodating former fighters in camps that included satellite television and food, UNMIL arguably designed a programme that encouraged the abuse of such a programme in one of the poorest countries in the world. The reintegration process also demonstrated inconsistencies. Former combatants were given the choice of where they wanted to be placed after the programme; approximately 45 % opted for Monrovia rather than their home towns, believing the capital would offer greater economic opportunities. Others may have been afraid to return home. However, overpopulation of ex-combatants in one area created a threat to national security. Additionally by November 2004 only '11,212 former fighters were registered in on-going projects with a further 4,681 registered for formal education, this left more than 82,000 unaccounted for' (Paes 2005, p. 258).

are rare and payment is still expected for treatment and is therefore a luxury for the few. Monrovia has a relatively modern USA-built hospital named J-F-K; however, the facilities within the interior of the country are basic and many use traditional forms of treatment for their ailments. Unemployment, illiteracy and unskilled workers present a continuous barrier to sustainable progress. Most significantly, however, the direct effects of a long and bloody civil conflict mean that tens of thousands of children are orphaned and many exist with the status of ex-child combatant in desperate need of guidance, support, medication and education.

Liberia may be unique as an African post-conflict state because of the almost unprecedented and virtually complete disappearance of the rebel forces from the political process after the 2003 Comprehensive Peace Agreement (Harris 2006, p. 375). After the main rebel parties were forced to withdraw from Monrovia, neither LURD nor MODEL survived the political change. In 2005, Liberia participated in 'free and fair' elections as recognised by the involved international organisations and community. In what ultimately became a two-way contest, a 66-year-old Harvard-educated woman, Ellen Johnson Sirleaf, defeated ex-World Footballer of the Year George Weah. Presenting himself as the young candidate beyond Liberia's traditional politics and its ethnocultural baggage, Weah's candidacy fascinated the world's media; however, the absence of any substance in his campaign and the violence of his young followers prevented Weah from becoming the first professional footballer to become Head of State (Armstrong 2007).

During the second run-off for presidency, Johnson Sirleaf took 59.4% of the vote whilst Weah finished with 40.6%; Weah claimed systematic fraud had cheated him of victory. The big story of the post-conflict election was The Woman versus The Footballer; the woman won and has so far sustained peace and tried to work with the international community towards development. Many Liberians I spoke to believe that Weah was cheated out of the election and blame his loss on a conspiracy involving the USA and the international community to elect Johnson Sirleaf. Weah once again stood for election in 2011 for The Congress for Democratic Change party as vice-presidential candidate and invited Winston Tubman to stand as the presidential candidate. He was again defeated by President Ellen Johnson Sirleaf.

References

Armstrong, G. (2007). The global footballer and the local war-zone: George Weah and the transnational networks in Liberia, West Africa. *Global Networks, 7*(2), 230–247.

Aronson, D. R. (1976). Ethnicity as a cultural system: An introductory essay in ethnicity in the Americas. *World Anthropology Paris*, 9–19.

Barth, F. (1969). *Ethnic groups and boundaries: The social organization of culture difference.* Boston: Little, Brown and Co.

Bellman, B. L. (1975). *Village of curers and assassins: On the production of Fala Kpelle cosmological categories.* The Hague: Mouton.

Bellman, B. L. (1984). *The language of secrecy: Symbols and metaphors in Poro Ritual.* New Brunswick: Rutgers University Press.

Beyan, A. J. (1991). *The American Colonization Society and the creation of the Liberian state: A historical perspective, 1822–1900.* Lanham: University Press of America.

Cassell, A. C. (1970). *A history of the first African Republic.* New York: Fountainhead.

Dalton, G. (1965). History, politics, and economic development in Liberia. *The Journal of Economic History, 25*(04), 569–591.

Ellis, S. (1999). *The mask of anarchy: The destruction of Liberia and the religious dimension of an African civil war.* New York: New York University Press.

Ero, C. (1995). ECOWAS (Economic Community of West African States) and subregional peacekeeping in Liberia. *Journal of Humanitarian Assistance.*

Gberie, L. (2005). Liberia's War and Peace Process: A Historical Overview. *In, Aboagye, F. & Bah, A.M.S (eds). A Tortuous Road to Peace: The Dynamics of Regional, UN and International Humanitarian Interventions in Liberia.* Pretoria: Institute for Security Studies, 51–71.

Harris, D. (1999). From 'warlord' to 'democratic' president: How Charles Taylor won the 1997 Liberian elections. *The Journal of Modern African Studies, 37*(3), 431–455. United Kingdom: Cambridge University Press.

Harris, D. (2006). Liberia 2005: An unusual African post-conflict election. *Journal of Modern African Studies, 44*(3), 375–395.

Hlophe, S. (1973). The significance of Barth and Geertz'Model of ethnicity in the analysis of nationalism in Liberia. *Canadian Journal of African Studies/La Revue canadienne des études africaines, 7*(2), 237–256.

Holsoe, S. E. (1971). A study of relations between settlers and indigenous peoples in Western Liberia, 1821–1847. *African Historical Studies, 2*, 331–362.

Howe, H. (1996–1997). Lessons of Liberia: ECOMOG and regional peace-keeping. *International Security, 21*(3), 145–176.

Indiana University. (2004). The Liberian Constitutions: The Liberian Constitution of 1847. http://www.onliberia.org/con_1847.htm.

Indiana University. (2015). William V.S. Tubman papers, 1904–1992: Biographical note. http://webapp1.dlib.indiana.edu/findingaids/view?doc.view=entire_text&docId=VAB6923.

Iweze, C. Y. (1960). Nigeria in Liberia: The military operations of ECOMOG. *Nigeria in International Peacekeeping, 1992,* 218–223.

Jaye, T. (2009, June). International justice and DDR: The case of Liberia. *International Centre for Transitional Justice.*

Jennings, K. (2007). The struggle to satisfy: DDR through the eyes of ex-combatants in Liberia. *International Peacekeeping, 14*(2), 204–18.

Jennings, K. (2008). Seeing DDR from below: Challenges and dilemmas raised by the experiences of ex-combatants in Liberia. *New Security Programme Report, 3.*

Liebenow, G. J. (1987). *Liberia: The quest for democracy.* Bloomington: Indiana University Press.

Lowenkopf, M. (1976). *Politics in Liberia: The conservative road to development* (Vol. 151). Stanford: Hoover Institute Press.

Moran, M. (2006). *Liberia: The violence of democracy.* Philadelphia: University of Pennsylvania Press.

Oritsejafor, E. (2009). National integration in Liberia: An evolving pursuit. *The Journal of Pan African Studies, 3*(1), 96–120.

Paden, J. (1970). African concepts of nationhood. In J. Paden & E. W. Soja (Eds.), *The African experience* (pp. 403–433). Evanston: Northwestern University Press.

Paes, W. C. (2005). The challenges of disarmament, demobilization and reintegration in Liberia. *International Peacekeeping, 12*(2), 253–261.

Ray, C. (2008). How the word 'tribe' stereotypes Africa. *New Africa, 471,* 8–9.

Schermerhorn, R. A. (1970). *Comparative ethnic relations: A framework for theory and research.* New York: Random House.

Smock, A. (1971). *Ibo politics: The role of ethnic unions in Eastern Nigeria.* Cambridge: Harvard University Press.

Staudenraus, P. J. (1961). *The African colonization movement, 1816–1865.* New York: Columbia University Press.

UN Resolution 1509. (2003). United Nations Security Council 2003-S/RES/1509. www.un.org/ga/search/view_doc.asp?symbol=S/RES/1509(2003).

UNMIL. (2012). UNMIL: United Nations mission in Liberia: UNMIL facts and figures. http://www.un.org/en/peacekeeping/missions/unmil/facts.shtml.

West, R. (1970). *Back to Africa: A history of Sierra Leone and Liberia*. New York: Holt, Rinehart and Winston.

Wurbel, T. (1971). Liberia: The dynamics of continuity. *The Journal of Modern African Studies*, 9(2), 189–204. Cambridge University Press.

3

Richie

My favourite time with Richie was in the evening after dinner. In the absence of electricity, we would sit outside in our yard catching the cool breeze in the darkness, listening to the evening noises. During this time, we would talk for hours covering an array of subjects from European football to his Zatti FC teammates to general life. It was during these times that Richie described his experiences of the war, his life before displacement and his ambitions for the future. His story would enlighten me on the experiences of being a child during the conflict, his journey to Monrovia and his life now. His story represents many young Liberian's experiences during the conflict and most significantly their position in Liberian society now.

Richard Toe was born on 5 January 1985 in Flehlah, Bong County. His mother was 18 years old when she became pregnant, still in school, and she had already lost one child. Richie was born and stayed with his mother in Flehlah. Flehlah is a Kpelle farming community set in the bushlands of Bong County. Richie's father was a school teacher and moved from Flehlah to Bhanga for work, so was not seen regularly in his life. When Richie was three his father returned and took Richie to stay with another woman in a neighbouring village, but he did not settle and

© The Editor(s) (if applicable) and The Author(s) 2016
H. Collison, *Youth and Sport for Development*,
DOI 10.1057/978-1-137-52470-6_3

complained of sickness. Richie's mother found him after 4 weeks and took him back. His father then relocated to Monrovia and wanted to take Richie with him but his mother refused and kept him in the village with her.

With his mother and her family in the village they made a swamp farm and planted rice. As a duo they were part of a group of farmers in the village who took turns to tend to each other's land. The women tended the farms while the men burnt the land before planting. As Richie grew so did the size of the land they used for farming. His mother found a man to help her and he became a stepfather teaching Richie how to climb palm trees and hunt. Richie had no formal education as an adolescent so his main pursuits revolved around farming, hunting and playing. Throughout Richie's early years his father continued to send for him to join him in Monrovia but his mother never agreed to the move.

Living in a Kpelle village Richie was brought up according to Kpelle customs and traditions. The only language he spoke was Kpelle. Children take on the indigenous affiliation of their fathers; Richie's father is Gruebo so Richie is Gruebo and not Kpelle despite his upbringing. That his why his father refused to allow him to join the Kpelle society and go to the *poro* bush school. Whenever the time came to recruit new members to join the society, his mother would keep him inside the house. The notion of the devil, poro and secret societies was fed into the hierarchical framework of the village. Through this function the village population attained adulthood, marriage, housing, employment and respect. Richie spoke of the 'society' often. His mother is a society woman and has marks on her back as a symbol of her membership. Whenever the village had meetings Richie would have to stay at home whilst his mother attended. Richie spoke with great passion and in great detail about his life in the village.

Becoming a Kpelle society member is an issue that is raised to this day and his maternal grandmother still offers to pay to send him to poro school. His response to this is that he does not want to be a society man and that the thought of it scares him. Reminiscing about his time with his mother he described many incidents when his lack of belonging to the secret society affected his life in the village. On one occasion, whilst helping his mother on the farm he heard three loud horn blasts; this meant the devil was coming. He ran and hid in the house to be sure he was out of sight. As a non-society member he had no protection. Richie described a number of events when devils would visit the village; some were bad and some were good. At Christmas time a good devil would come to the village to entertain the children. When a 'big person' in the village died another devil would arrive to cover the body but this devil would only interact with society people in secrecy. A bad devil with a mirror on his head and a rattan in his hands wearing large palm leaves would also come to the village from time to time to 'put things in order'. He would chase the children and beat their legs; sometimes Richie would interact with the good devil and they would dance with each other.

In 2011 Richie took me to Flehlah to meet his family. After a 2-hour drive by taxi we arrived in Bong County. The only way to reach the village was by foot or motorbike. The path through the bush was rocky, steep in places and narrow but Richie reassured me that the driver of the motorbike knew the road well; by foot it would have taken over an hour and the heat was already sweltering. So, wedged between the driver and Richie I made the journey. The contrast to Monrovia was vast; the lush green surroundings were breathtaking. Women walking on the trail with large bundles on their heads and babies on their backs looked on with surprise at the sight of a white woman on a motorbike. Above the noise of the engine Richie explained that this was interior walking; due to the narrow trails people always walked in a single line one behind the other. Before we arrived word had somehow spread to the village that I was on my way; children waited with anticipation whilst the men stood behind them. I was warmly greeted and surrounded by the inquisitive children who had never before seen someone like me. A male elder showed me around the village while Richie was alongside, interpreting. The village was smaller than I had imagined. Round houses made from mud, wood and bamboo encircled the communal buildings which lay in the centre. Richie warned me of the buildings that he and I were not allowed to enter as non-society members. His grandmother was tending to the farm and we were told to go and see her. I followed Richie as we walked through denser bushland; looking behind I was taken aback by the line of more than twenty children following me. After a challenging 30-minute walk we arrived on the farm and Richie was reunited with his grandmother who was working tirelessly. I was once again welcomed and talked through the farming process. After having food back at the village and spending some time playing with the children we made the journey back to Monrovia. I was struck by the contrast, the simplicity of design, the organic nature of life, the closeness of its population and the strong ties to the Kpelle tradition that had not been interrupted by the war. My mind shifted back to Richie as a child leaving this highly regulated environment for the chaos of the city.

In 1995 Richie's father made contact and again requested that Richie and his mother join him in Monrovia. By this stage the war had engulfed Liberia and chaos threatened the stability and seclusion of the village set in the bushlands. Richie and his mother made the decision to leave Bong County and travel to the capital. It was the first time that Richie had seen a car and been exposed to the world outside of the village. He remembers looking at the endless new sights with fear but felt protected under his mother's arm. His arrival at the city provided little security or stability. For 1 month the three of them stayed with an uncle in Jacob Town but food was in short supply and whatever they did have attracted rebels and was quickly stolen. He recalls moving from place to place and having to go through checkpoints. Young boys dressed strangely were looking for 'tribe's people'.[1] The Krahn checkpoints were looking for Mandingos and Gio and vice versa; those identified were denied access through the checkpoint and beaten, maimed or murdered. His Kpelle dialect provided protection. He recalls walking a long distance, as the rebels had taken all the cars, and for the first time he saw a dead body on the streets; he was confused and just stood still and stared until his mother grabbed him.

After a few months his father left them, despite his mother begging him not to. His father had set up home by the swamp area of Matadi, a suburb of Monrovia; he would fish and sell most of his catch to the rebels who resided there. The rebels told him to send for his family and that they would be safe, so Richie's father travelled back to Jacob Town to pick them up. Richie explained that he was scared when he first came to Matadi and the rebels always had guns in their hands. His father continued to sell fish and Richie was given the job of delivering the fish to

[1] By this Richie was referring to men and women of specific ethnic affiliation.

the estate houses. It was during one of his trips that he met Flomo, a 15-year-old Kpelle boy fighting for Charles Taylor. Although Richie was initially scared they became friends; they spoke the same dialect, which was comforting to Richie as this was all he understood. When Flomo was sent to fight, Richie would clean his house and prepare the place for his return. Flomo would feed Richie and protect him and his family from any problems with other rebels. One day Richie found Flomo's gun and ammunition when he was cleaning; scared, he ran back to the swamp and refused to leave. Flomo came and reassured him that he need not worry. Flomo was forced into fighting by the rebels who had enlisted young boys from his village by force. He tried to encourage Richie to join him and to become a soldier, claiming that 'You'll have lots of things, you'll benefit'. Richie explained that he did not want to and that his parents would not be satisfied with that.

In 1997 the Economic Community of West African States (ECOWAS) secured Matadi and Flomo decided to return to the interior. Richie describes this as a sorrowful moment. Flomo left behind the things that he had looted and Richie and his father sold the items for food. During this time the fighting stopped in the capital. His family supported Charles Taylor because they felt that the war would not start again if he assumed presidency. It was at this time that Richie attended the Central Matadi Community School and began his schooling; he joined Grade 1 at the age of twelve. Although it was relatively peaceful at this time Richie recalled that the disarmament process was not easy and that the rebels' activities were still occurring in what remained an unstable and violent society.

From 1997 Richie began playing football at the Don Bosco Youth Centre. The compound was in front of his house, and from 1991 this was a religious site, encouraging rehabilitation and reconciliation. The youth centre opened intermittently throughout the war when it was safe, and children were encouraged to play in the afternoons within the relative safety of the compound walls. From 1997 to 2000 Richie was part of a junior football team called Young Star that trained in the youth centre. The team proved invaluable to Richie as he was able to make friends his own age without the threat of conscription and this aided his ability to learn English. The youth centre also provided small meals. Between 2001 and 2003 there was no play due to the conflict in and around Monrovia.

One night as we sat eating outside in our yard he described the 'wickedness' that occurred during Charles Taylor's presidency, in particular the presence of the Anti-Terrorist Brigade (ATU), which was a parliamentary force established by Charles Taylor and led by his son Chuckie.[2] He claimed that 'the ATU were very wicked, no freedom of speech. They were Charles Taylor's eyes. They would flog you.' Richie described the expanding groups associated with Charles Taylor as 'complete rebels'. There were militias of boys aged between twelve and fifteen who would wear bandanas and dress in what he termed a 'foolish way'. They had strange names that would scare people and 'these guys never had mind,' meaning that these boys were drugged, given alcohol and were under the influence of JuJu to make them brave. The rebels at this time would occupy Matadi and make attempts at recruiting other young boys, including Richie, with the promise of US$300. Initially the presence of these militias in the capital and its suburbs was to ensure continued support for Charles Taylor, but Richie and his family were aware of the escalating conflict outside the city.

Richie was still attending school in Matadi but classes were only offered for a few hours a day. Classes would finish at midday and the children would be sent back home. Despite the end of the conflict in the capital Richie said, 'We were not in peace.' He would go home and stay with his parents, never leaving the inside of the house in case soldiers came and tried to take him to their base. Over the next few years the war escalated and the conflict travelled from the interior to the capital. Schools closed down, people hid and only ventured out of their homes in search of food. Richie described Charles Taylor as 'stubborn. People were dying and yet he still trying to force people to become soldiers, they would come and knock on everyone's door in the community.' During such time, scared by the desperation of Charles Taylor and his militias, Richie would hide in the swamp during the day and return late at night to his mother for

[2] The ATU (1997–2003) was a security force established to protect government buildings and embassies. In reality it acted as its own terror group. Nicknamed the 'demon forces' it caused fear and committed some of the most violent acts during the conflict. The group consisted predominantly of foreign nationals from Burkino Faso, the Gambia as well as the RUF combatants from Sierra Leone. Chuckie is now serving 97 years in a US prison (c.f. Armstrong and Rosbrook-Thompson 2012).

food. A community building Liberia Opportunity Industrialisation Centre (LOIC) in Matadi near his mother's house provided shelter for families during the day and during heavy fighting. Most of the houses in Matadi at this time were made from thin wood panels and Zinc so bullets would travel straight through the walls. The LOIC became a meeting place for the elders of Matadi who would discuss their strategies for protection and for finding food for the community. On one occasion children were taken by rebels from the centre so Richie remained in hiding in the swamp.

The male elders of Matadi formed a 'night watch group' to protect the community. They would patrol the main streets in Matadi and had knives and cutlasses, but in reality had little defence against the armed and fearless rebels. During the final months of the conflict the bridges in and out of Monrovia were blocked. Richie remembers that this was the time that food was in short supply: 'People ate leaves. My friend had a dog but the soldiers killed it and sold the meat back to us.' When the war was coming to an end Charles Taylor was 'tired and had no ammunition so people were a little free'. Richie remembers the day that the UN and The Economic Community of West African States Monitoring Group (ECOMOG) came to Matadi: 'It was fine, food came because the port was open again.'

In 2004 Richie returned to school to the third grade at the age of nineteen. He also returned to the youth centre to play football. He enjoyed school and worked hard. His school career did not progress without disruption and intermittently he dropped out due to financial problems. He sought work within the community and even at the youth centre, helping to clean the school and doing small maintenance work. From 2004 the youth centre entered a football team called Don Bosco Dream into the fourth division of the national league; they won the league and were promoted to the third division. They have since entered a team every season under the new name Zatti FC. Richie has captained the side for the last two seasons and many of the players in the team are still the original ones from 1999.

At the age of twenty-six Richie passed his final school exams and was awarded a high school diploma. Still living by the swamp with his parents he enrolled into a carpentry course in the LOIC which he successfully

completed in 2013. During this time his new skill as a carpenter and reputation in the community as a good, strong, hard-working, honest and committed boy helped him find small jobs for food or small pay. Often he did
not ask for compensation if he was helping an elderly community member.
Richie was known to be 'good' amongst the community: the younger children looked to him affectionately as he never treated them badly; those of a
similar age respected his moral fortitude and non-threatening manner; and
the adults and elders thought of him as an honest and hard-working boy.

As a child Richie was exposed to a decade of conflict, violence, instability and chaos. He had to teach himself English from the age of ten in
order to acclimatise and fit into his new surroundings and multi-ethnic
community. Through various strategies, support from his parents and
luck he survived forced conscription, starvation and violence. It is hard
to imagine the sights he describes through his eyes as a child. Whilst
combatants and opportunists took advantage of the DDRR process and
benefitted from financial reparations and trauma counselling the likes
of Richie watched from the sidelines and quietly began the process of
rebuilding a peaceful life in a broken society. Since the conflict he has
accomplished recognised education and training whilst building a good
reputation within the community. Many adults have employed Richie
for small odd jobs, cleaning their homes and fetching water. Yet his status
and position within his community has not changed. On the football
field he is the team leader and an authority figure within its structure but
off the field he is still referred to as a 'boy' or 'pekin'³ by adults and elders.
Whilst living with his mother without any means to sustain a relationship, marriage, children or any tangible tokens of adulthood his status is
stagnant. Any monetary gain from small work is used for the here and
now, for survival, not for the future. A good reputation may provide an
opportunity for acknowledgement amongst adults and small openings
for work but only for the short term and within the limits of youthhood.

Richie's story introduced me to his childhood experience of conflict
and the consequences he now faces. Many families migrated to Monrovia's
suburbs during the conflict. Many remained internally displaced after the

---

³ Pekin is a local term for boy or younger male. It is a pidgin word derived from the Portuguese
word *pequenino* or *pequeno*, meaning small.

conflict reached a state of peace. A very specific generation of youth lived their childhood during the conflict and this created very specific challenges for them. The newly formed and expanded post-conflict communities are full of youths into their late twenties and thirties who missed out on the opportunity of attending bush schools and traditional rites of passage into adulthood. Richie, like many others, missed over a decade of schooling. The inability for many to achieve recognised education and training prevented them from gaining formal employment and independence. In a broken society they have become stagnant and are caught in the consequences of Liberia's history and fragile present. For many youths, like Richie, gaining respect, recognition and a role is achieved on the community football field without the intervention of outsiders. Ageing within Liberian communities, it seems, is the most significant challenge to Liberia's youth population. Given that this group is the largest within Liberia, youth are particularly problematic within the society. Some are targeted through SDP projects and engaged with international and local NGOs but what about boys like Richie who were not actively involved in the war and are therefore not considered a priority by the policymakers and implementers. Football may still be the answer and connection between adults, youths and communities.

Reference

Armstrong, G & Rosbrook-Thompson, J (2012). Terrorizing defences: Sport in the Liberian Civil Conflict. International Review for the Sociology of Sport, 47(3), pp 358–378.

4

In Pursuit of the Winners: SDP and Football Interventions

Development

Development can be viewed as a powerful discourse within a set of institutions that gained momentum and was thrust into global politics post-World War II. Previous to this the International Monetary Fund and the International Bank for Reconstruction and Development were among a group of institutions established in response to growing financial uncertainties after the Great Depression and during the Cold War (Leys 1996). Escobar claimed that the emergence of development practices and development discourse in fact produced the 'Third World' (1995, p. 4). According to Escobar the less developed

> embarked upon the task of 'un-underdeveloping' themselves by subjecting their societies to increasingly systematic, detailed, and comprehensive interventions. As Western experts and politicians started to see certain conditions in Asia, Africa, and Latin America as a problem—mostly what was perceived as poverty and backwardness—a new domain of thought and experience, namely, development, came into being, resulting in a new strategy for dealing with the alleged problems. (p. 6)

© The Editor(s) (if applicable) and The Author(s) 2016
H. Collison, *Youth and Sport for Development*,
DOI 10.1057/978-1-137-52470-6_4

The adoption of development policies, practices and interventions became a concept and task bound by social consciousness and notions of duty as the developed sought to aid the less developed. Mair claims that '"development" refers to a process, and in contemporary contexts the process is a movement towards a condition that some of the world's nations are supposed to have attained' (1984, p. 1). Entwined in this sense of duty is the relationship between former colonial powers and those left in poverty, 'merged in a wider feeling that the rich countries collectively had a responsibility towards the poor ones' (ibid., p. 3). Colonial politics aside, one can progress with the understanding that the emergence of development came at a time when international politics, global security and a growing sense of duty towards the 'Third World' had gained momentum.

Anthropologists have long considered development as an important research area. Escobar concurred with Stacy Leigh Pigg's (1992) claims that 'anthropologists have been for the most part either inside development, as applied anthropologists, or outside development, as the champions of the authentically indigenous and "the native's point of view"' (in Escobar, 1995, p. 15). However, Grillo advocates that 'anthropology can illuminate aspects of development which other disciplines ignore, inevitably this stresses upon the social and cultural dimensions of development that incorporates indigenous perspectives' (Grillo and Stirrat 1997, pp. 5–6).

Anthropologists' interest in development (as opposed to their participation in it as consultant experts) has led them to focus on the social practice of development. These practices are typically opposed to or in tension with the stated aims of development, thus calling them into question. Ferguson (1994), for example, examined development projects financed by the World Bank in South Africa, specifically Lesotho. He considered ways in which development projects replaced the role of the government in attempts to provide technical solutions and gain state control and power. He concluded that 'it may be that what is most important about a "development" project is not so much what it fails to do but what it does do; it may be that its real importance in the end lies in the "side effects"'—in this case reinforcing and expanding state power (p. 254).

Maia Green provides an alternative stance to that of Ferguson and claims that Ferguson holds an 'alienated view of development as a reification of institutional practice in which human agency has a limited role to play' (Green 2003, p. 127). Despite this claim Green and Ferguson draw relatively similar conclusions. Green examined what development agencies actually do, what drives them and the process of policy directives. From her work in Tanzania she considered forums and spaces that brought donors and recipients together, for example, workshops, and she states:

> Development planning involves representatives and professional specialists from donor and recipient organizations, as well as personnel recruited to manage implementation and representatives of the local institutions with which a project is to work. Increasingly, representatives of the so-called beneficiary groups are invited to participate in design and management processes, for example the users of public services or members of farmers' groups who are intended targets of development assistance. (Ibid., p. 128)

This view highlights the importance of social practices when planning development interventions and not the outcome and its side effects; in effect, the multiple human faces of development.

Mosse (2005) focused his work on the internal politics of development and claimed that the existence of a development project depends more on its ability to represent itself as fitting within a frame of policy and funding opportunities than on its outcomes, which are rather marginal to its continuation. Hence, a development project exists upstream of its target population mainly as a series of shifting representations of itself, without any strong relationship to its actual effects. This inevitably overdetermines on-the-ground failure even in successful projects. Mosse states that 'policy models do not generate practices, they are sustained *by* them. Project failure is not the failure to turn design into reality. ... Failure is not a failure to implement the plan, but a *failure of interpretation*' (2005, p. 182). Evaluation and impact studies are important when considering any development project but as Mosse claims, 'This is not possible without close encounters with the administrative politics of development practice' (2005, p. 243). In his opinion evaluating development begins within the internal structures and bureaucracy of an institution before further considerations can be made. In other words, the outcome of development starts 'upstream' of actual projects on the ground and not at the final destination.

As these studies suggest, anthropologists overwhelmingly conclude that development fails. In many ways, assessing the outcome of any project in relation to success or failure can only be determined by the initial focus of inquiry. For anthropologists this presents numerous possibilities such as donors, recipients, implementers and agency staff, state institutions and broader social and economic structures.

Sport and Development

SDP: Adoption and Evolution

The idea that sport is good for society has been recognised for a long time. Recently, this notion has shifted from an educational to a developmental frame. While a great deal has been invested in sport, the outcomes of SDP are really unknown, and the notion has not been systematically applied (Coalter 2007, 2009, 2013). The UN's adoption of the SDP policy came at a time of increased scepticism towards its ability to resolve conflict, sustain peace and develop post-conflict civil societies. The UN needed to reform and rebrand to raise its profile and reassure its international members that they were still *the* entity for global security and development. However, this new direction needed to be sold to its international audience and partners at cost-effective prices—SDP became the logical choice and vogue policy for international peacekeeping and development.

The programmes that promote sport for the purposes of peace and development in the twenty-first century are a consequence of a wide variety of socio-political influences but draw fundamentally on the ancient belief that 'sport is good'. Philosophers as early as Plato and Rousseau noted the importance of sport for personal development. Rousseau's '*Emile*' states: 'Give his body constant exercise, make it strong and healthy in order to make him good and wise' (cited in Arnold 1997, p. 44). The past 40 years have seen collective protests around sport that, combined with individual initiatives, have placed sport and its practice and delivery high on the agenda of several entities: NGOs, governments, charities, faith-based organisations and the various notions that thrive under the title of Corporate Social Responsibility (CSR). It is relevant to research enquiries that we understand how sport has become an essential part of their post-conflict strategy. Whilst not denying the potential value and popularity of football in a developmental environment, I will argue that its adoption and evolution by the UN—which has spread over the past decade throughout the world of peacekeeping and philanthropy—are a result of failed military interventions and post-conflict reconciliation and rehabilitation programming.

The inclusion of sport as a tool to achieve development objectives provides cost-effective programming that can—and does—attract celebrity endorsements and also raises marketing. In a socio-political milieu invariably driven by 'value for money' how does a project—any project—based around sport bring proven cost-effective results? In the absence of effective rehabilitation programming, what can address the marginalised, unsatisfied and potentially volatile youth of a post-conflict society? This provokes us to ask: What are the primary intentions and priorities of aid agency sporting programmes? Crucially, we have to ask: What is considered a success and how is this measured? Amidst the enthusiasm for promoting the game we must examine whether the game reflects a wider post-conflict society and whether in the post-conflict milieu it merely reaffirms the position of the youth and their relationship to others. Inevitably we need to ask: What happens when the game—that is seen as an answer to so many people—ends? (Coalter 2010; Darnell 2012; Giulianotti and Armstrong 2014).

It has been argued that 'most of today's sport and development projects are merely spot solutions which as a rule reach only a limited number of people and hardly have any impact beyond their immediate surroundings' (SDC 2005, p. 77). Since the beginning of the millennium, the UN and, increasingly, local NGOs have considered sport as a method of assisting and realising ideals for peacekeeping, security and development. The value of sport has long been recognised by educators, philosophers and humanitarian agencies yet the UN's recent millennium promotion of sport is a somewhat radical tactic in its long-established peace and development programmes. The role of sport and its connection to development was formally recognised at an institutional level in 2003, as the

Amsterdam Conference[1] Report stated: 'The idea that sport and personal and social development are related is as old as society' (2003, p. 3). The value of sport as a practice tends to be the principle focus of many global development conferences, to sustain momentum and build partnerships. An acknowledgement of modern sport and a fundamental shift of recognition have influenced a number of local, regional and global partners when considering youth, development and rehabilitation—especially in post-conflict societies (UN 2013). Sport as directed by the UN as an ideal means for peacekeeping, development, security and reconciliation continues to serve as an unproven and unmeasured attempt to improve the lives of the underdeveloped; arguably this is an alternative to previously endorsed unsuccessful peacekeeping strategies.

The United Nations and SDP

Peacekeeping: Increased Demands: Increased Failure?

The UN serves as the principle advocate for SDP but this was not envisioned as part of its organisation or included in its philosophy at its conception. Since its formation in 1945 the UN has been a global organisation with the aim of facilitating cooperation in international law, international security, economic development and social equity. The principle directives of the UN are to settle disputes and undertake coercive measures against any state that poses a threat to another. Peacekeeping decisions are the primary role of the five permanent members (UK, USA, Russia, China and France) along with the ten non-permanent members elected by the General Assembly for 2-year terms. If armed conflict is already under way, the Security Council—comprising the fifteen members—appeals for military action to stop, encourages ceasefires whilst procedures are established and attempts to resolve the conflict. This system of peacekeeping was established early in the formation of the

---

[1] The Amsterdam conference was the first in a series of 'Next Step' conferences aimed to gather experts and advocates in the field of SDP. This included government representatives, development organisations and academics.

UN. The fundamental management of such a task has seen little change. Throughout its history the UN's success and failures in peacekeeping have gone largely unassessed. This absence may stem from the very nature of its existence, as one authority states: 'The organization suffers from a lack of accountability and difficulty in measuring its own performance' (Jett 1999, p. 178). This lack of audit has become a contributing factor to the decline in the confidence of international members in the UN peace-keeping programme. The process of peacekeeping has been criticised for both its time-consuming procedures and indeed its very assumption that the parties involved are willing to cooperate[2] (Jett 1999; Baehr and Gordenker 2005).

The early activities of the Security Council saw little by way of effective resolution of the conflicts it intervened in[3] (Howard 2008, Barnett 1997, Goulding 1999). However, in the absence of any other agency willing to take on such a role the UN continues to be the primary agency for world security and peacekeeping. Regional conflicts kept the UN's peace-keepers busy throughout the 1990s. In 1991 Somalia's dictatorial govern-ment collapsed, resulting in violence, famine and the huge displacement of persons.[4] The UN agencies and NGOs could do little to help those caught up in the fighting between a number of self-declared autonomous states. The desperation of such refugees and the extent of the violence was highly publicised to the extent that the UN Security Council was forced to send a peacekeeping force called United Nations Operations in Somalia (UNOSOM) consisting initially of only 500 soldiers as a response to the

---

[2] Louise Frechette, Deputy Secretary General of the UN claims: 'Our member states remain deeply divided on key issues—divisions which paralyse collective action and cripple multilateral institu-tions. ... We still lack adequate standby arrangements to enable quick deployment, with the neces-sary strategic reserve' (cited in Heinbecker and Goff 2005, pp. 11–13).

[3] Between 1960 and 1964, the UN Forces in Congo (ONUC) provided 20,000 personnel and soldiers to Congo. The mission was deemed ineffectual by many an observer when the ONUC-departed fighting resumed until the end of the cold war. It was a mission that nearly bankrupted the UN. Other campaigns followed in Somalia (1992), Rwanda (1994) and Yugoslavia (1999) and were all tainted with massacres and brutal civil conflicts that the UN could not and did not prevent.

[4] UN Security Resolution 733 and UN Security Council Resolution 746 formed a strategy to deal with the Somalian civil unrest. Since 1991 an estimated 350,000–1,000,000 Somalis died as a consequence of conflict and poverty. There were an estimated 1,000,000 refugees and almost 5,000,000 people threatened by hunger and disease.

growing humanitarian catastrophe. The failings of UNOSOM to have any impact on the situation saw continued fighting and an estimated 2.5 million people suffer from severe malnutrition and diseases. This provoked the USA to send in 28,000 soldiers under the factional title the United Task Force (UNITAF) to Somalia with instructions to use all necessary means to carry out the task and restore and maintain peace. The UN approved this action but in 1993 replaced UNITAF with UNOSOM II with an extensive mandate to rebuild the Somali state. UNOSOM II comprised of 28,000 personnel including 22,000 troops and 8000 logistic and civilian staff. However, the peacekeeping strategy used was unfamiliar to the UN; military force was used largely by the US Marines against violent but unarmed citizens. The cessation of hostilities that was hoped for did not happen, fighting never truly ended and at no stage was a common ground found for reconciliation or peace talks: 'The International intervention in Somalia failed ultimately because it was poorly conceived, poorly planned, poorly executed and was erroneously perceived to be a "quick fix" and a rapid exit operation' (Mohamoud 2006, p. 135). A US unit acting outside the UN command structure was later attacked by Somali militia and eighteen soldiers were killed. The USA withdrew its troops soon after and the UN ended its peacekeeping programme in 1994. The UN could not restore peace and withdrew. The campaign had failed.

The Need for a New Strategy

After the Somalia conflict the UN was forced to reconsider its peace-keeping and security strategies. From 1991 in an attempt to expand the functions of peacekeeping and enforcement the UN Security Council approved over 100 resolutions. Conflict in the former Yugoslavia during the 1990s forced the UN to approach its involvement in zones of conflict differently. The Yugoslavia crisis saw the Security Council create a UN Protection Force (UNPROFOR) of some 14,000 soldiers. At the height of the Yugoslavia conflict human rights violations and violence reached critical levels, and tens of thousands of refugees were left helpless. An arms embargo, a sea blockade and a 'no-fly zone' were imposed on Bosnia and Herzegovina by The North Atlantic Treaty Organization (NATO),

America and UNPROFOR. The situation escalated and became a military engagement. NATO air strikes were carried out in 1995 but reservations persisted among the commanders in charge as the repercussions were catastrophic for the ethnic minorities ostensibly protected by the UN. As a consequence of the NATO air strikes a Serbian battalion rounded up thousands of Muslim men from a UN camp and killed them in what was described as 'the worst violations of human rights in Europe after World War II' (Baehr and Gordenker 2005, p. 87). A ceasefire was called in 1995 and a peace agreement was signed by Yugoslavia, Bosnia, Herzegovina and Croatia. The Yugoslavia conflict exposed the limitations of the UN to deal with large-scale military conflicts. Its failure illustrated how the UN was unprepared for late twentieth-century civil wars and their accompanying ethnic conflicts. The situation was highly complex; ethnic cleansing, military atrocities and fleeing inhabitants typified such conflicts. The need for the UN to be supported by other international organisations became obvious. The involvement of NATO,[5] the Organisation for Security and Cooperation in Europe (OSCE), and the European Union in this conflict left the UN with less responsibility. UNPROFOR was a peacekeeping force without any peace to maintain— it was a force in limbo. The UN was mainly involved with the humanitarian effort of dealing with refugees through their The United Nations High Commissioner for Refugees (UNHCR) agency. This highlighted the UN's willingness to step back in large-scale, unfamiliar operations if alternatives were provided.

Whist the UN had achieved some success with security and peace-keeping, many operations were time-consuming, expensive and rarely achieved their aims. Some operations were abandoned by small UN agencies and international aid groups were sent in to represent humanitarian efforts. The 2003 outbreak of hostilities and genocide in Darfur is a prime example of the UN failing to fulfil its promises and allowing aid groups like the British Red Cross to carry out humanitarian work. MacQueen suggests the following:

---

[5] NATO was established upon the signing of the North Atlantic Treaty in 1949. Currently twenty-eight nations are members of NATO from North America and Europe, with the main purpose of creating an alliance amongst nations, protection and engagement in humanitarian global efforts.

A well-intentioned initial response by the local agency may prove unable to make a significant impact on the situation. In the meantime the United Nations, which is fundamentally reluctant to become closely involved, resists the logic of this situation and remains at a distance. Then, when circumstances reach a point where action becomes unavoidable, the UN response is inadequate to meet the needs of the ever growing crisis. (2006, p. 238)

The UN Security Council Resolution 1706 authorised a rapid deployment of a force of over 20,000 civilian police and troops. Ten months later only 200 UN technical personnel were employed and the number of conflict-affected civilians had grown to 4.7 million (Reeves 2007, n.p). The UN's reliance on peacekeeping partnerships allowed others to take the primary role in active conflict management and resolution. The UN took a step back in the immediate intervention of conflict and focused on seeking resolution and humanitarian involvement after a crisis. Conflicts that escalated despite local agency attempts for resolution created primary failings for the UN as its actions in active conflict were inadequate and ineffective.

The UN's reliance on local agency intervention during conflicts could also be seen in the case of Liberia, West Africa. The UN did not provide any military assistance throughout the civil conflict of 1989–2003, instead choosing to leave the responsibility to The Economic Community of West African States Monitoring Group (ECOMOG) and ECOWAS. This local agency provided the primary military resources and personnel to stop the civil conflict and bring about peace. The UNMIL did not begin its on-the-field observations until 2003 preferring to support the state of peace already established.

With such a history and a growing lack of confidence in its peacekeeping programmes and missions the UN needed a new direction, specifically one that could raise its profile, provide positive press and be integrated into tasks at a low cost. This was available in sport for peace programmes.

UN, the IOC and Sport

The UN's support for the Olympic Movement was not evident until 1993, when the International Olympic Committee (IOC) proposed a resolution to the UN General Assembly to observe the 'Olympic Truce',[6] entitled *Building a peaceful and better world through sport and the Olympic ideal*. The resolution proclaimed its interest in contributing to international understanding and the maintenance of peace whilst supporting the purposes and principles of the UN Charter[7] (UN Resolution 48/11, 1993). In 2000 the UN Secretary General, Kofi Annan, recognised the importance and similarities of the UN and the Olympic ideals and stated that 'Olympic ideals are also United Nations ideals: tolerance, equality, fair play and, most of all, peace. Together, the Olympics and the United Nations can be a winning team' (Annan 2000). Pierre De Coubertin, the founder of the Modern Olympic Games, was a key advocate of the value of sport. He declared that the 'aim of the Olympics was to place sport in the service of harmonious individual development and the establishment of a peaceful society' (cited in Schwery 2003, p. 16). In a sense the IOC and UN were made for each other; why they had not joined forces before remains a mystery.

One can argue that the UN's adoption of the SDP ideal is a reaction to the capacities of contemporary sport to engage and access populations and the increasing rate of commercialism, globalisation and celebrity endorsements, all of which sporting practice can bring to any humanitarian, development or philanthropic organisation. The Olympic Movement has been implementing this philosophy for some 100 years. Many organisations, for example, the Fédération Internationale de Football Association (FIFA), were well ahead of the UN in their sport for development work. The FIFA 'Goal Programme' began in 1999 under FIFA President Joseph Blatter and aimed to promote football projects and development work in the world's most vulnerable countries. The subtext was perhaps win-

---

[6] The tradition of the 'Truce' or 'Ekecheiria' was established in ancient Greece in the ninth century BC by the signing of a treaty between three kings. During the Truce period, the athletes, artists and their families, as well as ordinary pilgrims, could travel in total safety to participate in or attend the Olympic Games and return afterwards to their respective countries. As the opening of the Games approached, the sacred Truce was proclaimed and announced by citizens of Elis who travelled throughout Greece to pass on the message (IOC 2013, Olympic Truce).

[7] The UN Charter was signed on 26 June 1945, in San Francisco, at the conclusion of the UN conference on International Organisation. It is the fundamental treaty for the UN stating its purpose, defining criteria for membership and describing the structure and institutions of the UN and their powers.

ning Blatter votes for his future presidency campaigns. The artificial all-weather pitch laid at the Antoinette Tubman Stadium (ATS) in Monrovia in 1999 was funded by the Goal Programme. The involvement of governments in aiding those less fortunate, the media's attention to sport, international organisations' philanthropic obligations and athletes using their status to gain funding for sport in development projects has increased. This makes the inclusion of sport in development a safe option with huge international interest guaranteed and financial backing evident.

Evolution Within Sport and Development Practices

In 1992 the Norwegian Lillehammer Olympic Organizing Committee (LOOC) established 'Olympic Aid' in preparation for its hosting of the 1994 Olympic Winter Games. The aims of Olympic Aid were to provide financial and material support for war-torn countries and areas of distress, notably Yugoslavia at the time it was engulfed in civil war. The original partnerships included the Red Cross, Save the Children, the Norwegian Refugee Council and the Norwegian Church Fund. Athletes were the driving force behind both raising awareness and generating funding. Olympic athletes were chosen to be 'ambassadors' to assist the fundraising effort prior to and during the games. An initial $18 million was raised. The principal exponent of the scheme was Norwegian speed skater Johann Olav Koss, who donated a large portion of his prize money and challenged fellow athletes—and the public—to donate money for each gold medal won towards projects for peace in war-damaged Yugoslavia, Eritrea, Guatemala, Afghanistan and Lebanon. In 1996 Olympic Aid formed a partnership with UNICEF and raised $13 million through donations received from ten countries and athletes prior to and during the Olympic Games held in Atlanta. The funds assisted UNICEF in vaccinating some 12.2 million children. What such practices and procedures showed was that UN agencies were proactive in collecting their investments and forming partnerships.[8]

---

[8] The partnership between 'Olympic Aid' and the UN continued during the 2000 Sydney Games. Olympic Aid supported UNHCR efforts to assist Eritreans fleeing into Sudan by holding an

In 2002 the United Nations Inter-Agency Task Force on Sport for Development and Peace was established and Chaired by Adolf Ogi. The former Swiss President was appointed in February 2001 as the Under Secretary General and Special Advisor to the Secretary General on Sport for Development and Peace, and Carol Bellamy, Executive Director of UNICEF. The Task Force was to assess the role of sport within the UN system, critique its implementation to date and provide recommendation for future policy. In 2003 a document titled 'Sport for Development and Peace: Towards achieving the Millennium Development Goals' was produced by the Task Force. This recommended that sport should be better integrated into the development agenda, and used as a tool for development and peace but meanwhile required greater attention and resources from the UN and from governments for sporting programmes (UN 2003, pvi). The aim of the Task Force was to specifically manage and 'promote the more systematic and coherent use of sport in development and peace activities' (UN 2003, p. 1). The Task Force was also responsible for generating greater support for the UN's sport campaign amongst governments and sport-related organisations. This was not an easy task, and in its own admission, 'sport has yet to be mainstreamed into the development agenda or the United Nations system. In general, sports initiatives have been ad hoc, informal and isolated' (UN 2003, p. 1). Despite this, the Task Force personnel confidently proclaimed that 'the fundamental elements of sport make it a viable and practical tool to support the achievement of the MDGs' (UN 2003, pv). In March 2003 the UN decided to acknowledge the inclusion into policy of the use and importance of sport when the General Assembly proclaimed 2005 as the International Year of Sport and Physical Education (IYSPE) 'to encourage governments, sport-related organizations and athletes to help achieve the Millennium Development Goals'[9] (2005).

Olympic Festival and Coaching Clinics for children in refugee camps along the Sudan–Eritrea border.

[9] The Millennium Development Goals are to (1) eradicate extreme poverty, (2) achieve universal primary education. (3) promote gender equality and empower women, (4) reduce child mortality, (5) improve maternal health, (6) combat HIV, malaria and other diseases, (7) ensure environmental sustainability and (8) develop global partnerships.

Arising out of the appointment of Adolf Ogi, the first International Conference on Sport and Development was held in February 2003 at the Swiss Academy for Sport in Magglingen, Switzerland. The stated aim of the conference was to 'make all parties concerned aware of the possibilities that sport offers for development and the promotion of peace, to define a common ground and to launch strategies, initiatives and measures' (Ogi 2003a). Alongside the UN agencies of the World Health Organization (WHO), UNICEF, and United Nations Environment Programme (UNEP) stood Jacques Rogge, President of the IOC, as well as dozens of international government officials, sports federations, NGOs and a host of international athletes. Two significant items emerged: the Magglingen Declaration on Sport and Development, and a list of recommendations for the role of sport in development. The former spoke of 'sport's potential to improve physical and mental health that will help to heal emotional scars, and overcome trauma for people in situations of conflict, crisis or social tensions' (Ogi 2003b). It also proclaimed the generic ability of sport to overcome barriers of race, religion, gender, disability, social class and to develop societies in a respectful, fair and inclusive way. This introduced a concept—the development of society through sport—and a theoretical construct for all to follow. The aim of the conference was to build partnerships between the world of sport and development work as well as to attain support from governments, UN agencies, sports federations, the sports goods industry, businesses and NGOs to collectively contribute to a sense of development via sport or as the author stated to mark the 'first step to our commitment to create a better world through sport' (Ogi 2003a).

The UN 'Sports for Development' campaign emerged through the initiatives of other sports organisations, independent schemes and the utilisation of accomplished athletes. Collaboration between regional, national and international governments, development agencies, private organisations and athletes has seen the quest for development through sport become a multi-partnership project working under the umbrella of the UN. Practically the UN can provide facilities within its headquarters, access to UN personnel to support the necessary committees, financial assistance and most importantly the brand of the UN that attracts athletes and the sports industry, and provides a global audience. The UN has a huge capacity to help delivery.

A 2003 report on the UN Inter-Agency Task Force for SDP provides an insight into the efficacy and implementation of sport policies. The UN report states:

> The potential of sport as a tool for development and peace has yet to be fully realized. The use of sport remains outside the mainstream of thinking among United Nations agencies. While sport and play are repeatedly acknowledged as a human right, they are not always seen as a priority and have even been called the 'forgotten right'. Sport is seen as a by-product of development, not as an engine. (UN 2003, p. 2)

Clearly discrepancies exist as to the place of sport in the development world. An obvious absence of planning and implementation was and is recognised. So we can ask 'Was sport really being adopted by the UN peacekeeping and development agencies or is this a case of creating appealing rhetoric, tokenism and self-promotion?'

In Oct 2007 the Liberian President Ellen Johnson Sirleaf speaking of the possibilities that sport had for her country stated that 'programs (SDP) being implemented for the children of Liberia will set the basis for the future.' This was in response to 'Right to Play' initiatives in the country. But, in 2009 when I visited the 'Right to Play' headquarters in Monrovia, I was refused access to their work by the one employee stationed there because 'most of our projects have finished; the only ones left are in the interior.' Although present in Liberia from 2006, Right to Play programmes were in operation in just three counties: Montserrado, Margibi and Bong. The impact, accessibility and purpose of these projects were questionable. Certainly 'Right to Play' projects were not evident in some of the poorest and most war-affected locations in Monrovia. In 2010 I visited Bomi, Bong and Grand Bassa counties and still no form of UN Sport for Development and Peace projects were active. In 2008 the 'Right to Play' agency facilitated a workshop for football coaches in Monrovia. A participant described how the course focused on the role of the coach as a 'father, advisor and role model' located within football teams in communities, holding—in the words of 'Right to Play'—a parallel position with the church and preaching a moral ethos. The workshop attendee stated his frustration: 'I don't think it was a proper course, we didn't do any practical and there was no follow up.' A visitor could not walk in Liberia for more than 10 minutes without witnessing makeshift goalposts, children playing with rolled-up bags for footballs or people crowded around small televisions to watch international football, yet there were no SDP projects being delivered despite a substantial UN presence in the country.

Sport and Human Development?

Integral to the role of sport within the UN's framework is 'development', a word with no precise definition but insinuating a multitude of meanings. Rist regarded 'development' as a buzzword—a term in vogue for the last 60 years. He suggested that 'despite its widespread usage, the meaning of the term "development" remains vague, tending to refer to a set of beliefs and assumptions about the nature of social progress rather than anything more precise' (Rist 2007, p. 485).

How is development—whatever the definition—via sport meant to work? And what, we might ask, is sport meant to develop precisely? The answer is provided to some extent by The Swiss Agency for Development and Cooperation (SDC), UNDP and UN Inter-Agency Task Force who agree that 'to achieve maximum "development" all organisations, governments, sports associations, international organisations, the private sector, NGOs, the media and the scientific community work together, cooperate and incorporate their specific areas of expertise collectively' (SDC 2005, p. 20). But can sport become a principle exponent of the development process? A short answer perhaps is available from Mahbub Ul Haq,[10] founder of Human Development Report, an independent annual publication for UNDP, which states: 'The objective of development is to create an enabling environment for people to enjoy long, healthy and creative lives' (Human Development Report 1990, p. 9). Common sense tells us

---

[10] Mahbub Ul Haq was a pioneer of the Human Development Theory and founder of the Human Development Report for the United Nations Development Programme. From 1989 to 1995 he was Special Advisor to UNDP administrator and in 1996 he founded the Human Development Centre in Pakistan.

that sport and regular physical exercise is an essential element to living a long and healthy life, so it would be illogical not to incorporate sport into the development process.

The UN Inter-Agency Task Force offers further semantic anomalies when it defines sustainable human development as central to the UN sporting system. Encompassing the values of 'health and well-being, social integration among communities and individuals, education, knowledge and respect of environment and increasing social capital' leads ultimately to the promotion of human development. It does not state, define, or strategise the concept of sustainability (UN 2003, p. 3). In terms of economic potential, sport is considered by the UN and its partners as an effective low-cost strategy to achieving development goals; it is in their words 'a low-cost, high-impact tool' (Right to Play 2008, p. 249). Economic developments are considered by the UN Task Force when they state that the 'economic potential of sport is highlighted by its economic weight, resulting from activities such as the manufacture of sporting goods, sports events, sport-related services and the media' (UN 2003, p. 3). Hosting sporting events to raise money and awareness, and appointing sports stars as Goodwill Ambassadors[11] is how the UN has supported this claim.

Fundraising to Implementation: Evolution of the Ideal

In 2003 'Olympic Aid' evolved into 'Right to Play'; it developed from a fundraising vehicle to an implementing NGO. This evolution enabled Olympic as well as non-Olympic athletes to become sporting ambassadors and the acceptance of non-Olympic sports thereby increased the potential for partnerships. Arising out of this, projects in more than twenty countries in Africa, Asia and the Middle East are currently supported by elite athletes from some forty countries. The ambassadors include Chelsea

---

[11] UN ambassadors are appointed via invitation by the heads or individual agencies of the UN or by voluntarily showing interest in specific causes. UNICEF currently has over 150 ambassadors. UNDP's Goodwill Ambassadors include Ivory Coast and Chelsea footballer Didier Drogba, Brazil and Barcelona footballer Ronaldo, the Russian-born former Wimbledon tennis champion Maria Sharapova, former France and Real Madrid footballer Zinedine Zidane and star of American basketball Lebron James.

Football Club, tennis champion Martina Hingis and Ethiopian long-distance gold medallist Haile Gebreselassie. Principle supporters include numerous national governments, SDC and UNICEF. The organisation describes itself as an athlete-driven international humanitarian organisation that partners with athletes from around the world to bring sport and play to the lives of children affected by war, poverty, disease and illness (Right to Play 2006, pp. 1–5). 'Right to Play' focuses on four strategic programme areas: (1) basic education and child development, (2) health promotion and disease prevention, (3) conflict resolution and peace education, and (4) community development and participation. The organisation claims to be 'a global-scale implementer of sport for development and peace programmes and takes an active role in driving research and policy development in this area and in supporting children's rights' (Right to Play 2006, p. 4).[12]

The development strategy of 'Right to Play' is a multinational, multiyear programme titled *Basic Education through Sport and Play for Children in West and Francophone Africa*. Similar projects have been implemented in Benin, Ghana, Liberia, Mali and Rwanda. This programme focuses on a commitment by governments to provide a basic education, to work towards the MDGs and to work in line with the UN Convention on the Rights of a Child. Sport has been given a huge responsibility towards achieving the vast and complex desired outcomes. Without tried and tested strategies and tangible results the question of whether sport is working in line with UN philosophy remains.

In 2007 the Sport for Development and Peace International Working Group (SDP-IWG) hosted a conference in Accra, Ghana, entitled 'The Accra Call for Action on Sport for Development and Peace'. The purpose of the 3-day meet was to bring together ministers from forty-three nations in Ghana's capital to discuss ways to harness the power of sport to advance national and international development goals. Also in attendance were various UN agencies including UN Habitat, which is responsible for providing adequate shelter for all. UNHCR, intergovernmental

---

[12] One example of their work is evident in Rwanda. 'Right to Play' considered their remit in such a milieu to be 'conflict resolution, care of orphans, gaps in healthy child development, HIV and Aids and improved inclusion of girls and vulnerable children within society' (Play to learn, Rwanda). UNICEF supported the 'Right to Play' project by working with the Rwandan Government.

bodies such as African Union and European Commission, and NGOs. High on the agenda was the implementation of sport policies in national and international frameworks and ways to accelerate intergovernmental outreach and engagement. The outcome was a set of recommendations which include the request for 'Right to Play' to examine the feasibility and develop a strategy for extending the SDP-IWG mandate for 2008–2010 as well as urging UN agencies, programmes and funds to 'fully recognize, and provide tangible support to countries wishing to harness the peace and development potential of sport' (SDP-SDP-IWG 2007). The SDP-IWG also recognised the need to continue its work with the UN until 2015 if it were to contribute in the quest to achieve the MDGs. The role of the SDP-IWG is embedded in promoting the UN sport for development ethos and endorsing this to a global audience while constructing policies and recommendations that can translate to the Olympics and national and international agencies and governments. Such conferences confirmed not only the SDP ideal but the expectation of primary advocates and organisations for governments and local agencies to build SDP into their project frameworks.

Conferences and promotional events for SDP became fashionable within the development and aid world at the turn of the millennium. An interview conducted with an academic and SDP researcher in 2008 shed some light on the purpose and content of such events:

I expected more critical debates on sport and to which degree sport can develop local communities in ways which is actually beneficial for those communities. Sport and development conferences are not like academic conferences. Yet the realisation that this was more of a charismatic, evangelical NGO-rally to raise money for sport and development projects than a critical forum left me disappointed. It was mildly shocking to realise that during one of the conferences people discussed whether 'negative data', i.e. data suggesting 'sport doesn't work' should be included in research reports. ... From a political point of view it would be nice to see sport being used as more than publicity stunts. ... In post-conflict areas I think sport can unite and give kids a more positive outlook on life, but we need to cool down expectations of what 'sport can do'. (Interview conducted 29/4/2008)

If the SDP theory was driven by potential and assumption its advocates would be keen to drive the image and Victorian beliefs of muscular Christianity. The concept of muscular Christianity emerged from the English public school system; headmasters of prestigious public schools were, in the main, also ministers of the church—Christian values were inserted into the educational system to produce Christian gentlemen. Part of this curriculum was the pursuit of physical education and team sports:

> Team games, it was said, developed moral character, patriotism, and the courage to stand up for what was right; to defend the underdog, to champion fairness, and to exercise self-control. If a young man was strong in body; pure in heart; faithful and loyal to friend, family and country; knew his duty before God; put service to the team ahead of himself; and adhered to the rules of the game, he was a muscular Christian. (Morford and McIntosh 1993, p. 72)

In relation to SDP Giulianotti claimed that it was an 'evangelical argument regarding sport's innate goodness' (2004, p. 367). Those tasked with promoting the concept focused on the sport and presumed the outcome without measure or assessment. Sport was easy to sell and implement in challenging environments and this was its fundamental credential.

The Price of Sport

The assessment and evaluation of development projects through sport is a contentious area. Progress is generally intangible and almost impossible to quantify: 'The relative newness of the movement and its, until now, limited links with the mainstream development community, has resulted in little substantial analysis of how the impact of sport-in-development programmes on recipient communities should be evaluated' (Levermore and Beacom 2009, p. 254). In 2003 Johann Olav Koss, President of 'Right to Play', admitted as much, stating: 'We do not evaluate enough … we need to prove what we say that we do' (Amsterdam Conference report 2004, p. 15). Three years later, Alison Qualter Berna, a Sports for Development Officer for UNICEF stated that 'the need for the monitoring and evaluation (M&E) of sport for development initiatives has become apparent' (CCPA 2006, p. 36), which suggests that few saw the need before 2006. Many would argue that the need for M&E should have been obvious rather than ambiguous. Coalter suggests that M&E 'should provide the basis for a dialogue, both between organisations and sponsors and within organisations, and be as concerned with organisational development' instead of 'reflecting sponsors' need to discover if their desired outcomes have been achieved' (Coalter 2006, p. 150). The issue is complicated and driven by self-interest: summary findings and sustainability reports have focused on how to continue projects dependent on funding and international support rather than the assessment of their impact. Sports psychologist Auweele suggests a possible reason for the reluctance to evaluate: 'There may be some resistance to reflection, monitoring and evaluation because one feels controlled and patronized by donors and sponsors whose main interest is accountability, i.e. relating financial support with proof of efficiency and sustainable effects' (Auweele et al. 2006, p. 16).

Despite the criticisms, sport continues to sell to those responsible for the poorest and most vulnerable populations in the global south. There is a strong link between economic underdevelopment and potential for actual violent conflict. According to the World Bank, in 2003 there were forty-one countries affected by conflict, of which thirty-two were low-income countries. The World Bank has stated bluntly: 'During the past 15 years some 15 of the 20 poorest countries have had violent conflicts' (2003, p. 2). In 2005 Julie French, a Research Assistant for the UN Institute for Disarmament Research, stated that 'an economic solution must be the first step in meeting human development needs' (French 2005, p. 62). Despite this claim, Ban Ki-Moon, current Secretary General of the UN, supports the beliefs of Adolf Ogi that 'the United Nations can make full use of sport as a cost-effective tool' (Ogi 2007, p. 1). This fascinating claim may explain the UN's adoption of sport. The SDC claims that 'sport can improve economic development by creating employment and income opportunities as well as contributing to a more productive economy by improving people's health and lessening the burden on public services' (SDC 2005, p. 15). It did not elaborate on the nature of such opportunities; nor did it mention the injuries that would inevitably occur from sporting participation that would burden the scarce health services of many nations. At the same time the 2006 SDP-IWG sought to explain the reason for shortcomings in some SDP projects as part of the MDGs stating: 'Common reasons for shortfalls in the attainment of the MDGs include poor governance, poverty traps with local and national economies unable to make investments, unequal distribution of economic development within countries' (SDP-IWG 2006, p. 15). These were big issues. What seems to be argued here is that if people could not eat, many did not want sport projects, however well intentioned they were.

A cycle seems evident here: conflict and the need for development tend to arise in poor countries; costly interventions have been the first step to help these countries, yet the UN has historically had severe financial problems due to numerous, long, expensive peacekeeping and security operations as well as significant fees not being paid by large financial contributors (Baehr and Gordenker 2005, p. 58). Sport is suddenly targeted as a cost-efficient approach to aid development, yet such projects need financial backing to secure effective implementation and sustainability. So in the absence of funding and any assurance of effectiveness, what do the policymakers do?

Currently the UN still heavily endorses sport and continues to proclaim how in post-conflict situations, UN peacekeeping operations' sporting programmes cannot, on their own, stop or solve acute conflicts: 'It represents a flexible and cost-effective medium for post-conflict relief work and peace building as well as conflict prevention' (UN 2012). Current Under-Secretary-General and Special Advisor to the United Nations Secretary General on Sport for Development and Peace, Wilfried Lemke, continues to advocate increased support, partnership and implementation of development within and through sport during the post-MDGs era. This is particularly evident within the *UNOSDP 2014 Annual Report* and the conversations surrounding the 2015 Sustainable Development Goals.

Within the Liberian context sport for peace programmes were adopted by UNMIL. On 2 March 2007 a 5-week-long 'Sport for Peace' tournament was launched by UNMIL with the support of the government of Liberia, the IOC, sporting associations and NGOs. This culminated in over thirty games of football, volleyball and kickball in various parts of the country. During the tournament's launch, IOC President Jacques Rogge stated the philosophy behind the programme:

> This project is an excellent example of how different organisations and institutions can create synergies to achieve a shared objective—the promotion of a peaceful society in Liberia. Sport is, in essence, the only language understood by everyone and has a huge as well as educational impact: sports activities promote interaction, tolerance and the spirit of fair play. If youngsters learn through sport to respect each other, they will be well equipped for their role in contributing to a better society. (UNMIL 2007a, n.p)

It is unclear how many people had access to these events but it is estimated that an average of 2000 people attended each of the games (UNMIL 2007a). The tournament was combined with 'sensitization in support of community initiatives that promote peace, reconciliation and recovery, as well as awareness of HIV/AIDS, rape, sexual exploitation and other forms of gender-based violence' (UNMIL 2007b). Sport provided an opportunity for education and aided the work of partner agencies. I was unable to observe any UNMIL-managed 'Sport for Peace' projects or any form of planned sporting activity for youths implemented by the UN or its partners. By 2009 they were no longer active. The lack of any relationship, communication or friendliness between UN peacekeepers and the Liberian people supported the assumptions made during the early phase of research: that SDP projects in post-conflict environments lacked sustainability and potentially acted as token gestures that constructed desired images.

A primary question then develops: What happens when the footballs are taken away and the projects move on? In a post-conflict setting the lack of facilities, amenities and sheer poverty acts as the most significant barrier to change; football can act as a gatekeeper for access as long as there is something meaningful and substantial to back it up within the context of intervention. Otherwise we can assume that football provides access to playing games and little else. The history and evolution of the SDP theory and its inclusion in the development policy is what has driven the initial research interest. Liberia represents a country in turmoil as a result of conflict and an environment sustained by one of the largest UN peacekeeping forces in history. Consequent NGO activity has also increased since 2003 as a response to the post-conflict need. It was an obvious choice for such a research interest and the images presented on many development publications and SDP web sites suggested it was an appropriate decision. My field observation between 2009 and 2012 steered the research into different directions, but at the core there remained the theory, belief and use of football for SDP and youth rehabilitation, reconciliation and reconstruction.

SDP for Success Stories: Images in Black and White

Over half the population in Liberia is under the age of twenty-five. In the absence of structured and well-financed state interventions to support young people and without sustained and appropriately resourced provisions in place for education and guidance there is a severe lack of infrastructure to engage and develop young people. In 2009, the United States Agency for International Development (USAID) conducted a Liberian youth fragility assessment and claimed that 'Liberia fits the description of a fragile state. A fragile state is defined as "Governments and state structures lack capacity and/or political will to deliver safety and security, good governance and poverty reduction to their citizens"' (USAID 2009, p ix).

The consequence of this fragile state is the overwhelming influx of international aid, humanitarian assistance and peace-building agencies in Liberia. In 2008 an estimated 180 foreign charities were active in Liberia, most focusing on marginal groups such as women and youth (Fuest 2010, p. 7–8). The momentum behind building a peaceful civil society in Liberia posed an opportunity for agencies to incorporate SDP—and specifically football—in line with its evolution and inclusion in the development policy over the past decade. UNICEF claims the following:

The sport is more than just a game. It's a positive lifestyle. It's a way to promote a peaceful approach to conflict resolution. It's a tool for wooing a young body away from the lure of drugs, unsafe sex, or violence. It's a way to help ensure that young people grow up healthy, fit and full of self-esteem. (UNICEF, n.d, n.p)

It was recognised that sport could seduce and lure young people to NGOs and intervention programmes whilst addressing social problems in broken societies. Overwhelmingly sport, and football in particular, is used by aid agencies for self-promotion, fund-raising, access, engagement and questionably intervention. Can the problem of 'youth' in Liberia be addressed with football?

The heavy reliance on foreign aid intervention has created numerous partnerships between donors from the Global North and locally managed NGOs. The relationship between the two parties can take many forms but generically provides expectations, requirements and 'give and take' from both sides (Green 2000, p. 68). Overall what is required is the sense and evidence, in the form of images and success stories, that the organisation is doing 'good' in return for which the donor continues to fund projects. Football in many instances is the face and tool of such projects and the evidence of their success. Thus, when considering aid interventions and the use of football, what is defined as success and who are the winners?

Don Bosco Homes and Its Partners

Liberian-run NGO Don Bosco Homes (DBH) described a Liberian football team called 'Millennium Stars FC' on their web site. The squad had toured the UK in 1999. The image endorsed football as a medium to achieve their aims of using sports to bring young people together to engage and discuss issues and advocate their work on child protection. A product of the philanthropic aspect of the Catholic religion's Salesians missionary work, DBH initially responded to the needs of young people during the civil conflict (1989–2003); sheltering and informal counselling progressed to structured programming with vocational training centres, and educational and interim care (Armstrong 2004). By my first fieldtrip in 2009 it was an NGO with multiple international donors and revenues secured from the UK, Ireland and America. DBH's ethos was clear: a focus on children and youth with interventions relating to child protection, vocational training and peace-building. Their core ideal was that 'All children belong in the family home.'

The Salesians of Don Bosco (SDB) is an international Roman Catholic religious order founded by Father John Bosco in Italy during the nineteenth century. From 1979, its purpose in Liberia was to 'transform idle hands and minds into active contributors to community and national development initiatives. Help young people discover their potential so that instead of depending on hand-outs to survive, they could become independent and productive people' (Monibah, n.d.). As well as Catholic missionary work SDB responded to the needs of young people during the civil conflict and expanded their mission to rehabilitation and skills training programmes. The outcome of such work was the Don Bosco Homes (DBH) NGO, which was officially founded in 1992. The post-conflict milieu also saw SDB personnel put up temporary night shelters to provide food on the condition that street children and young fighters should attend literacy classes. Vocational training centres were also established during the conflict for outreach and protection work. The idea behind this enterprise was to entice young soldiers to train and be productive.

It was not until the aftermath of the war that the Catholic Agency for Overseas Development (CAFOD) became an official sponsor for SDB projects and provided assistance to make them a recognised NGO.

> CAFOD exists to bring about lasting and positive change in the lives of some of the world's poorest and most disadvantaged people in the global south, while challenging those of us in the North to transform our lives for the common good. This change is underpinned by our faith identity and our commitment to partnership. (CAFOD 2010a, p. 4)

Established in 1962 by the Catholic Bishops of England and Wales, CAFOD's intention for Liberia and for the world was to provide assistance to small-scale charitable efforts. In 2000 CAFOD changed its status from a 'fund' to an 'agency', thus placing itself beyond the role of fund-giver and becoming an official member of partnerships. Raising money from the Catholic community, the UK Government and the general public, CAFOD puts these funds into development projects in over sixty countries. CAFOD claims to work within the core values of compassion, hope, dignity, solidarity, partnership, sustainability and stewardship (CAFOD, Our standards and Commitments). CAFOD seeks 'trusted, local groups staffed by local people, and our aim is to strengthen partners through improving skills, resources and systems so they can better help those in need'. In the aftermath of the first Liberian civil war in 1996 CAFOD helped to set up three interim care centres for the rehabilitation of ex-child combatants, but only one of these remains today in Monrovia; the others in Tubmanburg and Buchanan have been closed and the focus has turned to child protection, peace-building and vocational training. CAFOD continues to be one of the partnerships that facilitate Don Bosco's work most significantly by writing funding proposals and developing plans for larger donor organisations such as the UK-based Comic Relief and UN agencies. In 2011 CAFOD obtained £15 million from grants. In 2010 Liberia received three CAFOD grants totalling £408.00 and in 2011 six grants equalling £671.00—a very small amount that highlights CAFOD's role in providing administrative support and promoting their projects to secure larger financial partners.

The focus within the CAFOD–DBH partnership is heavily biased towards administrative support for seeking funds elsewhere. This is a long-distance hands-off arrangement whereby monies and funding applications are sought and processed by CAFOD whilst the Liberian staff control their best practice initiatives and projects without donor directives, except for annual visits from donor staff. Liberians managed and staffed the NGO and utilised its local knowledge without any inhibiting structures or project instruction from the funder. Instruction from its UK partner comes merely in the form of direction to align its ethical, moral and religious foundations.

The need for aid, education and establishing livelihoods is great and the programmes and projects endorsed by such an organisation need to consider demand, sustainability, impact, appropriateness and priorities. The DBH outfit had a unique structure. Firstly its foundations are in Catholic missionary work that was established in pre-conflict Liberia by religious figures and volunteers. Such people (active priests and nuns in Monrovia) now form the Board of Directors for the DBH NGO alongside the DBH senior management. Based in Monrovia and its suburbs this network of religious figures manages all Don Bosco and Catholic ventures, for example, the Mother Pattern College, the Don Bosco Polytechnic School, the Don Bosco Youth Centre (DBYC) as well as other Catholic-run schools and churches. They are the governing body for DBH and regular meetings are held between DBH management and the Board. Although answerable to such an entity the authority of the board showed little involvement in the day-to-day running of the organisation. During my 4 years of intermittent placements, no board members ever observed their practices, visited any of the sites or intervened in or directed any of their projects.

The DBH headquarters is situated in New Congo Town, a 20-minute drive from Monrovia's city centre. Its personnel—numbering thirty—are divided into sections: peace-building, vocational training and child protection. The staffing structure from 2009 consisted of Director David Konneh appointed by virtue of his voluntary work during the conflict and his previous ambitions of priesthood—he was given a choice by the established religious order in Liberia between priesthood and youth work. He chose youth work. Supporting David was the Deputy Director Joe; additionally there was an administrator, three section managers with volunteer and employed youth and social workers attached and two drivers and six security staff (covering their headquarters and two of their sites).

It was the peace-building team who claimed to be involved in football projects as a way of bringing young people, children and communities together. International and domestic football was discussed constantly by the DBH staff; my interest in the subject and knowledge of European football cemented my acceptance amongst the staff. Football images were seen within the headquarters; an Everton Football club table cloth covered a side table and paraphernalia were visible in department offices to show support for one's club, with Premiership clubs and Barcelona and Real Madrid being the dominant choices. Despite this interest, passion and ideology regarding football, accompanied by all the rhetoric associated with football for peace projects in the development setting, structured football projects managed by DBH were not evident. Informal football was constantly visible within the interim care centre but this was ad hoc and self-governed by the young people who were endorsing nothing other than the 'jumper for goalposts' principle. Football was also observed within the schools and communities visited by DBH staff but such staff were merely spectators to the game. Surely, if the CAFOD programmes were being implemented, football projects and interventions would have consisted of the DBH staff being the initiators, officials, coaches, advisors, teachers or at least referees. Additionally, there was a lack of actual football equipment; neither the peace-building team nor any DBH department had any footballs, shirts, whistles, bibs, cones or structured football project plans. At the minimum a football project required a ball. My placement with DBH continued despite the lack of SDP projects. I was able to gain invaluable insights into the lives of young people and had access to communities inside and outside of Monrovia when I was accompanied by their staff. My intention of observing any formal SDP projects in Monrovia had disappeared with the realisation that they were simply not happening—until visitors in the form of international partners and donors arrived from the UK.

A Goodwill Gesture: Shirts for the Children, Photos for the Donor

In May 2010 DBH received guests from England. The son of former manager of Barcelona, Newcastle United and England, Sir Bobby Robson, accompanied representatives from the Catholic Aid Charity, CAFOD, on a week-long visit. On the morning of their arrival all DBH staff were told by the manager and director to gather in the meeting room of the Headquarters in Congo Town. An itinerary and the Bosco Homes child protection policies were handed out. This was the one and only time these policies were consulted during my tenure with the organisation. The itinerary ensured that all staff were aware of their roles over the next few days and the logistics involved in 'pulling off' a successful visit. The official policies provided credibility for them as an active NGO that adhered to European rhetorical expectations and standards.

A DBH driver brought the visitors from their four-star hotel in the project's newest vehicle. The CAFOD representative had brought a dedicated photographer from the UK to record their trip. As they took their seats in the meeting room Joe was instructed by David to discuss safety issues with the new arrivals. They were instructed not to take taxis if they wanted to see the city, not to walk around Monrovia unaccompanied and if they needed to go anywhere DBH would provide the transport and security. On many occasions when such visitors were not present and when money was not available to buy fuel for cars, DBH staff walked for hours doing follow-ups and talking to young people not attending school. The rules and normal operating procedures were altered to show a model of best practice in line with what DBH management thought would be expected.

Regardless of this incongruity about staff safety the newly arrived Paul Robson[13] explained the purpose of his trip. His father was a former Premiership football manager whose death in 2009 led to thousands of Newcastle United football shirts being displayed at the Newcastle St James Park Stadium by fans as a tribute to him. Paul (and his absent brother) knew that their father had met the Don Bosco Liberian 'Millennium Stars' football team that travelled to England in 1999, and that his father had a photograph of that meeting in his study. Now the brothers thought it fitting to donate the shirts that were displayed in his honour. Approximately 6000 shirts were collected and distributed to various charities in different parts of the world. Some were to go to DBH projects in Liberia and Paul's brother Mark donated shirts to 'KitAid' projects in Kenya. Paul spoke with great affection for his father and came across as a gentleman who was taking the trip seriously. The CAFOD representative accompanying Paul learned more about the work of Don Bosco through introductions made at the initial meeting by Joe and David.

DBH Director David Konneh responded to Paul. A large figure always wearing a suit and usually at his desk working on his laptop or in

---

[13] It should be noted here that I intend no criticism and under no circumstances is the intention of Paul Robson or his family under scrutiny. This gesture was one that had particular meaning to the Robson family and was done out of kindness. Anonymity seems pointless considering the record of Paul's visit on the CAFOD web site. www.cafod.org.uk/News/international-News/Liberia-football-2010-07-30

meetings, Konneh combined paperwork with picking children up from police stations. A caring man with previous ambitions in the Priesthood he turned his attentions to the need of children during the late 1990s war in Liberia. With his image as a 'big man'—a man in a high position with formal employment—David commanded respect and attention and described to his visitors how Don Bosco were operational during the civil conflict, communicating with children particularly in the port areas of Monrovia where they gathered seeking food and informal income. He described the involvement of children both as combatants and victims of the conflict and how Don Bosco placed themselves within refugee camps to give pastoral support and care. Football played an important role for the youth workers and fatherhood who risked their personal safety to engage with young combatants. Football encouraged them to leave their violent surroundings for brief periods of time to play and communicate with those who attempted to educate and counsel.

During the post-war rehabilitation stage, and once the UN began providing assistance in 2003, Konneh revealed that he had questioned their strategies of paying ex-combatants for handing in their arms and ammunition to UN-established weapons camps. He had suggested that such money would be better invested in long-term rehabilitation programmes, notably schooling and vocational training courses. The UN sympathised with David's suggestions but as the money had already been allocated to the 'Disarmament Programme' they were not able to redirect its strategy. David's contentions proved correct as the Disarmament, Demobilisation, Rehabilitation and Reintegration (DDRR) programme did not provide significant results. Initially suspended for 4 months due to lack of planning, care and peace-training the courses that were offered were reduced from 3 weeks to 5 days. On top of this many ex-combatants waited for months for entry into the training camps, and the incentive of cash for ammunition meant that up to an estimated 60% of participants were not affiliated to a fighting force. Young people selling weapons to the UN for cash and interim care was a thought-provoking image. Cash incentives, training and a safe house attracted civilians and encouraged corruption. Consequently the UN's failure in its initial interventions for rehabilitation meant that for the young combatants who experienced war little had changed. The money they received had gone but their post-war position remained much the same as it had been before the war. Children who survived the war remained uneducated, unskilled and held little position or power in society. They continued to look to DBH for protection, reintegration, peace-building and vocational training courses.

This grim message—or plea—was delivered. The visitors sat listening whilst holding onto the notion of donating football shirts to help these young people in crisis. The visitors were scheduled to observe a number of different Bosco sites within Monrovia and accompany all three DBH departments throughout the week. All site managers and children and young people within structured groups[14] that work with Don Bosco staff had been warned and prepared for the visit prior to their arrival. Paul was attentive to the staff and children he encountered; he listened to their stories and thanked them for their time. He was a humble man, unassuming and genuine; he was interested in people's lives and he asked non-invasive questions and showed interest in the support being offered by the Bosco projects. In contrast, the CAFOD representative had a separate agenda, instructing the photographer at each site and seeking out success stories for the good news publications they would inevitably end up in.

DBH put on a show, leading the visitors around notorious sites where street children gathered and worked. They were escorted around small and dimly lit local police stations that incarcerated young people until DBH staff could release them. They were taken to communities renowned for poverty and high numbers of working children who did not or could not attend school. The bleak image of Liberia and its impact on children and young people was intentionally exposed by DBH and the distribution shirts lit up their dull faces. Donors need emotional causes to justify funding and success stories to raise awareness of their work (Green 2000, Shutt 2006). The work of DBH was also portrayed in its most idyllic form; the timetabled events ran efficiently, and the cars transporting staff, materials and the visitors ran on time. Projects and interventions were implemented during the week to ensure maximum development work was occurring. This was not the norm; visits to schools and night visits

---

[14] DBH worked in selected schools in Monrovia. They established focus groups of students whom they worked with on an ad hoc basis.

to street children were generally ad hoc but they occurred like clockwork the week that CAFOD visited.

Football was the all-encompassing theme of the CAFOD visit. Hundreds of football shirts were distributed throughout the different sites. Most unusually and most significantly a football match was organised for the visitors. At 8 am I was driven to West Point[15] with members of the protection team to pick up a gazebo, which was to be constructed at the pitch to provide shade to the visitors. A music system, chairs and refreshments were also brought to the pitch. Young boys were enrolled to mark out the pitch lines in the sand. The Millennium Star team was transported by Don Bosco to a community field near Chocolate City to play a local team. Paul was given the opportunity to distribute some of the shirts to the players and speak with the few in the group who had visited England and met his father.

For the next 3 months there were no football events or visits to any Don Bosco team. Football played a part in the Don Bosco schedule and they presumed the interest in the game was what prompted Robson and CAFOD to visit and give away the shirts. The Bosco project thus cut their cloth accordingly. They put on a football-related event and in return got hundreds of football shirts and, crucially, continued support from CAFOD. This support was confirmed during the 'final feedback session' when the CAFOD representative claimed 'I don't have a negative' and described the project as 'impressive'. The main headline on the CAFOD web site weeks later read 'Liberia: Football's legacy of Hope'. The article described the visit and stated that Paul believed that 'football has the potential to transform the country's fortunes' (CAFOD 2010b). The CAFOD staff and Robson had been wooed by the events during their visit. The images they saw were interpreted as SDP projects at their best, engaging vulnerable youths, building relationships with each other and the specialised skilled staff—a source of happiness and hope.

In its history Don Bosco had created a football image in its quest for engaging young people and attracting European donor support. In the eyes of the donors and DBH staff, football projects made them a legitimate youth-orientated organisation: 'Theorists argue that organisations

---

[15] A slum area in Monrovia.

adopt practices in order to increase their legitimacy which may actually *reduce* efficiency' (Meyer and Rowan 1977, cited in Rauh, n.p, 2010). Football was arguably a distraction to impact the monitoring and evaluation: 'Legitimacy is crucial for any donor organisation but is not necessarily linked to performance or other attributes' (Scott, 2008, cited in Rauh, n.p, 2010). The legitimacy of DBH for its donors was created through the images, the adoption of SDP practices and superficial props and performances, with little attention given towards tangible results or success.

Within the Liberian context a number of conclusions can be drawn with regard to SDP projects. Sporting programmes were not sustained by the UN and NGO aid agencies. These programmes were token gestures by the organisations and popular one-off events to engage large populations and affirm their presence. Football was used to attract and retain support from the Global North, and therefore it aimed at donors, not youth. Images are powerful tools for promotion and for encouraging donor support. Young people playing football makes up the perfect post-conflict African image. When assessing impact within the development setting, intervention, sustainability and capacity-building are principle themes for aid agencies, and football and sport are promoted as the answer. Despite the overwhelming presence of the UN, and foreign and local aid agencies—most with Western stakeholders—SDP projects were not occurring until one looks for projects and evidence of such organisations on web sites and other promotional media.

In this case DBH and CAFOD were the winners whilst the Liberian youth's newly acquired football shirts were now probably sold or stolen. Meanwhile back in the UK donations were sought with the help of the latest article describing DBH and its use of football for reconciliation and peace. In reality the core and crucial work of DBH was to free young people from prison, engage with street children, reintegrate displaced young people back into their communities and provide education, yet this was not given the attention it deserved. In the absence of infrastructure and national bodies for child protection and social work DBH was the body dealing with a very visible problem. Sport played an important role during the conflict for the Don Bosco youth workers who risked personal safety to engage with young soldiers via football, but this form of intervention was lost when the need outweighed their capacity. Structure and sports programming were secondary to the action needed on a day-to-day basis.

References

Amsterdam Conference Report. (2004). The quote and report can now be accessed at: http://www.toolkitsportdevelopment.org/html/resources/0E/0E00BE53-2C02-46EA-8AC5-A139AC4363DC/Report%20of%20Next%20Step%20 Amsterdam.pdf

Annan, K. (2000). Olympic Games: A true celebration of humanity, secretary general says. Press Release SG/SM/7523 31/08/2000. www.un.org/news/press/docs/2000/20000831.sgsm7523.doc.html.

Armstrong, G. (2004). Life, death, and the biscuit: Football and the embodiment of society in Liberia, West Africa. In G. Armstrong & R. Giulianotti (Eds.), *Football in Africa: Conflict, conciliation and community*. London/New York: Palgrave Macmillan.

Arnold, P. J. (1997). *Sport, ethics and education*. London/New York: Cassell Education.

Auweele, Y. V., Malcolm, C., & Meluders, B. (2006). *Sport and development*. Tielt: LannooCampus.

Baehr, P. R., & Gordenker, L. (2005). *The United Nations: Reality and ideal* (4th ed.). Basingstoke: Palgrave Macmillan.

Barnett, M. N. (1997). The UN Security Council, indifference, and genocide in Rwanda. *Cultural Anthropology, 12*, 551–578.

CAFOD. (2010a). Just one world. http://www.cafod.org.uk/content/download/3036/21931/version/1/file/JustOneWorld.pdf.

CAFOD. (2010b). Liberia: Football's legacy of hope. http://www.cafod.org.uk/News/International-news/Liberia-Football-2010-07-30.

CCPA. (2006). Cross Cultures Open Fun Football Schools 2005 sustainability report. www.ccpa.eu/data/files/annualreport/ccpa05.pdf.

Coalter, F. (2006). Sport-in-development: Process evaluation and organisational development. In Y. V. Auweele et al. (Eds.), *Sport and development*. Tielt: Iannoo Campus.

Coalter, F. (2007). *Sport a wider role: Who's keeping the score?* London: Routledge.

Coalter, F. (2009). Sport-in-development: Accountability or development? In R. Levermore & A. Beacom (Eds.), *Sport and international development*. Basingstoke: Palgrave Macmillan.

Coalter, F. (2010). The politics of sport-for-development: Limited focus programmes and broad gauge problems? *International review for the sociology of
sport, 45*(3), 295–314.

Coalter, F. (2013). *Sport for development: What game are we playing?* London/
New York: Routledge.

Darnell, S. (2012). *Sport for development and peace: A critical sociology.* London/
New York: Bloomsbury Academic.

Escobar, A. (1995). *Encountering development: The making and unmaking of the
Third World.* Princeton: Princeton University Press.

Ferguson, J. (1994). *The anti-politics machine: "Development", depoliticiza-
tion, and bureaucratic power in Lesotho.* Minneapolis/London: University of
Minnesota Press.

French, A. J. (2005). The private sector's share in peace: Education to provide
social stability in conflict-affected areas. www.peacestudiesjournal.org/docs/
july05French.pdf.

Fuest, V. (2010). Contested inclusions: Pitfalls of NGO peace-building activities in Liberia. *African Spectrum, 45*(2), 3–33.

FrontPageAfrica (2013). 'Defining Community in post-war Liberia: Challenges
and Opportunities'. http://frontpageafricaonline.com/op-ed-editorial/comm
entary/4966-defining-community-in-post-war-liberia-challenges-and-
opportunities.html.

Giulianotti, R. (2004). Human rights, globalization and sentimental education:
The case of sport. *Sport in Society, 7*(3), 355–369.

Giulianotti, R., Armstrong, G. (2014). The sport for development and peace
sector: A critical sociological analysis. In N. Schulenkorf & D. Adair (Eds.),
Global sport for development: Critical perspectives. Jones et al - Basingstoke,
Hampshire: Palgrave Macmillan.

Goulding, M. (1999). The United Nations and conflict in Africa since the Cold
War. *African Affairs, 98*(391), 155–166.

Green, M. (2000). Participatory development and the appropriation of agency
in Southern Tanzania. *Critique of Anthropology, 20*(1), 67–89.

Green, M. (2003). Globalizing development in Tanzania: Policy franchising
through participatory project management. *Critique of Anthropology, 23*(2),
123–143.

Grillo, R. D., & Stirrat, R. L. (1997). *Discourses of development: Anthropological
perspectives.* Oxford/New York: Berg.

Gberie, L. (2005). Liberia's War and Peace Process: A Historical Overview. In, F.
Aboagye and A.M.S Bah (eds). A Tortuous Road to Peace: The Dynamics of
Regional, UN and International Humanitarian Interventions in Liberia.
Pretoria: Institute for Security Studies.

Gluckman, M & Gluckman, M. (1977). On Drama, and Games and Athletic Contests. In, S.F Moore & B.G Meyerhoff (eds). Secular Ritual. Assen: Van Gorcum.

Heinbecker, P., & Goff, P. (2005). *Irrelevant or indispensible? The United Nations in the 21st century*. West Waterloo: Wilfred Laurier University Press.

Howard, L. M. (2008). *UN peacekeeping in Civil Wars*. Cambridge: Cambridge University Press.

Human Development Report. (1990). *Published for the United Nations Development Programme*. New York/Oxford: Oxford University Press.

IOC. (2013). Olympic Charter. http://www.olympic.org/Documents/olympic_charter_en.pdf.

Insight (2005–2013). Insight News Online: 'French Embassy Tourney Makes Impact'. http://www.insight.com.lr/story.php?record_id=184&sub=37.

Jett, C. (1999). *Why peacekeeping fails*. Basingstoke: Palgrave MacMillan.

Jaye, T. (2009). Transitional Justice and DDR: The Case of Liberia. International Center for Transitional Justice, June.

Levermore, R., & Beacom, A. (2009). *Sport and international development*. Basingstoke: Palgrave Macmillan.

LACC (2011). 'Profile of the LACC'.http://www.olympic.org/Documents/olympic_charter_en.pdf.

Leys, C. (1996). *The rise & fall of development theory*. London: James Currey.

MacQueen, N. (2006). *Peace-keeping and the international system*. London/New York: Routledge.

Mair, L. (1984). *Anthropology and development*. London: Macmillan Press.

Meyer, J. W., & Rowan, B. (1977). Institutional organizations: Formal structure as myth and ceremony. *American Journal of Sociology, 83*(2), 340–363.

Mohamoud, A. A. (2006). *State collapse and post-conflict development in Africa: Case of Somalia (1960–2001)*. West Lafayette: Purdue University Press.

Morford, W. R., & McIntosh, M. J. (1993). Sport and the Victorian gentleman. In A. G. Ingham & J. W. Loy (Eds.), *Sport in social development: Traditions, transitions, and transformations* (pp. 51–76). Champaign: Human Kinetics.

Mosse, D. (2005). *Cultivating development: An ethnography of aid policy and practice*. London/New York: Pluto Press.

Ogi, A. (2003a). International Conference on Sport and Development. Press Release ORG/1374, 29/01/2003.

Ogi, A. (2003b). Sport and Development International Conference: The Magglingen Declaration and Recommendations. www.sportanddev.org/data/document/document/50.pdf.

Ogi, A. (2007). Achieving the objectives of the United Nations through Sport: SDC and United Nations publication. www.sportanddev.org/data/document/document/421.pdf.

Pigg, S. L. (1992). Constructing social categories through place: Social representations and development in Nepal. *Comparative Studies in Society and History, 34*(3), 491–513.

Right to Play (2006). Right to Play Annual Report 2006. www.righttoplay.org.uk/moreinfo/.../2006%20Annual%20Report.pdf

Right to Play. (2008). Harnessing the power of sport for development and peace: Recommendations to governments.

Rauh, K. (2010). NGOs, foreign donors, and organizational processes: Passive NGO recipients or strategic actors? *McGill Sociological Review, 1,* January 2010, 29–45.

Reeves, E. (2007). The UN's bloody failure. www.theguardian.com/commentisfree/2007/jun/20/thefailuresoftheun.

Rist, G. (2007). Development as a buzzword. *Development in Practice, 17*(4), 485–491.

Right to Play (2006). Right to Play Annual Report 2006. www.righttoplay.org.uk/moreinfo/.../2006%20Annual%20Report.pdf .

Schwery, R. (2003). The potential of sport for development and peace. *Bulletin 39.*

Scott, W. R. (2008). *Institutions and organizations: Ideas and interests* (3rd ed.). Los Angeles: Sage.

SDC. (2005). Sport for development and peace. Swiss Agency for Development and Cooperation.

SDP-IWG. (2006). Sport for development and peace: From practice to policy. www.righttoplay.com/site/docserver/Right_to_Play_from_Practice_to_policy_book.pdf.

SDP-IWG. (2007). The Accra call for action on sport and development and peace. https://www.un.org/wcm/content/site/sport/home/unplayers/memberstates/sdpiwg_meetings.

Shutt, C. (2006). Power in aid relationships: A personal view. *Institute of Development Studies Bulletin, 37*(6), 79–87.

SDC. (2005). Sport for Development and Peace. Switzerland: Swiss Agency for Development and Cooperation.

Tylor, E, B. (1879). 'The History of Games'. *Popular Science Monthly, Volume 15, June 1879.*

UN. (2003). Sport for development and peace: Towards achieving the millennium development goals. Report from the United Nations Inter-Agency Task

Force on Sport for Development and Peace. www.un.org/wcm/.../sport/.../
sport/.../2003_interagency_report_ENGLISH.pdf.

UN. (2012). Sport for development and peace: The UN system in action. www.
un.org/wcm/content/site/sport/peace.

UN. (2013). Sport for development and peace: The UN system in action: Why
sport? http://www.un.org/wcm/content/site/sport/home/sport.

UN Resolution 48/11. (1993). UN general assembly: Observance of the
Olympic Truce. www.un.org/documents/ga/res/48/a48r011.htm.

United Nations. (2005). Sport as a tool for development and peace: Towards
achieving the United Nations Millennium Development Goals. http://www.
un.org/sport2005/resources/task_force.pdf.

UNMIL. (2007a). IOC latest news: Sport for peace project brings together thousands of Liberians. http://www.olympic.org/content/news/media-resources/
manual-news/1999-2009/2007/04/12/sport-for-peace-project-brings-
together-thousands-of-liberians/.

UNMIL. (2007b). UNMIL, Government of Liberia and partners end sport
for peace programme. http://reliefweb.int/report/liberia/unmil-government-
liberia-and-partners-end-sport-peace-programme.

US AID. (2009). Liberian youth fragility assessment. Report produced for the
USAID/Liberia under task order 9 of the global evaluation and monitoring.
Prepared by the Aguirre Division of JBS International Inc & Associates for
Global Change. http://pdf.usaid.gov/pdf_docs/PNADQ258.pdf.

Zakaria, Y. (2006). Youth, conflict, security, and development. In, The Reality
of Aid Management Committee, *The Reality of Aid, London: Zed Books*.

5

Matadi: Structure and Power in a Post-Conflict Urban Community

Community

The notion of community evokes many traits, meanings, presumptions and images of people cohabiting in harmony: 'Community is tradition; society is change. Community is feeling; society is rationality. Community is female; society is male. Community is warm and wet and intimate; society is cold and dry and formal. Community is love; society is, well, business' (Berger 1988, p. 324). Yet observations made in what people call the community of Matadi, a suburb of Monrovia, would suggest otherwise. Anthropologists such as Barth (1969), Goodenough (1971, 1976) and Hannerz (1969) questioned notions of homogeneity amongst collective cultures and focused on inequalities and the uneven distribution of power, knowledge and wealth within. Arising from their studies was a new theme of 'individuals attempting to make the best of complex situations, jostling for position and denotation. And with this emphasis came an almost inevitable problematization of community' (Amit and Rapport 2002, p. 16). This analysis appreciates the problems that any notion of community brings with it. At the same time it needs to be understood that the Matadi community—the primary research site—is a

© The Editor(s) (if applicable) and The Author(s) 2016
H. Collison, *Youth and Sport for Development*,
DOI 10.1057/978-1-137-52470-6_5

consequence of an enormously complex situation wherein contemporary issues of jostling and denotation are minor when one considers the history, traditions and circumstances that conceived the establishment of this Liberian community.

Local knowledge is of paramount importance when considering and describing development sites as communities and this is why the notion has become particularly problematic. In 2004 The World Bank aptly described the problematisation of the notion of community:

> Participatory projects are typically implemented in a unit referred to as a community. Most of the literature on development policy uses the term community without much qualification to denote a culturally and politically homogeneous social system or one that, at least implicitly, is internally cohesive and more or less harmonious, such as an administratively defined locale (tribal area or neighborhood) or a common interest group (community of weavers or potters). This notion of community is problematic at two levels. First, defining the geographic or conceptual boundaries of a community is not always straightforward. Administrative boundaries can be meaningless where settlement patterns are distinct from such boundaries or where increasing mobility or temporary migrations have transformed community boundaries. In many cases, factional, ethnic, or religious identities may further complicate the picture. Second, an unqualified use of the term often obscures local structures of economic and social power that are likely to strongly influence project outcomes. (The World Bank 2004, p. 8)

The concept of 'community' is to many Liberians very real and pivotal to their sense of belonging and indeed of survival. An African media source noted: 'Even today, the idea of community is central to most things that happen in Liberia' (2013, FrontPageAfrica, n.p). This is true in light of the regularity of its usage by Liberians when describing local issues, politics, development, religion, football, security, business and life in general terms.

However, underneath the ideal lies an arena for disconnected people battling for personal gain, status and opportunity. Berger states:

The dark side of community is the eternal internal power struggle over always limited resources and over the authority to interpret the ultimately ambiguous, shared culture in a way that ensures optimal conformity and continuity of members… community actually hides the internal conflicts within each of these groups behind an implied rhetoric of shared culture. (1988, p. 326)

Continuity is the leitmotif of post-conflict Liberia. Conformity is needed to avoid division. Internal conflicts are best concealed around and behind common enthusiasms. With this understood it is important to analyse the concepts which Liberians and specifically those who reside in Matadi promote. Amit and Rapport believed that

it is a mistake (factual and moral) for anthropology to take cultural ideologies of collectivity, homogeneity, boundedness and distinctiveness at face value,[1] and to further translate this into so-called rights of cultural difference; a serious failing for anthropology to describe and prescribe community—its relative cultural reality—without admitting the universality of underlying individual consciousness and creativity. (2002, p. 139)

Expressions of community need observation and scrutiny. This requires fieldwork, participation and a form of membership to challenge it as a global notion and pursue it as a local term with a specific conceptualisation. Many theories surround the concept of post-conflict 'communities' as Delanty describes:

There are many themes that have emerged in the nineteenth century among these is the notion of nostalgia trying to recreate traditional living patterns, or the recovery of traditional and an organic unity of state and society i.e. to reconcile community to the conditions of modernity. By contrast the utopian ideal of community as expressed in the discourses of communism, socialism and anarchism where community is an ideal to be achieved, rather than being simply recovered from the past. (Delanty 2003, p. 19–20)

---

[1] The 'face value' that Rapport refers to here is really a translation of indigenous concepts of community into a romantic ideal of 'community' pointing to a notion of 'primitive communism'.

Welter proposes that 'communities are depicted as shining beacons of a new social order in the otherwise harsh urban surroundings of society' (Welter 2010, p. 65). His research on community in Weimar Germany suggests that communities are often formed to overcome social transformations; therefore community acts as a common denominator of highly diverse change (ibid, p. 65). The work on Weimar Germany has many similarities to the situation the Liberian citizens found themselves in post-conflict:

> Whatever salvation community ideas promised, modern society was rejected because of its detrimental effects on human beings, which it alienated from either their origin in nature—the assumed security of traditionally arranged, tightly knit communities. ... Instead society thrust its citizens into the public domain where life was ruled by artificial social codes and reduced to the pursuit of material and economic gain. Redemption seemed reachable only through the conscious return to the primeval origins of humanity in a community-based life. (Ibid, p. 70)

One of the most visible legacies of the 1989–2003 conflict in Liberia was the demographic and spatial changes in Monrovia (Williams 2011, p. 5). This is no surprise as civil conflicts have always led to major population shifts and Liberia was no exception. Many internally displaced persons (IDPs) (approximately 500,000) sought refuge in the capital city and its suburbs. The novelty of urban life drew many to its newly established settlements. Post-conflict many chose to stay in the pursuit of better living standards, business, schooling and 'modernity'. This relative 'modernity' here is an indigenous perception and is used in local context. Yet evolved social practices, alienation (possible fear) and nostalgia for their safer and more accepting former homes encouraged those displaced to form familiar living patterns known as communities. For those who had never left the direct vicinity of their villages before the war years this post-conflict existence was a whole new freedom that could be fully explored when the conflict ended in 2003. This reality created a new form of multi-tribal urban community, nostalgic for what they had lost yet drawn to new possibilities.

Community development projects have rapidly become an important tool for targeting the less developed—'Community-based development and its more recent variant, community-driven development, are among the fastest growing mechanisms for channelling development assistance' (The World Bank 2004, p. 2). The World Bank claims to have a portfolio of $7 billion specifically for community development projects. According to The World Bank's 2004 Critical Review, community development is viewed as a mechanism for enhancing sustainability, improving efficiency and effectiveness, making development more inclusive, empowering poor people and building social capital (p. 2). The same report also claims that 'community based projects have not been particularly effective at targeting the poor and that most community projects are dominated by elites' (p. 1). Hence, Olivier de Sardan criticised the concept of community development as 'profoundly ideological, a myth, based on assumption and used as a smokescreen' (2005, p. 73). Despite its increased usage as a strategy for development those who have attempted to evaluate such projects are not convinced by its results and the presumptions advocated by the implementers. According to Cochrane:

> Community development is not the place for the expert of for massive financial assistance. It should be thought of as an abnormal and unusual form of development. Expert-led-and-executed showcase schemes which have usually only minimally involved local people neither develop a community in its best interests nor do they provide a blueprint for broader application. (1971, pp. 53–54)

The problematisation of both development and community has seemingly been identified by researchers and those tasked with monitoring and evaluation; despite this, community development has secured its place as a mode for development. This chapter seeks to construct a better understanding of community and development in Matadi, by considering such notions as ethnographic terms.

The above selected concepts all expose problems with their usage in the language of development. What connects them is the effect and impact they have upon those they serve to inform and attract—in essence they are all seductive. Football is a global phenomenon that unlike other concepts is universally codified and understood; football draws millions of participants and spectators daily across the world. Any inclusion of football for any purpose is almost guaranteed to serve a purpose. Youth serve as a seductive generational category, primarily for the images they produce but also for their cause, their dynamic nature and, specifically in Liberia, for the stories they produce of conflict, struggle and survival. Cochrane claimed that '"development" is an emotive term; it appeals to feeling rather than intellect' (1971, p. 3); the same can be said for 'community'. Such terms conjure images of inclusive progress, unity and all striving towards a common goal as equals for the benefit of all. Football, youth, development and community all operate via seduction, and a cycle of seduction sees SDP projects progress from inception to implementation. Throughout this book seduction is the concept that steers the theory and is supported by ethnographies.

Non-governmental organisations in Liberia focus much of their attention towards talking about community engagement and project implementation and this in turn amplifies the problems associated with the notion as the ideal becomes affirmed in everyday language by local people and Liberian-run organisations. The use of the term 'community' in the aid sector—in its general usage and promotion—considers communities as units of people. The dilemma then is understanding the social effects and functions of a Liberian post-conflict community. A detailed description of Matadi will provide context and conceptualisation to the notion and will consider language, housing, economy, leisure time and security. I will ethnographically demonstrate the notion of community as it is structured in Matadai and will empirically examine the function of this residential space whilst positioning the youth within it. In turn this will offer an alternative to the unproblematic uses of the concept (Amit 2001).

Don Bosco personnel frequently explained to me that community residents and groups were highly important to their work, especially when returning a young person home. I observed many reunifications and all were carried out in a similar fashion. The white 4 × 4 vehicle would attract onlookers as we drove to the young person's house and within minutes a crowd would emerge as the parents were found. Chairs would be offered to us outside the house and the crowds were welcomed to witness the handing over of the young person with the signing of an official document accepting the child back. The youth workers would tell the story from the initial pickup to temporary housing to reunification and this would follow with a lecture on parental expectations, safeguarding and the role of the community in ensuring child protection and supporting each other. Usually a community elder would be called to officially witness the handing over and would be asked to monitor the family and contact Don Bosco youth workers if there were any concerns. Don Bosco's projects with school children were also focused towards educating those in their community and spreading their knowledge and skills training. This form of participatory development, 'community-based action' and project implementation has become the trend and a main strategy for sharing information, sustaining implementation and empowerment (cf. Cooke and Kothari 2001). The term 'community' has become a powerful term for aid agencies and the abundance of development project work in Liberia.

Running alongside this network of development activity is the strategy of football for peace and development. The game's governing body FIFA claims:

> Football has become a vital instrument for hundreds of social development programmes run by non-governmental and community-based organisations all around the world. These programmes are providing children and young people with valuable tools that make a difference to their lives and, by addressing the most pressing issues in each community, they are contributing to positive social change on a global scale. (FIFA 2013, Football for Hope)

This message had become part of the rhetoric of the LFA and during many discussions with their coaching staff and project personnel the concept of community football was central to their ideals. With the limited resources that the LFA claimed to have they relied on community football teams and coaches to produce future league players despite being unsupported and masked under the ideals of peace and development. In the NGO and football governing bodies 'community' was central to their rhetoric, ideals and strategies. The problem I faced was the images that the notion provoked did not always match the images and results I saw. Community was a key term used by all I spoke with but I suspected that the concept and reality of living in a post-conflict community was far more complex and socially, culturally and economically significant for its various members. Potentially being part of an urban post-conflict community could pose new challenges, opportunities and exposure to different actors and networks—especially for young people.

The Concept of Community: Those Like Us?

Community is a significant concept used by the aid sector and those tasked through corporate social responsibility towards peace and development initiatives. Community is also a familiar notion to Liberians but the post-conflict conditions of poverty, displacement and trauma have directed much responsibility towards community when considering survival, access and project implementation. Many IDPs—approximately 500,000—sought refuge in the capital city and its suburbs. The novelty of urban life drew many to its newly established settlements. For those who had never left the direct vicinity of their rural villages before the conflict this post-conflict existence was a whole new freedom that could be fully explored when the war ended in 2003. This reality created a new form of multi-ethnic urban community, nostalgic for what they had lost yet drawn to new possibilities. When examining post-conflict football and youth the impact, resources, functions and internal structures of 'community' become of paramount importance—not only to the analysis of Liberian youth but to the consideration of football for development and peace in Liberia.

Neighbourliness and Forming Groups

Being a 'good' neighbour is part of Liberian culture; the pressure of living in close proximity with little privacy insists upon generosity and sharing in order to live safely and harmoniously. Arising out of this food is often shared by those in close proximity. My neighbours were families in the immediate vicinity of my house, with whom I would exchange pleasantries every day. Families living beyond my house were recognised as fellow community members but not referred to as neighbours. Despite this, when a community member dies in Matadi it is the residents and not just the immediate family and neighbours who support and finance the funeral by collecting monies in the surrounding streets.

Living in the post-conflict environment has exposed many who migrated to Monrovia to the NGO-driven trends for forming support groups and associations. Most Monrovian communities have organised youth groups, 'Old Timers' associations, and ethnic and political organisations that bring residents together in more formal ways which indeed brings formality and structure to the new community. This trend promoted by NGOs as a community function is the only function that encourages separation and ethnic, generational and religious divide.

Many Monrovian communities emerged and expanded haphazardly during the conflict due to mass migration from the interior. In some areas of a community there are families and clusters of people belonging to the same indigenous group that reside together although this is not always the case. Affiliation to indigenous groups is, in some instances, of little relevance to one's membership in a community and generally the only reference to ethnic identity is the use of descriptive or mocking stereotypes. Many elders and families converse in dialects with people of the same indigenous group, yet such conversations cause no apparent separation between communities of different origins.

Palava Versus Lecture

Adejunmobi claims that the term 'palava' is derived from the Portuguese word *palavra* meaning 'word' or 'speech'. In West African pidgin its usage includes discussion, dispute, trouble, argument or calamity (2004, pvii). The act of 'palava' has been commented on by many observers of West African modes of speech, yet the term 'lecturing' in opposition to 'palava' has not seen the same level of consideration. These opposing forms of speech are a structural feature of language in Matadi and indeed an important component of the characteristics associated with youths and adults in Liberia. Much attention seems to have been given to the concepts that insight opposition, potential violence and aggression but not towards its controlling mechanisms that harness potential disputes. This may provide an indication towards the focus of research conducted within post-conflict societies. Distinctions have been made, however, in relation to varying forms of language used by adults and youths during initiation rituals. In this scenario elders and ancestors are identified as cold and youths as hot and this provides continuities with the varying usage of language in different generational categories (cf. Bloch 1975, 1986, see also De Heusch 1980 and Turner 1969).

Palava is the act of arguing, of having a dispute or animated discussion. It is not just an act of verbal aggression but is also a form of entertainment. In a society with few visual forms of entertainment palava acts as a direct theatrical performance. Gesturing, mocking, baiting or challenging each other, for many, is fun, playful and generally a way of interacting, asserting pecking orders and passing the time. Palava can be seen everywhere; in the markets, on the streets, on the football field, in schools and in any available public space. The subjects for palava vary from arguing about football teams, discussing whether a penalty was rightly or wrongly awarded in the previous night's Champions League game, love rivalries, establishing seniority within a group or debating politics. The subject of dispute is never too inconsequential or small to allow a major debate. Due to its trivial nature the act of palava is associated with adolescents and those without seniority and status. Palava requires two participating parties; otherwise one is just scolding or mocking without challenge. Two people engaged in palava means the two people are looked upon equally as juveniles. One person verbally challenging another without response asserts a higher position. A person who responds with composure, gives advice or provides a solution, or talks as a calming mechanism is viewed as a good *lecturer* who has a higher status. Therefore, palava and modes of speech highlight hierarchy within a community and between its residents.

Whilst palava involves confrontation I rarely witnessed actual public violence; the result of palava is usually adults intervening and converting potential conflict into lecture. As previously stated the art of conversing in any manner is enjoyed and participated in with extraordinary vigour.

To give advice, guidance or converse openly is known locally as *lecturing*. While judging a dispute the elders will lecture the accused describing the wrongdoing and stating the behaviour that should be demonstrated in the future. Elders and established adults are thought of as good lecturers. Those in positions of responsibility, for example, football coaches and religious figures, partake in lecturing as part of their role within community. Speech is potentially the most powerful tool any Liberian may or does possess. An effective orator can attract an audience with ease and for many being heard is a rare opportunity for self-promotion to gain recognition. One can become a powerful figure and thereby status and social worth increase.

By contrast, the use of futile palava is associated with adolescence and merely the act of juveniles with little else to do other than quarrel and debate non-issues, while lecturing is the high-status speech of elders. Therefore, modes of speech have the ability to heighten or weaken social standing: religious preachers and political figures attract listeners and this aids and maintains high social standing, whereas young people who create much noise, gesturing and performance are confirmed as idle community members with little worthy social function. Palava is the language of the young and those lacking status, and predisposes one to crime and dysfunctional behaviour. Lecture is the language of the wise and elderly associated with security, protection and authority. The use of language is a controlling mechanism for hierarchy within the community system.

Others' perception of one's social status is crucial. As the generational categories are not defined by chronological age this can lead to confusion and add to the instability and tension running through the community. The need to address residents with the appropriate title can become competitive in a quest to be distinguished and acknowledged in public, which further generates internal conflict. A negotiation of establishing status occurred during a football training session when one player referred to another as 'my pekin' during a debate surrounding the previous evening's Champions League match. My pekin would generally be considered a fond and acceptable address by an older youth to a younger male. The player stopped the other mid-sentence to argue that 'I am not your pekin! I am older than you!' This caused palava, which drew many of the other players in. Chronological age was not discussed but the protesting player (although visibly younger) claimed 'I am in the 10th grade at high school you are in the 9th'.[2] The palava continued until Richie made light of the situation and claimed that they were both younger than him so there was no need to argue. As the game continued girls watched from the sidelines partaking in *chi chi pulley*[3] about the boys who were arguing, deciding who they thought was the most desirable and ultimately who they considered was the lowest on the pecking order. At the end of the session the players sat together discussing the game they had just played; the coach lectured them on how they needed to be more serious and not embarrass themselves in public by engaging in palava. The player who initially referred to his teammate as pekin stood and claimed, 'Coach, he's my brother there's no problem.' The need to establish hierarchy amongst the players was inherently important and took up much of their time but the debate could be ended quickly without any residual emotion—proof that this was a superficial and essentially futile youthful spat.

This ambiguity of status provides a platform for different language use; arguments or having palava about who is the eldest (meaning who has the highest social standing) provides images of two immature people negotiating seniority. A person who gives advice to settle the dispute regarding age claims higher status and wisdom. Such forms of communication provide subject matter for gossip, or participating in *chi chi pulley*, about palava or individual social status.

Youth and Adults

Community in Liberia has a hierarchical structure of male elders held with the highest regard. The majority of community residents fall into a vast category of 'youth', namely males and arguably females (see Chap. 6) without independent living and employment. Crucially, 'elders' is a term associated not only with chronological age but is strongly linked to status. One would not be labelled an *elder* unless one is looked upon

---

[2] Due to the civil conflict many young people missed 14 years of education, so age has no factor in the school year one attends. It is not unusual to see men in their late twenties in high school.

[3] Slang term for gossip.

by one's community with respect. A man gains this respect by having a good moral reputation, living wholesomely and independently and being generally open to others and conducting himself with honourable beliefs and practices like going to church, and sharing food with neighbours.[4] Elders are the first to be called upon to deal with conflict or criminal acts and at times to intervene in domestic disputes.

Women may also be elders, but their role is different. Female elders are often approached by younger families and individuals for guidance and counselling, usually with regard to relationships, parenting or money issues. In return for advice they are helped with chores. Married couples are well respected within community structures as the ability to get married highlights the male's success in acquiring bride wealth to secure a wife. Only men with formal respectable employment have the assets necessary to secure a wife and support a family and this provides status. This status is only maintained by consequently obtaining a family home, providing schooling for children and financing the wife, who in turn is expected to behave 'respectfully' by maintaining the house, attending to the children and looking after the family unit. Not all married women are exclusively housewives; many are also expected to seek employment, be it working in the community market, selling food or working for government ministries. Couples were not getting married due their inability to financially adopt the position of formal martial status. Elders and adults are essential to the everyday functioning of Liberian community.

The acknowledgement of hierarchy and status is highly important. Not respecting another resident's position publicly is considered to be rude and is associated with adolescents. However, a problem surrounding this acknowledgement is that chronological age is not a factor in defining status and therefore other indicators need to be observed, for example, clothing, jewellery and physical size. The need to be addressed in specific ways can cause confusion, insult, palava or mutual respect. Elders are greeted with the title 'ol ma' or 'ol pa' or 'papaye'. This is seen as respectful; youths will refer to male adults either by 'Mr' followed by

---

[4] Communities can be large in size and highly overpopulated; neighbours are seen as those in the direct vicinity of one's home. Whilst residing in a compound my neighbours were other families living inside the compound, and this acknowledgement did not go beyond those walls.

their surname or 'uncle' if they know them on a more informal capacity. Older male youths will expect to be greeted by their peers either by nickname (which most youth football players have) or 'brother'. An older youth or man will address a younger youth as *pekin* or 'boy'. Titles like pekin implicitly mean the recipient is lower than the giver. Brother means they are equals. The same can be said for greeting females, a married women[5] would be referred to as 'Mrs' followed by her surname and if more familiar, aunt or auntie. Younger girls are acknowledged by their first name or the term 'sister'. Young girls will be referred to as 'girl' by those trying to get her attention—provocatively or otherwise—but have no relationship or familiarity with her. During my time in Matadi the football players would refer to me as 'Sister Holly' (implying to others that we had a close relationship). Players would also call me 'auntie' (as a term of respect). When some players came to me on a personal level for advice or guidance they would call me 'Ma'. Members with recognised occupations like 'coach', 'Father' (a religious figure in the church) or member of Government would be addressed by acknowledging their position, for example 'Mr Senator'. These hierarchies are continuously evident in everyday speech.

Spaces

Hansen (2005) claimed that space, money and social relations encompass an urban geography of inequality and social exclusion in Lusaka, Zambia (p. 4). Spaces and housing organisation in Liberia has a direct relationship to social status. Those who become generationally stuck tend to also be stuck in the spaces they reside and this acts as a social marker and indicator (ibid; see also Schlyter 2003). Social and spatial organisation here acts as a guide to the generational divisions and social order in Matadi (cf. Oldfield 2004).

---

[5] Being classed as a married person doesn't necessarily mean an official marriage ceremony has taken place. The majority of adult couples residing together as a family are unmarried but are referred to and viewed by the community as married.

Matadi comprises New Matadi and Old Matadi separated by a 'T' junction that gives access to Monrovia or 'in town'. Old Matadi (right of the 'T' junction when coming from town) was formed by a housing project in the 1970s initiated by then President William Tolbert. New Matadi (left of the 'T' junction) was formed as a consequence of its new post-conflict residents. New Matadi has very few houses of formal permanent structure: most homes have been built ad hoc. Off the main street that runs through both sections of Matadi (new and old) there are no planned streets or apparent order or shape. Vehicle tracks and footpaths have been created in the sand via use. Houses face in all directions and are of different dimensions. Buildings tend to be multi-purpose; schools can become meeting houses or churches. A market is located in New Matadi halfway up the main road on the right hand side. Approximately fifty uneven wooden tables lined up in rows are occupied by women and their younger female assistants. The majority of sellers trade the same produce: peppers, onions and other condiments and spices, fish, coal, oil, rice and chickens that roam the sandy ground. It is a vibrant space of noise, colour and competition. Other sellers place themselves on the roadside on either side of the market to flaunt unique items like bananas, cooked corn, second-hand footwear and clothing, soap and hygiene products, sweets and Tupperware. The main road that runs through New Matadi is lined with sellers. There is a sense of chaos yet functional order as little seems formalised, permanent or definite (Jacobs 1961; Scott 1998; see also Simone 2004).

Every 'community' has a name; these are often derived either from physical or visible characteristics. For example, 'Chocolate City' is so called because of its dark brown sand, which turns into a chocolate-like substance during the raining season. A community called 'Rock Hill' was named thus because of the rock-breaking work carried out in the hilly area in which its people resided. Others like Matadi had names that were established long ago that had no relevance to their physical make-up and whose origin was not fully known.

Matadi had a number of churches; the most visible was the Parish of Holy Innocents Church situated within the DBYC. The DBYC is located beyond the market and the line of street sellers, to the left of the main road. The high walls that encircle the site begin at the road's edge and present Matadi's largest compound and landmark. The half-built school within the grounds is on two floors and the shell of the building asserts itself above the outer compound walls.[6] A two-storey building is a rare sight in Matadi; the housing block for the priests is also on two floors and can be seen from the roadside. Other churches are randomly placed within New Matadi and generally occupy communal spaces and multi-purpose buildings. Churches were not always obvious until they could be heard and identified on Sunday mornings or in the evenings during the week. Church services were loud as preaching was the tool used to communicate with its followers. Microphones powered by generators ensured the messages were heard and the crowd responded with apt acknowledgements. Music, singing, clapping and dancing were a frequent part of church services that were intermittently combined with the preaching. In Matadi there was a catholic church within the youth centre, a Korean church, multiple-denomination Christian churches and others that provided worship in specific ethnic dialects. Some churches were known as 'money-making churches'. Richie explained to me that his family used to attend a church in Matadi and the preacher would call out each member's name for attendance and they had to come one by one to the front of the church to put money in a collection box. He claimed that 'this would embarrass people who didn't have money and cause pressure.' Preachers would also claim that if contributions were given God would bless that person. From my house in Matadi I could regularly hear the preachers during their services saying, 'For 50LD[7] God will bless you.' Richie and his mother now attend the 'Korean Church'[8] and are under no pressure to pay money at every service. Crucially, religion was the binding factor amongst the Liberian population transcending any sense of community and ethnic boundaries. Attending one church over another is not important; one could attend many as long as one believed in the faith.

---

[6] The school building project ran out of money halfway through construction but has been used for classes in the last few years despite not being completed. The breeze block shell stands without windows, doors or any finishing to the rough brick work. Wooden scaffolding aids to stabilise the building.

[7] 50LD (Liberian dollar) converts to £0.35p. In Liberia 50LD would buy ten small bags of water or a large cup of uncooked rice.

[8] The 'Korean Church' in Matadi is a Christian church led by a Korean family.

Housing

Houses in Matadi varied in size, shape and structure ranging from single-room homes made from wood and metal sheeting to multiple-room houses made from concrete and breeze blocks. The more expensive high-end properties had surrounding concrete fencing for security. All these forms of housing could be seen integrated together in the community, whereas some communities in more deprived areas had only the most basic forms of housing. Most rented their properties; finding a house to buy was almost impossible in Matadi. Buying land was very expensive and virtually unavailable due to the high demand, and this made the housing system increasingly competitive.

For the young people of Matadi their place of residence was a tangible indicator to status, prospects and future possibilities of independent living. Richie lived in the swamp area behind the DBYC with his mother and other extended family members. The house was a temporary wooden structure protected with metal sheeting. It comprised two separate rooms for the sole purposes of storage and sleep, a toilet positioned by the swamp catered for all the families who resided in this area. His status as a youth was confirmed by his living arrangement with his mother, and his lack of financial wealth was evident by his basic living conditions in Matadi's lowest form of housing. Richie's teammate Lawrence lived within a high-walled compound. His uncle was a politician and that status was extended to his family who resided with him. Lawrence's housing arrangement represented opportunity and a pathway to education and future employment which was gained through family networks.

Matadi has three housing types which reflect community hierarchy. The poorest (and usually largest) family groups occupy the zinc-roofed structures usually consisting of one or two rooms that housed up to eight people. The land behind and beyond the DBYC consists of swamps and creeks, where lie the foundations for galvanised iron-roofed houses (referred to locally as 'zinc'). Generally, they do not include furniture other than wicker stools; food is prepared outside where coal fires are burned on the ground. The small strips of land separating these houses are communal spaces for sitting, playing, washing and drying clothes and cooking. The average price for such housing is US$5 per month. It is common for the landowner or extended family to live in the same community to manage the properties and collect the rent. There is no electricity supply or running water to these houses, and communal toilets are situated next to open swamp areas. Zinc house residents tend to share washing lines to hang clothes, and partly due to their proximity to each other, they share outside space without claim. Although adequate during the dry season, the zinc houses flood during the rainy season and cause great health risks for the families which occupy the space. Many of these houses are filled beyond capacity. This form of housing is also found sporadically throughout Matadi as any available space has been built upon. Clusters of Zinc houses surround larger and more stable properties adding to the disorder.

Another type of housing is called 'estate'. These are larger houses made up of breeze blocks and cement. They are situated around and within the main areas of zinc-roofed houses and spread across the majority of the land that is considered Matadi. They have their own bathroom either within the house or as a separate outhouse. Although many such homes include a washbasin and a toilet, such artefacts normally do not function and water for sanitation and bathing is still collected from communal pumps. These domestic manual chores are completed by the children and young people of the home. Some of these houses are connected to generators for electricity supply, but their working depends on the occupiers' ability to afford petrol. There are no perimeter fences or specific boundary markings for such houses, albeit the land around the house is referred to by the owner as 'my yard' signifying a strong sense of ownership in comparison to that of zinc houses. Residents in estate houses have their own inside and outside cooking areas where they can also wash and dry clothes and socialise. Families which reside in estate houses have at least one member working full-time usually in government ministries in central Monrovia, or in hotels and supermarkets catering for foreign aid agencies and UN officials. Depending on their size most estate houses would be priced between US$25 and US$100 per month.

Those referred to as 'compounds' provide the most luxurious form of housing. Pellow studied compounds in Accra and believed they are significant because of the activities they are able to facilitate, their flexibility and the relationships they anchor (2003, p. 173). For Pellow compounds represent a microcosm of the social systems of which they are a part (1991, pp. 187–188). A compound is a house or building surrounded by tall bricked walls with barbed wire or broken glass resting at the top to deter the curious and the criminal. The entrance is a large metal gate usually only opened to allow cars to enter but locked at all other times to keep away outsiders. These houses usually have multiple bedrooms, a communal area, a cooking area and a bathroom. Most have electricity supply. Water is still collected from hand pumps but the majority of compounds include their own wells. There can be three or four houses within one compound. Larger houses can be over two floors. Many occupants employ locals to wash their clothes and clean their houses, some even employ 'house-boys' for security and labour-intensive duties. The residents of such housing include foreign-born UN employees, Liberian-born government ministry officials, parliamentary candidates, elected senators and representatives and business owners (usually involved in rubber, palm oil or large supermarkets). These are 'big men' to the youth and residents of Matadi. Compounds are usually built on the outer boundaries because of the space needed for such housing but are also scattered amongst zinc and estate houses. They can be rented for anything up to US$800 per month depending on one's occupation; it is known that UN employees can afford to pay more.

The housing system in Matadi thus represents a distinct social hierarchy. Those residing in compounds are more likely to receive high school and university education and are therefore more likely to become financially independent. They are amongst the most eligible bachelors. Living in the lowest type of housing meant that young people are more likely to share space with family members, not attend school or slowly progress through schooling when finances allowed it. Their development into a respected status could be indefinitely deferred, thus affecting official employment opportunities, independent living and bride wealth. Community living meant no one could hide their family's financial status.

Employment, Money-Making and Hustling

Living in Matadi provided opportunities for employment. Every Monrovian community has a marketplace that whilst seemingly randomly placed take advantage of any open space, usually a rare commodity in densely populated settlements. This provides small business opportunities primarily for the women of the community who sell goods at a small profit. Whilst living in Matadi I was expected to purchase my food from my community market, as buying food from elsewhere would be frowned upon and cause *chi chi pulley* amongst the sellers. Part of having a 'good' image was investing and supporting community businesses. *Kobo* shops provide cooked food; many are run by young girls under the instruction of senior female family members and are placed along the main road through Matadi. The need for charging mobile telephones encouraged charging booths powered by petrol-fuelled generators. Money-changing stalls,[9] converting American dollars into Liberian dollars, and mobile-phone scratch-card vendors all encourage entrepreneurial ventures. Facilities like churches and schools provide maintenance tasks and skilled and administrative jobs.

Most male youths gain money through 'hustling', petty trading of small goods such as mobile phones and clothing, stealing or performing manual labour for local residents (cf. Munive 2010). Making money is another way to assert status. In Liberia and within community structures money equals power, power equals status, being a successful entrepreneur (illegally or legally acquired) means being respected and branded a 'big man'. Being a 'big man' navigates a clear path to becoming an elder. Sahlins (1963) claims that 'big man status is attained as a result of a series of acts which elevate a person above the common herd', in the case of Liberia—youth (p. 289). Big men need to be identified in order to mark a distinction between themselves and the lower social status of youth. This in part is achieved through status symbols and the ability to fill the big man role according to social criteria (cf. Nugent 1995). This in turn can convert economic resources into political authority or provide entry into formal institutions, thus widening the division between the informal and formal economic and status-defined ventures of youths and adults (see also Medard 1992; Simone 2004).

Hustling is therefore a petty version of entrepreneurship and a youth behaviour that is constructed from previous experience of adult practices to gain status. Roitman claims: 'Hustling, illegal and licit activities are a

---

[9] These were small wooden boxed structures secured by a padlock and always watched over by men sitting on plastic chairs next to it.

form of work for the marginalised' (2006, p. 258; see also Chabel and Daloz 1999). Hustling is a form of non-regulated economic exchanges. Such exchanges can cross the somewhat blurred boundary from legal to illegal. Distinction here is not important as the majority of money-making practices are considered hustling. In the case of Liberia, and specifically Matadi, licit practices are defined by normal behaviours in the context of community, not by morality or informal law and culture. Similarly, Janet Roitman considered the ethics of illegality in the Chad basin and claimed: 'Ultimately, while viewed by most as illegal, unregulated economic activities and violent methods of extraction are also described as legitimate; most often, these alleged exceptional practices are elaborated by local people as rational or reasonable behaviour' (2006, p. 249). Hustling is therefore crucial to the urban economy. According to the 2009 Rapid Impact Assessment on the global economic crisis in Liberia, 'The share of working poor is extremely high with more than 85 % not earning a sufficient income to lift themselves and their families above the US$1 a day poverty line' (International Labour Organization, p. 32). It is estimated that only 16 % of all employment can be considered to be formally paid (ibid, p. 33). This shortfall is thus supplemented by the act of hustling.

Hustling is the model for all business in Liberia; 'Big men' also hustle but do so whilst wearing a suit under the guise of a formally employed citizen. Corruption and morally questionable forms of business are part of Liberian society. The Liberian Anti-Corruption Commission (LACC) claims that corruption 'is a universal phenomenon that transcends culture, nationality and race. In Liberia, the practice is endemic and alarming' (LACC 2011). Unofficial practices are part of the bureaucracy of business and making money for all generations. Being arrested for an illegal act like stealing is another form of money exchange; freedom can be bought in Liberia. This nexus of relationships forms the trail of those who benefit from hustling; it can be seen as economic redistribution. An explanation for this comes from Roitman who argues as follows:

> The idea that theft is work is more than just a rationalisation of illegal practice; it is a reflection that is grounded in particular notions about what constitutes wealth, what constitutes licit or proper manners of appropriation, and how one governs both wealth and economic relations. (2006, p. 256)

Women have their own form of hustling. They form relationships with men, sometimes multiple, in return for money, clothes, food or other items. The more money a man has, the more desirable he becomes. Hustling is vital for survival. Within youth culture and the wider society there is a rationality of illegality; corruption is endemic in politics, business and day-to-day life. As illegal practices become the norm and are expected in money-making pursuits the local view of morality and ethics becomes blurred, especially if the opportunity to profit becomes apparent. Some churches are known as money-making churches and demand financial contributions for the exchange of blessings, health and financial good fortune. If the customs of the church, police, politicians and businessmen promote money-making schemes and endorse vague official procedures, then hustling can be viewed not only as a product of the post-conflict environment but as an initiation of essential skills into adulthood. Hustling is critical for survival, gaining power and raising status, yet its lack of moral, ethical or legal boundaries creates another chaotic concept in an already anarchic space. Community is therefore an essential part of livelihood and survival and acts as a platform for economic opportunity. A critical function of community is to provide economy for its residents. In this pursuit, adults and youths both prescribe to similar practices under the umbrella of hustling; however, the manner and perception of others in the community towards both groups is distinctly different.

Free Time

Walking through the main road of Matadi it is overwhelmingly common to see groups of young people and youths loitering, sitting or simply walking up and down aimlessly. At night most of the youths gather at Central Matadi Junction, at the 'T' junction connecting New Matadi to Old Matadi and Central Monrovia. Here there is a bar known as a *club*, a betting booth called *winners*, and areas that sell alcohol and play loud music. Many use this as a social gathering point. *Video clubs* are another gathering point for young people. Wooden structures covered with metal sheeting house rows of wooden benches for seating with all the paying occupants focused towards large projectors at the front. International football matches prove the most popular as hundreds cram inside to be part of the entertainment. African movies and news events are also shown. Large men secure the video clubs, collecting money, ensuring no palava turns into violence and protecting the equipment; long wooden clubs are their weapon of choice. Prices range from 30LD [10]) to 100LD depending on the prestige surrounding the event. For some, given the choice between eating and watching a Champions League Match, their stomachs would lose out.

The use of these spaces and the interactions within them proved an indicator of social status not only for me as an observer but also for the Matadi residents. Adults and elders do not loiter and socialise on the streets aimlessly; their movements are purposeful and engaged. Video clubs and bars are places for youths to interact, hustle (in this environment by betting) and have heated discussions, debates or arguments about what they're watching. They compete by outperforming each other by their behaviour and the use of props to attract the most desirable girls. Big men also occupy these spaces but their manner is distinctly different. They sit unchallenged surrounded by submissive and willing supporters flaunting their wealth by ordering others to get drinks and food. Free time is a time for enjoyment and pursuing leisure and social activities; the activities that community residents choose to participate in and the manner in which they conduct themselves whilst doing so is directly linked to their status.

In this highly socially competitive environment, leisure time is spent by adults and elders pursuing activities afforded to them through the fruits of formal employment. Sport is not considered a pursuit of the established hierarchy; only on occasion will men gather on a Sunday after church for an informal football game, and youths are not invited. This is known as an 'Old Timers' gathering and is a rare event. Sport is pursued by those without responsibility and those who have plentiful free time; this excludes adults who have more obligations, responsibilities and purposeful ways of spending their weekends.

---

[10] 1LD is the equivalent of 0.01penny and 30LD = £0.21p.

Community Organisation, Security and Its Effect on Youth

The post-conflict environment in Liberia has created numerous security risks. The number of arms in circulation and the weapons that evaded the disarmament process have created real concerns for personal security. As one of the world's poorest countries Liberia faces daily struggles for sustenance. This state of survival, desperation and the need to obtain wealth for social worth and status combined with the availability of arms has increased the rate of armed robbery. Poverty has also increased the incidents of petty theft. Being part of Matadi's community provided certain residents with a sense of relative security. Neighbourhood-watch groups were common in the absence of street-level police. Smith-Hohn (2010) states that 'with the rise in crime and the lack of adequate state-led responses to the problem, community-based neighbourhood watch teams have become more prevalent in Liberia' (p. 141, see also Baker 2007, 2009; Basedau et al. 2007). At night if someone was in trouble and called for help, neighbours would be obliged to investigate and assist. People tended to calls for help when a house had been entered by robbers with the call of *rogue rogue*. Houses were also susceptible to fires from candles, which could burn curtains, mosquito nets and wooden panels. Sickness and motorbike accidents were also reasons to call for help within one's community. Some communities formed groups of men to patrol at night to prevent armed robberies perpetrated by outsiders.[11] It was well known that a community situated on the main road was more at risk from such armed robbers as it was easy for them to escape. Residential settlements based off main roads usually had only one road of access in and out and so 'rogues' could be easily caught. Such 'community policing' dealt predominantly with crime that had been committed by an 'outsider'. Retribution would be administered to the culprit there and then usually in the form of beating or *flogging* the *rogue* who would then be escorted—post-beating—to the police station. Beating was rarely so severe to the extent of needing medical assistance; it was done as a means to scare the

---

[11] An 'outsider' is someone who lives outside of the community or a stranger.

perpetrators, to pacify and restrain them so they could be taken to the police station without too much opposition. The weapon of choice was usually a wooden cane. The eldest member of the group would supervise; giving orders and ensuring that their actions were 'appropriate'.

Non-governmental organisations endorse the illusion that communities act as a safety net for Liberians from a violent post-conflict society and function as a collective unit of people who provide security and safety for all. However, trust is virtually non-existent amongst Liberians; secrecy is used to protect possessions and finances. Richie would hide money in the sand close to where he slept to protect it and would not even inform his father of any financial gains. He would sleep with valuable items near his head or underneath his mattress on the floor. Family and friends were not necessarily trusted companions when it concerned money or tangible wealth, as he had learnt from previous experience. Once, a young cousin of his came to visit our house. He looked tired so I encouraged him to rest on Richie's mattress in his room. The boy left half an hour later without saying goodbye to Richie. When I told Richie he had left he ran to his room and then ran out of the compound without explaining anything to me. I presumed the cousin had forgotten something and Richie was running after him to return it. Soon after Richie returned and explained that his cousin had stolen some money from under his mattress and he had to beg his younger relative to return it, which he did. Richie's analysis was simple: 'You can't trust anybody. He's a bad pekin.' Gaining wealth and therefore social recognition was much more important than maintaining social relations and meaningful family ties. These could be rebuilt once status had been gained.

Other crimes would gain less attention, especially crimes against women. Rape and domestic violence was and remains commonplace in Liberia. Rape was endemic during the civil conflict and was used not only as a weapon but for ritualistic purposes and male initiation into rebel factions. Rape continues to be rife, especially towards young adolescent females. In 2011 'Doctors Without Borders' treated many rape victims and claimed that nine out of ten were under 18 years old, almost half of them were under twelve and one was under four (Toral 2012, np). One of the first acts by President Johnson Sirleaf in 2005 was to strengthen Liberia's previously weak rape legislation. A special court was formed to deal with rape cases. In 2011, 1475 rapes were reported, but this is a small percentage of how many actually occur. Many victims stay silent due to social pressures and the shame that can be brought to the family. Fear and the stigma attached to such crimes lead many to turn a blind eye. Men are also the principal enforcers of informal community complaints and this reinforces internal hierarchy and unequal justice in a wider patriarchal society. Women and the young persist as the main victims as well as the perpetrators. Conflict within the marital home is pursued behind closed doors and incidents of domestic violence are largely ignored. This reinforces wider gender-specific social hierarchical processes in Liberia and maintains them at the community level.

Violence amongst young people and youths are also seen as petty criminal acts that should be managed by the involved parties. Only when help is sought by the citizens involved does any intervention occur. This is usually led by the elders of the community in a private or public space. Conflict amongst adults is frowned upon and not expected to be publicly displayed. Again in extreme cases elders are called upon to aid negotiations. This is rare and would usually involve land disputes or marital infidelity. There is a clear distinction between adults and youths and the perception of others of violence; youth involvement in conflict and violence is not considered serious but adults who are involved in identical circumstances are frowned upon, and this will potentially incite intervention by elders who are expected to rectify the situation in private.

Stealing is the most frequent crime, committed by both community members and outsiders. Due to its frequency the level of tolerance is limited; it is a nuisance, and at times violent and always immoral. As in many circumstances and potential scenarios within Matadi, and the wider society, the rhetoric surrounding ethics, behaviour and morals (generally based on Christian teachings) is clear but the practice is inconsistent and blurred. Within the community there is a definite contradiction between words, lecturing, preaching and action by both adults and youths.

Those whom we might call community citizens, residing in Matadi, caught committing a criminal act are usually punished in a similar fashion but afterwards the family is called upon by the elders to ensure correct measures are enforced in the home to prevent recurrence of this behaviour. If the family is known in the community and the offence is minimal, the police will not be called. The threat of harsher punishment or police involvement is usually the binding factor to prevent further crime, although an elder or religious figure is called upon to counsel the individual and provide moral guidance. A community member having a reputation for such behaviour is looked down upon by neighbours, gossiped about and distrusted. In many instances young boys are either the heroes or the villains within the community. This neighbourhood resource opens up avenues for abuse towards young people as well as protection. Either way, on many occasions, young boys are not to be trusted and are openly accused without question.

The following are effects of the key aspects of community that were discussed: neighbourliness, housing, trust, informal employment and hustling, as well as security, crime and punishment are conducted under the premise of a functional, inclusive, progressive community setting. Yet, the need to claim and assert status causes facades, competition and mistrust. Analysis will suggest that the principal community functions are directed, conducted and enforced by adults and elders for the benefit of adults and elders. Youths are pushed to the margins of the community system. They are seen as the perpetrators of crime who cross the border from informal employment to illegal ventures known as hustling; they then become the victims of community policing and the main focus of mistrust. The community function of providing relative safety to residents ultimately victimises women and the young.

Money-Making, Status, Safety and Survival

Liberian society does not have state provisions for the poor, the sick, the hungry or the unemployed. Furthermore, education, healthcare, housing and welfare are not subsidised. Therefore, the role of the community and one's family and neighbours are of pivotal importance in an individual's existence. The primary functions of a community include providing for housing, economic opportunity and relative security. Residents' use of free time and modes of speech combine with these functions to determine status, establish adult, elder and youth roles, influence others' perceptions of social standing and generate money-making opportunities.

The DBYC personnel in Matadi also believe in this claim and provide intervention and support exclusively for those within the community of Matadi.

I have analysed the case in order to cast doubt upon formal and informal procedure, relationships and behaviour, creating a degree of scepticism concerning the notion of community in Matadi used by Don Bosco and other NGOs. Evidently community structures do encourage youth stagnation and the broader hierarchical nature of Liberian society. Yet, the community provides relative security and its own policing and penal system, support and guidance from elders, food from neighbours when in need, and it serves the collective requirements of its residents in bad times and good. The most important aspect of a young person's life lies not solely in the hands of his or her family but within the strength and support of one's community. But community is also the place that creates tension and harbours internal conflict. It secures hierarchy and prejudices others. The discrimination faced by youth in the community is disabling but still living in such an environment is essential for survival and provides the slimmest of opportunities to progress and prove social worth. If one were to strip back the concept and weigh up its functions and workings, 'community' would be seen as an associational identity with some sense of collective identity and common purpose based on residence. Money making, status and survival are the significant functions of any Liberian settlement, but community is what provides the opportunities, allows access, encourages development and serves to supply security, amenities and a platform for acknowledgement. In a post-conflict urban community individual identity takes precedence over collective identity.

As an ethnographer researching rehabilitation and football strategies I needed to focus on community if I were to truly understand the trilogy of post-conflict society, youth and Liberian culture. One thing was clear: community had the capacity to encourage youths to live moral lives with integrity and with resources such as churches, community organisations, sports grounds and the customs of helping neighbours, sharing, protecting each other and supporting one another. However, community structures encouraged youth stagnation by highlighting their status as dependents. Elders and accomplished individuals were seen as all-powerful and were openly able to assert this authority upon young people, at times leading to abuse without question. It seems that in a community young people can thrive within the social and cultural networks or be open to prejudice, abuse and dependency and thus stagnate. It would seem that 'community' creates a problem for young people whilst football exposes the concept for SDP projects. This dual notion of community and football for development and peace underpins the problems being examined for the specific generation of Liberian youth who lived their childhood through the conflict. Youth-focused SDP projects endorse and promote the notion of community. NGOs direct policy and programming actually becomes conflictual to local functions of community, which in turn exacerbates conditions for young people.

References

Adejunmobi, M. (2004). *Vernacular palaver: Imaginations of the local and non-native languages in West Africa* (Vol. 9). Buffalo: Multilingual Matters.

Amit, V. (2001). Youth culture, anthropology. *International Encyclopedia of the Social & Behavioral Sciences, 24*, 16657–16660.

Amit, V., & Rapport, N. (2002). *The trouble with community: Anthropological reflections on movement, identity and collectivity.* London/Sterling: Pluto Press.

Baker, B. (2007). Post war policing by communities in Sierra Leone, Liberia, and Rwanda. *Democracy and Security, 3*(2), 215–236.

Baker, B. (2009). A policing partnership for post war Africa? Lessons from Liberia and Southern Sudan. *Policing & Society, 19*(4), 372–389.

Barth, F. (1969). *Ethnic groups and boundaries: The social organization of culture difference.* Boston: Little, Brown and Co.

Berger, B. M. (1988). Disenchanting the concept of community. *Society, 25*(6), 50–52.

Bloch, M. (1975). *Political language and oratory in traditional society.* London: Academic.

Bloch, M. (1986). *From blessing to violence: History and ideology in the circumcision ritual of the Merina of Madagascar.* Cambridge/New York: Cambridge University Press.

Chabal, P., & Daloz, J.-P. (1999). *Africa works: Disorder as political instrument.* Oxford: James Currey.

Cochrane, G. (1971). *Development anthropology.* New York: Oxford University Press.

Cooke, B., & Kothari, U. (2001). *Participation: The new tyranny?* London/New York: Zed Books.

De Heusch, L. (1980). Heat, physiology and cosmology: Rites de passage among the Tonga. In I. Karp, & C. S. Bird (Eds.), *Explorations in African systems of thought* (pp. 27–43). Bloomington: Indiana University Press.

De Sardan, J. P. O. (2005). *Anthropology and development: Understanding comtemporary social change.* London/New York: Zed Books.

Delanty, G. (2003). *Community.* London/New York: Routledge.

FIFA. (2013). Social responsibility: Football for hope. http://www.fifa.com/sustainability/football-for-hope.html.

FrontPageAfrica. (2013). Defining community in post-war Liberia: Challenges and opportunities.

Goodenough, W. H. (1971). *Culture, language and society.* Reading: Addison-Wesley.

Goodenough, W. H. (1976). Multiculturalism as the normal human experience. *Council on Anthropology and Education Quarterly, 7*(4), 4–7.

Hannerz, U. (1969). *Soulside: Inquiries into ghetto culture and community.* New York: University of Chicago Press.

Hansen, K. T. (2005). Getting stuck in the compound: Some odds against social adulthood in Lusaka, Zambia. *Africa Today, 51*(4), 3–16.

Jacobs, J. (1961). *The death and life of great American cities.* New York: Random House.

LACC. (2011). Profile of the LACC.

Medard, J.-F. (1992). Le "big man" en Afrique: esquisse d'analyse du politicien entrepreneur. *L'Annee Sociologique, 42*, 167–192.

Munive, J. (2010). The army of 'unemployed' young people. *Young, 18*(3), 321–338.

Nugent, P. (1995). *Big men, small boys and politics in Ghana: Power, ideology and the burden of history, 1982–94.* London: Pinter Pub Ltd.

Oldfield, S. (2004). Urban networks, community organising and race: An analysis of racial integration in a desegregated South African neighbourhood. *Geoforum, 35*(2), 189–201.

Pellow, D (1991). Spaces that Teach. *Human Behaviour and Environment*, Vol 12, pp187-210.

Roitman, J. (2006). The ethics of illegality in the Chad Basin. In J. Comaroff, & J. L. Comaroff (Eds.), *Law and disorder in the postcolony* (pp. 247–272). Chicago: University of Chicago Press.

Pellow, D (2003). The Architecture of Female Seclusion in West Africa. In, Low, S, M and Lawrence-Zuniga, D (2003). The Anthropology of Space and Place: Locating culture, pp160-183. Malden, MA: Blackwell Publishing.

Sahlins, M. D. (1963). Poor man, rich man, big-man, chief: Political types in Melanesia and Polynesia. *Comparative studies in Society and History,* 5, 285–303.

Schlyter, A. (2003). *Multi-Habitation: Urban housing and everyday life in Chitungwiza, Zimbabwe* (Vol. 123). Uppsala: Nordic Africa Institute.

Scott, J. C. (1998). *Seeing like a state: How certain schemes to improve the human condition have failed.* New Haven: Yale University Press.

Simone, A. (2004). *For the city yet to come: Changing African life in four cities.* Durham/London: Duke University Press.

Smith-Höhn, J. (2010). *Rebuilding the security sector in post-conflict societies: Perceptions from urban Liberia and Sierra Leone.* Münster: LIT Verlag.

The World Bank. (2004). Community-based and -driven development: A critical review. *The World Bank Research Observer,* 19(1), 1–40.

Toral, A. (2012). History of violence: Struggling with the legacy of rape in Liberia. http://world.time.com/2012/04/30/history-of-violence-struggling-with-the-legacy-of-rape-in-liberia/.

Turner, V. (1969). *The ritual process: Structure and anti-structure.* New Brunswick/London: Transaction Publishers.

Welter, V. M. (2010). The limits of community-the possibilities of society: On modern architecture in Weimar Germany. *Oxford Art Journal,* 33(1), 63–80.

Williams, R. C. (2011). *Beyond squatter rights: Durable solutions and development-induced displacement in Monrovia, Liberia* (p. 5). Oslo: Norwegian Refugee Council.

6

Becoming Somebody: Escaping from Youthhood

Youth

A developing theme throughout this book is the continued usage of broad and ill-defined key terms by development practitioners. These terms are used to seduce, mask reality and appeal not only to potential partners but to local populations. The notion of youth is central to this theme; *youth* is a broad, vague definition of a person who, one presumes, has not achieved adulthood. This would potentially suffice; however, it would be wrong to accept such terms as universal without considering the cultural and socio-economic conditions of the specific population being examined. Ethnographic evidence in this book considers youth in Monrovia as a social category judged by social worth, the ability to acquire financial independence and displaying the tangible riches of adulthood. Youth is a social status in Liberia and one that relies heavily upon adult acceptance and recognition, entrepreneurial skill, acquisition of a home and family and the ability to sustain such wealth, power and stature.

The consideration of youth has gained momentum in an era of increased national conflict, modernity, globalisation and economic instability. Many anthropologists have examined youths in order to gain a greater

© The Editor(s) (if applicable) and The Author(s) 2016
H. Collison, *Youth and Sport for Development*,
DOI 10.1057/978-1-137-52470-6_6

understanding of this controversial social category that is centred around issues of local politics, economy, culture, national security and society in general (Mead 1928, Evans-Pritchard 1969, Malinowski 1929, Amit 2001, and more recently De Waal and Argenti 2002, Gable 2000 and Weiss 2002). Anthropology is very useful in this regard as Mary Bucholtz states: 'Youth is a flexible and contestable social category…Anthropology is well situated to offer an account of how young people around the world produce and negotiate cultural forms' (2002, pp. 526–528).

The term 'youth' has particular masculine connotations and invariably describes males: 'Many scholars consider youth culture to be a male preserve almost by definition, and some even maintained that the primary purpose of such cultures is to work out issues of masculinity' (Bucholtz 2002, p. 537). Throughout this work the terms young people, young men and youth are recognised, used, unpacked and contextualised and, on rare occasions, conflated. This illustrates firstly the fluid and social conditions placed on such terminology and also the changing acknowledgements of status dependent on the space and specific interaction or activity. Going forward it should be recognised that *youth* in Liberia are male, the term *young people* tend to describe mixed groups of adolescents or females and *young men* demonstrates the spectrum of Youthhood. *Young men* can be used as a term to describe males who physically symbolise adulthood but lack status and adult authority; in this regard young men are part of the Youthhood spectrum and should not be confused with those considered adult. A growing trend in the Global North is to use the term 'young people' as a positive description of adolescents and 'youth' when presenting a negative image (Jones 2009, p. 145). It would seem that some are recognising the negative message attached to the term but this acknowledgement has not impacted its use by international development and peace agencies in Liberia. One cannot ignore the presence of youth; in any given society youths are both symbols of the past and indicators of the future. This point leads to the core issue youth presents for Liberia: If youths are not becoming adults what consequences will this hold for Liberia's future?

In Liberia generational categories are part of a struggle for influence, social worth, authority, position and power. As such, generational categories shift according to socio-cultural contexts. These realities have implications: the challenge and difficulty of ageing in Liberia has constructed hierarchical relationships and informal boundaries between generational categories. In contemporary Liberia, the difficulty of achieving and maintaining socially acceptable adulthood has resulted in the creation of a paradoxically rigid boundary between adults and youths. Beyond a certain point, these are not stages in a single life cycle, but increasingly operate like class distinctions: a huge swathe of Liberian youths face a whole life stuck in that category, without the capacity to advance to the status of elder—or even adult. This has very specific implications on males who are expected to adopt certain roles and duties as adults. These expectations are largely being financially dependent, securing a wife, providing for children and maintaining a family home. Relationships can at times actively prevent youths from ageing and thus confirm and affirm their low status in the eyes of their communities and the broader Liberian society (cf. Utas 2003, 2005; see also Sommers 2012). Large numbers of community members are locked into 'Youthhood' and implicitly denied access to adulthood, power and status. The relationship between youth and adult and youth and elder was a prominent feature on the football field within the youth centre.

Ageing in Liberia: Traditions

Ruling elites and chiefdoms have always governed community structures in Liberia since its origin. In rural areas of Liberia chiefdoms are still active. This style of social control has seen little change in tribal villages or suburban communities. Internal leadership within communities based on defined status levels has been a principal element of community living in pre- and post-conflict Liberia. The hierarchical organisation of community and its residents has intensified during the post-conflict era, as has the definition and categorisation of people to highlight status and pecking orders.

In Liberia the ability for young people to pass from adolescent to adult has always depended on elders granting terms and channels for access to adulthood. As George Harley's discussion of Kpelle 'bush schools' (1941) claimed:

No boy or young man is considered a member of the tribe unless he has been initiated by suitable rites into the company of his elders. The adolescent must undergo certain ordeals to prove that he is ready and worthy to take on the responsibilities of citizenship—until then he does not count. (Cited in Maclay and Ozerdem 2010, p. 344)

In traditional indigenous societies formal rites of passage via the *Poro* and *Sande* bush schools are the facilitator for initiation into adulthood (cf. Bellman 1984). Post-conflict youth who reside in the capital of Monrovia have found themselves removed from traditional styles of living and rites of passage and exposed to Liberia's 'modern' city culture. But even in this environment Liberian youths remain dependent on elders to be considered, confirmed and acknowledged as an adult.

There are two schools of thought concerning the post-conflict scenario. On the one hand, young people are characterised as victims of a conflict which has prevented them from fulfilling their potential. On the other, they are portrayed as revolution-seekers at best characterised as impulsive, violent and irresponsible. The marginalisation of youth in Africa is commonplace and widely acknowledged and accepted: 'Children and youth are often placed in the margins of the public sphere and major political, socio-economic, and cultural process despite accounting for the majority of the population in Africa' (Honwana and De Boeck 2005, p. 1). The marginalisation of youth in Liberia was a recurrent theme during fieldwork: 'Disconnected from broader society many young Liberians are actively marginalized' (Maclay and Özerdem 2010, p. 344). Henrik Vigh believes that 'the predicament of not being able to gain the status and responsibility of adulthood is a social position that people seek to escape as it is characterised by marginality, stagnation and a truncation of social being' (2006, p. 37).

Matts Utas studied youth in Liberia extensively and claims: 'As the category of youth is constructed upon notions of social age, social markers such as marriage, or at least a stable relationship with a woman, are requirements for moving out of the youth category and into adulthood' (Utas 2005, p. 141, see also Utas 2008). He further explains that older men during the conflict were classified as youth: 'They were mature men lacking the wealth and power required to cross the border between youth and adulthood' (ibid). Although in Utas's view the war was seen as a means of social mobility towards adulthood in the quest for respect and status, this was only short lived; 'once war is over marginal souls are once again deported to the margins' (ibid). This created what he termed 'youthmen'. This confirms that *youth* is a social category in Liberia that deems age insignificant. The issues of social mobility and marginality of youths before the conflict have returned and the quest regarding age remains a primary concern for many males in post-conflict Liberia, as Cote argues:

> For large numbers of people, prolonged adolescence—and more recently 'youth' —now takes up much, if not all, of what in earlier society would have been 'adulthood' ... it appears that an increasing number of people are not 'growing up' in the traditional sense of the word. (Cote 2000, p. 1)

The current position for many Liberians is bleak. The majority of young people reside in an indefinite state of powerless 'Youthhood' in what Richards called 'a crisis of youth' (1995) and others a 'lost generation'. These phrases imply an acknowledgement of the vulnerable state of the youth category as well as their lack of recognition and at times rejection from mainstream society. Adulthood was always socially defined in Liberia, but now it seems that the means by which youth can achieve that status has been withdrawn. Therefore, today youths are locked into social categories exacerbated by extreme poverty within a chaotic post-conflict environment. Those considered adult meanwhile fight to sustain their superiority and acknowledgement whilst others struggle to climb the ladder and join this chaotic game. In Liberia sustaining status is just as consuming as the journey to acquire it.

Governmental Perspectives

The term *youth* is freely used by governments and aid agencies and also in Liberian conversations. Officially the UN defines youth as anyone between the ages of fifteen and twenty-four. The Liberian government considers youth as those between the ages of fifteen and thirty-five because 'the government's rationale behind such a broad definition of youth is that 14 years of warfare have left "over-age youth" ill equipped to cope in a post-conflict society' (USAID 2009, p. 5). Observing the ways in which the term is applied a pattern begins to emerge. The 'European Youth Forum'[1] provides information regarding youth NGOs and key words are ever evident: 'disadvantaged, marginalised, challenged, deprived, exclusion, disengaged, homeless, poverty, unemployed' to name but a few.[2] The term 'youth' is problematic and provides assumptions about the population it is describing. There is a clear stereotype of 'youth' which carries many expectations or in most cases lacks expectation for their contribution to a civil society.

Youths are deemed a threat by the international development community: 'A well-educated, skilled and productive youth portends a bright future for any nation. Conversely, an unskilled and poorly educated youth whose indulgence is hard drugs, crime, and violence is a great threat to societal security and sustainable development' (Zakaria 2006, p. 52). This understandable sentiment needs to be disputed. Uneducated and unskilled youths are not implicitly disengaged, dysfunctional and a risk to civil society; such statements and judgements only encourage prejudice. Honwana and De Boeck (2005) argue that children and youth in Africa are the 'makers and breakers' of society and are the focal point between crisis and renewal (ibid., p. 2). The assumption too is often that youths are the extremes within society; both the light and the dark, the future and the threat to the future.

Considerations of Youth

The international aid community uses the term 'youth' as a global classification of units of people to be targeted. Lacking acknowledgement of the depth of meaning of the notion—historically and culturally—in the local context could potentially cause harm or encourage prejudice or prolong the problems associated with ageing, as Durham suggests:

---

[1] The European Youth Forum represents ninety-nine youth organisations, both National Youth Councils and International Non-Governmental Youth Organisations across Europe.

[2] Information gained from www.youthforum.org article titled 'Report on Youth NGOs'. Accessed 15 May 2012.

To pay attention to youth is to pay close attention to the topology of the social landscape—to power and agency; public, national and domestic spaces and identities, and their articulation and disjunctures; memory, history, and a sense of change; globalization and governance; gender and class. (Durham 2000, p. 113)

What precisely constitutes 'youth' provides considerable debate amongst many disciplines: sociologists, psychologists, cultural scientists and anthropologists all present different definitions. It has been argued that 'the sense of youth's absence in anthropology suggests that in the 1990s, as anthropologists began to recover "missing" youth, older approaches to youth and childhood no longer seemed central to sociocultural anthropological analytics' (Durham 2004, p. 590). The identity of 'youth' transforms and emerges in new cultural formations and during periods of change. Anthropology is therefore ideally suited to offer an account of how young people around the world produce and negotiate cultural forms (Bucholtz 2002, p. 525–528). Issues surrounding youth are important to any consideration of society; therefore the methods for this investigation must pay attention to power, behaviour, agency, politics, moral configuration and social mobility.

In Liberia relationships are constructed according to status and this enforces wider hierarchical social constructs. Such a pursuit is supported by Wyn and White who claim that youth are 'a rational concept, which refers to the social processes whereby age is socially constructed, institutionalised and controlled in historically and culturally specific ways' (1997, p. 11). Jones's 1988 'Secondary Analysis' argued that youth are neither a homogeneous group nor a static one; considering young people otherwise would be inaccurate and misleading (p. 707). A multitude of elements need consideration when examining current Liberian youth, as Adams (2009) and Durham (2004) report: '"African youth" occupy an awkward place in anthropological studies, sliding between analytical frameworks that approach them either as long-neglected social agents or as historically composed, modern social products' (Adams, p. 798).

Perspectives on youth notably differ as Mary Adams notes. Anthropologists such as Reynolds (1995) view youth as passive receptacles of cultural value and socialities, whereas radical anthropologists consider youth as a product of intergenerational relationships. The difficulty of conceptualising youth is compounded by the treatment of this category by governments and NGOs. Liberian youth are seen as controversial subjects: active and volatile in some ways due to their involvement in the conflict yet stagnant and vulnerable in others as they struggle to establish livelihoods in the post-conflict era. They are engulfed in a tragic history yet lost in the present; no other demographic group encompasses so many factors involving intergenerational relationships, community, society, politics, culture and character. They are present yet removed, heard but not listened to, constantly watching and waiting whilst time continues to pass them by.

As with 'community' the term 'youth' is problematic. The concept of this general category is broad, vague and used generally as a global notion. It carries little insight into the culture and meaning of specific groups of people in the local context. As with 'community' it is the aid sector and local NGOs that have used the term in Liberia with great vigour and regularity. Its use within the International Aid Community has encouraged and influenced its use at the local level, amongst community populations and Liberian-run institutions. FIFA also contributes to and endorses the notion of 'youth' in Liberia. Collaborating with the aid sector and national football governing bodies, for SDP projects, youth and football have become a national phrase and concept: 'Since 1999, UNICEF and FIFA have expanded their partnership to focus on country-level collaboration, encouraging national partnerships to use football to achieve goals for children and youth' (2007, UNICEF, Sport for Development).

The engagement of youths in the local context will provide for a richer understanding of the social position they find themselves in, in post-conflict Liberia. My observations made from participation in football will identify youth's experiences of interactions with community members, adults and each other as well as their position within the Liberian society. It is well documented that football has the ability to unite and divide, but in this context is its use by NGOs and local aid institutions empowering players or drawing attention to their youth status? Is football a youth activity for the benefit of youths or for the benefit of its facilitators and sponsors? The relationships footballers experience within and out of the fence[3] in Matadi highlight the complexities of Youthhood and the impact that varying interactions with varying generations can have upon a footballer's status.

The Question of Youth

Father L is an American-born Salesian priest whose vocation had placed him in Liberia for over 15 years. He was present every day at the youth centre where he would walk slowly greeting children and youths. He never sat and would occasionally stop and observe the activities taking place on the main football field. He enjoyed the banter between the spectators and players and sometimes joined in or playfully—and provocatively—asked questions as to what was happening. Of all the SDB he was the most respected by the players not only for being the eldest and white, but for his ability to speak fluent Liberian English, and he was considered by most to be a 'Liberian'. During one training session Father L conversed about the team and the players' characters and as two players began palava on the field and the spectators began to mock he sighed and said: 'This is the only place I know where a 35-year-old man can still be a 15-year-old boy.' This religious site, engulfed as it was in preaching of the next life and the muscular Christian principles, was a space where men were reduced to boys and all regardless of age were by virtue of what they were participating in viewed as youth by their audience and community around them.

Matadi Youth Inside the Fence

> Young people in Liberia have typically had little independence or agency over their own lives, and even less influence in the community around them. (Maclay and Özerdem 2010, p. 344)

---

[3] Zatti footballers referred to the youth centre as being in or out of the fence.

Youth and their passion for football needed to be considered at the community level. It is at this level where teams formed, trained and played—and strategically—where NGOs targeted much of their interaction with young people. Matadi was my home, and my main informant, Richie, was the captain of the DBYC team 'Zatti'. Our common interest in football was what bonded us and he was keen that I come and observe their training sessions within the youth centre.

The main football field within the youth centre was the focal point of the site and the first thing one noticed when walking through the large blue entrance gate. The walls of the centre were high; people on the outside could only see the roof and the wooden scaffolding supporting the half-constructed school building. The gates were opened by the security staff daily at 4 pm. Children rushed to be the first to enter the play areas to access the swings and other rides in the playground. Others ran to be the first at the water pump managing skilfully not to trip over the large water containers they carried.

The majority of those who attended the youth centre were Matadi residents involved around the football field either playing, spectating, refereeing or just lingering and socialising. There was less haste or sense of urgency among the football players. They arrived casually from 4 pm usually strolling onto the sandy pitch to the far corner where concrete steps provided for a team bench and place to dress and change. Not all had football boots and the ones without would *improvise* and play in socks or casual shoes. The process of preparing to train was accompanied by good-natured palava, usually disagreeing about recently broadcast Premiership or Champions League performances; others spoke quietly about their days' activities, which were usually focused on issues of school or hustling. Generally, it was a jovial atmosphere of banter amongst boys that easily made the transition into animated palava. Once Richie and other senior members of the team beckoned the players from the concrete steps to the middle of the sand field, the players would form a circle and sing a song, either a religious hymn or one adapted to become a Zatti song. Their favourite was

> Build the ark O build the ark O Noah
> Build the ark O build the ark O Noah

O papa papa Noah build the ark let Zatti go
O papa papa Noah build the ark let Zatti go
O papa papa Noah build the ark let Zatti go

The players would then hold hands in a closer circle and a volunteer would lead a prayer. The training then began under the instruction of their coach but internally supervised by the captain and other senior players. This group of senior players (seniority was determined by the number of years they had played for the team) kept younger, newer recruits focused and policed them to ensure they were doing things properly. If a player was not keeping to task or going too slow, they would be heckled and called *lazy o* by their teammates. Eventually if their effort did not increase, the insults would become more personal about their ability as a player. Running laps was the principle method of 'training' followed by a match played between the Zatti squad and most often the *outsiders*. These *outsiders* were Matadi residents who played for different teams but enjoyed playing on their community ground against the local set-up.

Coach J was in charge of the team. He was appointed coach for several previous seasons and was paid for his services by the youth centre. As my presence became more obvious, regular players began to become inquisitive. They would greet me upon their arrival with the Liberian handshake asking, 'What's up?' in their mock American accents. I introduced myself to Coach J and explained that I was a student from London interested in Liberian football and youth. I strategically added that I was an Arsenal supporter—not a lie, but I had seen him in an old Arsenal shirt the day before and thought this would hold me in good stead. He overexcitedly welcomed me, called all the players to come and sit in front of him and introduced me saying, 'This is Coach Holly. She is from Europe, London; she is enjoying the team and wants to help us improve.' The players clapped. Henceforth I was known as 'Coach Holly', and trained the team from 4 to 6 pm every day and went with them to games at the weekend.

The relationships between the players, facilitating adults and supporters that formed from the game of football proved significant in Matadi. By its very nature football draws a range of people of varying backgrounds together for a multitude of purposes. Many of these relationships (including my own) were constructed because of Zatti FC and were apparent only within the confines of the youth centre. Such interactions between the team and players and persons of varying generations, statuses and roles gave insights into the complexity of football in Liberia and the nature of Youthhood, hierarchy and ageing.

The Youth Centre Rhetoric and Vision

Father M was the Youth Centre Director and engaged young people in their activities. He provided funds for materials and when necessary counselled the players through challenges. Nigerian-born, he was placed in Matadi 2 years previously. He was particularly passionate about Zatti, having both encouraged and paid for them to register for the third Division National League. To sustain their profile, he provided money for transport to games and sometimes food for the players upon their return. A friendly fixture was arranged between Zatti and the National under-20 Liberian team in 2010. Father M played with them and advised the players on their behaviour and attitude towards each other and the game. He appealed to them not to have palava between each other or the opposition and not to be scared of players who were bigger than them— in status, not size. Father M's main goal for the youth centre was to one day replace the sand pitch with artificial grass because the pitch is unplayable for long periods during the rainy season (June–October) and as there is no drainage, the water is retained on top of the sand. In addition, any boots the players manage to acquire quickly *spoil*[4] due to the sand, forcing the players to sew them back together. In a project-proposal to renovate the pitch Father M wrote:

> Our mission is to facilitate the physical, intellectual, spiritual, personal/ social and career development and progress of each youth through football.
> Objective: To facilitate an environment of peer support amongst the young people of Matadi through football. To meet with young people in

---

[4] Liberian English slang term meaning broken or ruined.

Matadi on a regular basis, through football, so as to constantly influence their life choices, options and behaviours.

Specific Outcomes: Gain self-awareness and improve self-esteem, make healthy choices and effective decisions, assume responsibility for their own behaviour, respect individual differences and cooperate and learn to resolve conflicts constructively.

Ultimately the Fathers of the youth centre see sport as a way of character building and shaping the behaviour of the youths in their charge, providing an escape from the realities of being young in Liberia and an opportunity to give moral, ethical and spiritual guidance. The DBYC can be viewed as a local internal SDP organisation. Father M follows muscular Christian teachings be it whilst *lecturing* the players or applying for funding grants from international institutions such as UNICEF. The youth centre was able to appeal to the International Aid Community by their exclusive focus on youth; it provided the already established notions ideal for global partnerships. However, this creates tension with the young people who play at the centre: they do not necessarily share their objectives.

Quick to be Satisfied: Youth Opportunities in the Game

Money-making pursuits and claiming status are major priorities for youths in Liberia. The consequence of this is mistrust between youths and adults. For those who dedicate their time to youth this becomes a source of much frustration—especially as making someone say 'sorry' seems to be the only source of acknowledgement of wrongdoing. The Fathers are deemed powerless to discipline—they do not condone or participate in violence against young people and are aware of the corruptive and potentially violent strategies of the police force and elders in the community, so therefore do not refer cases to outside authority structures.

Father M explained to me how he has to negotiate and meet the challenges of being in a position of power in Matadi:

The young people know I will listen to them and try to help. I brought a bike so the youth could learn now to cycle, like during the war until the rebels stole all of the equipment. One boy asked to use the bike so I said 'yes'; he stole the bike and sold it for small money. I asked him 'why did you do that?' he said 'because I was hungry'.

Father M spoke with obvious frustration as he continued, 'They know when they are really in trouble they can come to me and I will try to help, even with food or medicine.' He then described another incident to prove his point that he no longer fully trusted the young people he works with:

Two older youths from the football players asked if they could borrow plastic chairs for a graduation party in the community, so I said fine. They sold the chairs. Again I asked, 'Why did you do that?' They did not say anything to me, just 'sorry o'. You see that is the problem, you do not know if they are sincere.

Father M was part of a game he could not win. Dedicated to working with the youth in his community he had to provide in order to engage but hustling and individual gain was more important to most of the youths than appreciating his gestures of investment. And he had no resources by which he could enforce compliance.

In 2012 Jackson, a Zatti player, was suspended from the team by Father M for stealing a pair of football boots. Father M had purchased several pairs of boots for players to wear for their league fixtures. These were carried to the league venue in a laundry bag. Two young boys aged twelve who watched every training session came to every fixture and became the unofficial team apprentices, would fetch water for the players, look after their possessions and help to carry the equipment. These boys together carried this bag into the school grounds where league fixtures were played. However, once the bag touched the floor the boys would be pushed aside by the players and the tussle for the best boots and kit would begin. *Plenty* of palava occurred whilst players fought for what they would claim were 'their' boots—even borrowed boots carried some weight in gaining status amongst players from other teams and spectators. At the end of the match each player would change back into their 'civilian' clothes and return the kit into the bag to be washed. On one occasion one player did not return his boots. The team quickly established who the player was as no one tried to protect the culprit and all wanted to prove their innocence from the accusation of 'theft'. The culprit was sent for by Father M and Coach J and was suspended until he could either return the boots or pay to replace them.

A few weeks later as I walked home from training with a group of Zatti players, Jackson called after me on the main road; he ran and greeted me, simultaneously separating me from the group. His voice was soft and his shoulders hunched and head lowered to avoid eye contact. Such a posture epitomised players who had behaved badly and were looking for forgiveness. I asked him why he had taken the boots and he replied: 'To pay my school fees. I had exams at school and if I didn't pay my fees they wouldn't let me take the test. I had pressure.' I asked him why he had not gone to Father M for help. He looked away and answered: 'I had pressure to find the money quick, the school would have failed me. I wasn't thinking too clear. Father M helps with medicine if we get sick but not money or school fees. It's only me and my Pa. I don't have support.' I suggested he explain to Father M and maybe he could still train but not play games, and meanwhile promise to try and replace the boots. I knew he found it hard to see his teammates play from the sidelines. Meanwhile he had taken his exams and would progress to the next year, a small milestone towards completing high school. In this case the desire for education and ageing was stronger than his loyalty towards both the football team and indeed the youth centre. Upon admitting his crime to the youth centre staff and saying sorry his punishment was suspension from playing. He was still permitted to watch them train, which he did every day.

Hustling the youth centre and the football team was a big risk. Shunned by both youth centre staff and the team he would be left without any support and this would weaken his position as a youth without the credentials of being a football player and part of the community team. Regardless, his dilemma was one which many of the players sympathised with and—despite the initial tension and palava—the team agreed with the suspension but continued to interact with him as a teammate during training sessions and off the field. His actions ensured instant results to the immediate problem he was facing and significantly took precedence over any concerns of loyalty or morality; Father M's muscular Christianity is systematically undermined by youths' need to hustle and the inability of the centre staff to discipline them effectively for wrongdoing.

A stereotype amongst elders and adults is that Liberian youth are 'too quick to be satisfied', meaning they seek instant gratification. This adds to the image of young Liberians being untrustworthy and impulsive. The moral codes spoken about by the Zatti players is evidence of their constant exposure to religious preaching and lectures by elders and adults and figures of authority including the International Aid Community. Such ideas are also apparent both in Father M's applications for funding for DBYC and in his informal comments on the conduct of youth. Many of the players are enrolled in some form of high school education. Their day begins with *devotion*[5] and this remains an element of their daily education and routine. At the youth centre all pray before and after training. A common element of lecturing is religious guidance. Players are continuously spoken to by adults, elders and authority figures, be it scolding, mocking, lecturing or offering religious guidance. As a consequence, many can recite biblical texts and give 'appropriate' Christian-led responses upon moral questioning. The frequency and direction of such guidance, however, means it has little meaning and impact on many of these players. The frequency of crime and hustling and the absence of a consistent and functional policing system mean tension exists between youths and adults. Yet acknowledging wrongdoing and preaching moral and religious verses suffice in many instances and are an acceptable response to wrongdoing. The tension between adults and youths remains; the reputation and stereotype of the youth is confirmed as a 'rogue' and someone who cannot be trusted, but the retribution is insignificant and in many cases inconsequential to a youth who lives for today and not for tomorrow.

In Matadi words speak louder than actions. Saying 'sorry', no matter what the crime is, is seen as a sincere albeit flimsy response to wrongdoing, and such an apology is generally accepted. This is also seen as a response of youths as elders and adults are held not to commit petty crime and have little to apologise for. Adults defend their wrongdoing as the rights of a superior person, no matter what the action. In 2009, the 'Truth and

---

[5] Local phrase for pray.

Reconciliation Commission' (TRC) in Liberia endorsed a local restitutive programme based on 'traditional' community justice mechanisms called the 'The Palava Hut Programme' for reconciliation but inadvertently created a culture of acknowledgement and saying sorry. Many believed that ex-combatants were rewarded after the conflict ended and the palava hut system was seen as a way of bringing such actors to justice. Acknowledging and confessing wrongful acts underpinned the purpose of this local conflict resolution mechanism. The overwhelming desire for peace meant that accountability and retribution was limited. Rosalind Shaw claimed that this was the process of 'forgive and forget', which is a post-conflict addition to the youth culture (2005, p. 9). Without significant measures in place to deter the young from petty crime they will continue to pursue money-making schemes, but in turn this will continue to establish them as youths by adults and elders of the community.

The impact of this is internal conflict as youths compete for money-making opportunities—even at the cost of their peers—and this creates tension and mistrust between youths and adults and between themselves. Players steal from each other, hustle each other and sleep with each other's girlfriends. On the field they *play foul*[6] and cheat to gain advantage and therefore football-related status; winning in any capacity forms a hierarchy. This is accepted amongst the players but if caught, they are expected to acknowledge their wrongdoing and say sorry for their crime or indiscretion. The coach and players regularly shout at each other to say 'sorry' for rudeness or fouls to keep the game going. This places the youth centre staff, the wider community and the society in a chaotic state as ethical boundaries are blurred and not followed; crime is a broad term with little local significance and moral codes are spoken but not adhered to. There is no trust as the reconciliation between perpetrator and victim is completed with a simple phrase 'sorry o'. In this context, the SDP programme supervised by Father M can have little effect. Youths' need to hustle, and combined with a permissive attitude to infractions of moral codes this makes football ineffective as a disciplinary mechanism of 'character building'. Instead, it operates as an extension of systems of hustling and ways of gaining status.

---

[6] Liberian slang term for deliberately fouling each other.

The Commander, the General and the Coach

Whilst Zatti were training or playing one voice was always prominent. This was the loud, husky, aggressive screams of Coach J who began coaching at the youth centre after the conflict in 2003. Well known in Matadi for his involvement in the war as a commander for the militia of Charles Taylor, within the community and amongst team members 'J' was best known as 'The General' or 'Wire' (his military names). The scar on his arm was evidence of a bullet that had travelled through the limb and unprofessionally removed and stitched, leaving an 8-inch protruding wound. He was neither embarrassed nor shy about his former employment and had no problem when people addressed him with this title. That said he was quick to lose his temper in any situation on and off the field, and his voice was at a constant shout.

He had knowledge of football but his coaching skills were limited. The players had more interaction with him than any other adult outside the youth centre compound. For many, contact with him was the most significant 'male adult relationship'[7] they had. Most days the team would warm up and play matches with no technical instruction or system. Coach J would publicly make the players aware of their mistakes and punish them by ordering them to run laps whilst play continued for the others. The verbal insults he gave to the players were personal, such as 'you stupido?' Players responded in a number of ways. Some would give a thumbs-up sign acknowledging their mistake and the insult, and others would shout back gesturing their account of the mistake. On some occasions players would remove themselves from the game and sit aside in protest. This would inevitably be the focus of the lecture at the end of training and potentially lead to a day's suspension from training or punishment of running laps.

The relationship between coach and player was hard to understand. Many respected J as a person who had coached them since they were 'small' players and had been a constant elder figure in their lives. Some described him as being like a 'pa to me'. Yet most of the Zatti players had a turbulent relationship with J that formed a chronology of respect, fear, resentment and anger. Whilst he was in charge, they knew he had

---

[7] Most players lived with a single mother or grandmother; fathers were largely absent.

ultimate control. Acts of anger against him or palava would lead to suspension or public disciplining and humiliation. The undertone of resentment was always present. This caused tension in every training session
but aided—ironically—levels of solidarity between players; the resentment felt from the youths towards the adult was a unifying factor.

J facilitated access to football. Because of this, many would tolerate his
verbal abuse and rudeness. He in turn encouraged—even relished—his
position of power. After practice he made players sit on the floor in front
of him and hit them on their backs with his fists if they delayed the meeting and his lecture. He would, on occasion, threaten to flog them if they
did not hurry up and sit quietly, despite his general tardiness and noisi-
ness. He talked to them about field issues; this would usually centre on
their bad behaviour and losing their temper or their lack of respect to the
referee, and his favourite mantra 'no one wants to take responsibility.' In
this he was correct; players were quick to place blame after a loss or goal
scored against them and rarely looked at themselves for the answers. This
caused much palava amongst the players during analysis. Placing blame at
the time was encouraged by the coach who picked players out constantly.
At times, and in stark contrast to his lectures on discipline, J would remi-
nisce about his playing days, claiming he was never scared of any opposition and went in hard for tackles and when the opportunity presented
itself, he would hurt the opposition with his elbows or poke fingers in the
opponent's eyes. His constant lecturing on 'discipline', however, would
be one of the contradictions he would continuously make. Football gave
this man an income, status in the community, power over the youth in
his community and social worth in the aftermath of the conflict. In contrast to Father M's aspirations for a game that would build character and
gain independence for the good of youth, for J football seemed to be a
powerful tool for adults to assert their positions over youth.

It Is a Money-Making Game

Coach J was a prime example of how corruption worked in Liberian
football. To Liberian men money means power, respect and a route to
women—which in turn gives a man status. Football was a tool for cor-

ruption and the creations of 'Big Men' (see Utas 2012). That is, it promoted power above age-based—and status-based—hierarchies rather than 'youth development'. The following incident illustrates this to some extent.

After a training session a number of players standing around Coach J were discussing in hushed tones. They walked away from me so that I may not overhear. Later, Richie confessed: 'We need to qualify for the second round of the league, it's a little bit tough, so we put our money together and pay the ref to help us.' Such 'money-making games' were commonplace: referees would be paid by team coaches, managers or senior players before the game to ensure key decisions went in favour of the paying team. If this failed to impact on the score, a late penalty was often given, usually causing big palava as people knew the background to such a decision. This was especially evident in the lower leagues where referees were usually elderly and had retired from higher-level games and so were not adequately paid by their FA districts' subcommittees. In such money-making games all players were asked to contribute 50LD to pay the referee. The coach knew who the referee was and was tasked with making contact with him the evening before the game to confirm the arrangement. Some players were against the idea, possibly because they did not have the 50LD rather than out of moral outrage and therefore trying to prevent embarrassment. Bernardo, in particular, disliked the arrangement. 'We've got force, we can make it,'[8] he argued, but the majority ruled and the reality of corruption was so commonplace that it almost seemed the acceptable and sensible thing to do. Besides, the other team was bound to be attempting the same arrangement.

The LFA financed the subcommittees but did little in the way of monitoring the leagues and the management of players. The players accepted that despite the league being financed they had to provide match balls, pay fines for lateness and disciplinary issues, and tolerate adults working for the FA league and teams to enhance their personal incomes and buy success. Being part of the structure of competitive football provided an enhanced income and power for officials and referees. The players did not get rich, but those above them might have.

---

[8] Meaning 'we're strong, we can win.'

Zatti needed to win the game to progress to the second phase of the competition and then stood a chance for promotion to the second division. On the day of the game, whilst talking to the players, I noticed Coach J and two of the players walk into the small room opposite the playing field. My chair had been positioned as far from this meeting as possible. I asked Richie what was happening, and he said, 'They go to pay the money, if they see we have a white coach they ask for more.' I played ignorant to the money exchange and continued to converse with the rest of the players telling them they needed to warm up well and start to focus. On this occasion the other team did not show up and the points were awarded to Zatti. I asked what happened to the money, but Richie was vague in his response; possibly the other team was warned of Zatti's arrangement with the referee and split the money with the official so they did not waste their time and the referee still got his share without having to work; or perhaps Coach J still had it. It was accepted amongst the majority of Zatti players that Coach J would have 'eaten the money' as he was a corrupt man. No player challenged him or enquired about the final destination of the money, and knowing that the Fathers of the youth centre would not approve of this plan there were no other adults from whom to seek restitution.

Nor was this the only time such petty corruption was apparent in the team's organisation. Towards the end of my 2011 fieldwork I thought of surprising the team by arranging a game either against a higher division team or at the ATS. In pursuit of this I asked Coach Tamba, Head of the Liberian Football Coaches Association, if he could help. He agreed to make some calls but assured me it would not be hard as news of a white female coach in Monrovia had spread and there would be no shortage of teams wanting to challenge 'my' team. The next day he confirmed we could play at the ATS that Friday against the National under-20 team. The arrangements of the friendly match caused excitement, clapping, shouting and laughing amongst the Zatti squad. Most had not played on Astroturf before and some were strangers to the pitch based in Central Monrovia as financial constraints prevented them from spectating at the ground. The next few training sessions saw numbers swell as news of the game travelled. Coach J and I had to draw up a list of players for the friendly match. I wanted only regular players who were registered as Zatti players for the National League.

The small van arranged to transport us to the ATS on the day was cramped; the squad sat five to a bench in a vehicle no wider than 5 feet for the 20-minute drive to the stadium. Observing a senior national team in training session built up the excitement. I suggested to Coach J that we arrange the starting line-up and get the players' kit ready. This was done democratically between us and I suggested the substitutes who should change into the leftover kits. Soon after, Coach Tamba arrived and asked to speak with me and then introduced me to the under-20 coaching staff. When I sat back with the Zatti team I sensed a different atmosphere, the players who did not have the kit were evidently unhappy, especially because a few players who had not been training regularly were proudly dressed in the Zatti uniform. I questioned J as to why he had not gone with my suggestions, but he refused to listen; this was the first time he had used his authority as a local adult over me. There was nothing I could do but to explain to the disgruntled players that it was not my decision.

I suspected that the majority of players in the under-20 squad were not in fact under twenty. Most Liberians do not have passports, identification or birth certificates; therefore, determining age can be impossible. Coach Tamba assured me that at least six were 19 or 20 years old, and then admitted that the rest were older. This provided an indication of the LFA classification of age.

Not used to playing on a flat surface the Zatti players struggled with the pace of the ball and the opposition. They quickly conceded three goals but continued to play their hardest whilst Coach Tamba and I advised them. Coach J began to shout and chastise the players, but Coach Tamba turned to him and said, 'Be quiet, let the boys play,' to which J replied, 'Sorry o, but Coach Tamba, they really make me vex.' At half-time the team had done well not to concede any further goals but they were clearly tired. The pitch was five times the size of what they were used to and the surface much faster. All the substitutions were made so that all players had an opportunity to play. Two regular players refused to play as they had not originally been given a uniform and sat in the stands on protest. I felt for them; Coach J had put uncommitted and unregistered players before them.

The event would not have been complete without palava and in true Zatti style they did not disappoint. One player who had refused to play entered the bus and in a cramped condition, which was not aided by the mid-day sun and seventeen sweaty players, he sat in his unchanged jeans and T-shirt as the players pushed against him. With a raised voice and finger pointing to the sky, he stated, 'My man, you sweating up on me,' which caused the players to respond saying, 'What you want me to do, I can't help it. Stop your talk.' The players began pushing each other until the player who had started the dispute was dragged from the bus by his T-shirt by Pa K, the youth centre manager, who took him to the side of the street and beat him on his back with his fists. Pa K then approached me and asked if I had small money. I gave him 50LD and the player was given money to transport himself back home without the team.

I asked Bernardo what he thought regarding the team selection—after all he was always bluntly truthful. He had no sense of loyalty towards Coach J; in fact, he was probably his biggest critic. Bernardo liked to challenge Coach J and was ever quick to identify contradictions in his punishments and selections. It was always amusing—to myself and the other players—when Bernardo went off on one of his rants in his mocking and humorous manner. Although I did not like the suspensions that sometimes followed for Bernardo, his rants gave fuel to the players and further highlighted the unfair way J coached. Bernardo would say, 'What if I gave money then you play me' and 'what about the money for the game we pay, where's that, you eat the money or go video club I see you all the time plenty women and liquor.' Sometimes in response, the coach would laugh and shake his head, but sometimes Bernardo would push him too far and they would both continue shouting at each other after training whilst walking down the main street. Bernardo looked at me with a grin asking, 'You don't know? The others guys played cos he pay the coach money.' It all became so clear. He was a corrupt coach who accepted and actively pursued 'money making'. As with the youths J put hustling before loyalty and morality—before the values Father M and SDP practitioners would hope to instil through football, values such as responsibility, loyalty, respect and sportsmanship.

Coach J did not hide his money-making ventures from the players; they were fully aware of his corrupt ways and the manner in which he flaunted his income in the community. Football provided this man with pathways and networks to money making and exchange. The players became indispensable accessories to his ventures. Youth football players in such relationships are pawns in the adult pursuit of personal gain and sustained status. In the case of football, having a title as 'coach' is not enough; money remains at the heart of an adult's social worth. Youths are trapped by their desire to play and enjoy the team and so tolerate being used in this manner. The consequence of this is that whilst J's status is being maintained and subsidised through football, the players continue to be youths without any access to adulthood through the game.

Zatti and the White Coach: Youth–Adult Relationship Reconsidered

The introduction of my coaching sessions was a world away from what the players were used to. I put high emphasis on fitness and skills training and taught them how to play with different strategies and playing systems. Every session was harder than what they were used to physically and mentally. When I first began my role as Coach Holly I expected to work with Coach J, assisting with fitness drills and imparting my knowledge of playing systems and tactics. It soon became obvious that this was not what he had in mind. He began turning up later and later for training and sometimes not turning up at all. If he was present he would hand me the whistle and gesture for me to begin the session. The boys' excitement and anticipation of being coached by a European was obvious by the increasing numbers of players, spectators and a renewed sense of enthusiasm. I did not want to disappoint them. I unofficially assumed the role of Head Coach.

My style was very different to that of Coach J. I would not raise my voice or scold when mistakes were made; I was able to give technical direction and make the sessions fun with different forms of game play and by embracing the players' characters. During the post-training meeting I would ask for their opinions on what went right and why mistakes had been made. They enjoyed blaming and speaking freely. But this caused another problem. Whilst Coach J had some questionable methods and interactions with the players he was all the same able to stop palava and could deal with discipline issues by virtue of the threat of his—male, elder—scolding voice. I was more of a technical coach and less of a disciplinarian. The inevitable issues of discipline and incidents of 'playing foul' and heated arguments escalated.

As a team, Zatti would train hard under my instruction and in confined and controlled scenarios they reacted well. The problem arose in game situations against outsiders or when playing different teams during training. In competitive league matches Zatti had a good discipline record so I knew they could be disciplined and could control their emotions. When Coach J was asked for his opinion, his response was simple: 'These are African players. They need African discipline and be treated in the African way.'

Being 'African' was a recurrent way the players and J described the identity of footballers. A training session was once abruptly finished by Father M and me after continuous acts of indiscipline and fighting on the field. Despite my best efforts to reinstate order the final whistle blew with conviction to indicate that the referee had had enough of the chaotic and unruly situation. The SDB Fathers were aware of the incidents occurring and spoke with me as the players gathered on the concrete steps. Two players from opposing sides were called as the main protagonists and asked to apologise to each other. The Fathers expected me to oversee the reconciliation to prevent any suspensions. Coach J appeared for the team's debriefing and began lecturing the players on the need for African discipline and how 'when you give an inch…' and the players responded together, 'you take a mile'. He continued: 'Gentlemen I guarantee to you I will flog you, I'll end up in South Beach.'[9] The players grinned but understood the traditional disciplinary method. Then J turned to me stating, 'These boys are all the same, EVEN in school you have to whip them to make them learn. They are stubborn.' The players willingly accepted this accusation.

I felt disheartened. The players' biggest issue when I began coaching them was the scolding that Coach J gave them and his lack of respect.

---

[9] South Beach is a prison in Monrovia.

One player argued: 'When the coach shouts at me it makes me feel too bad. Then my mind feels disturbed, my mind isn't on the game.' At one time or another each player had referred to feeling bad due to the coach's style. After a few weeks of coaching, some players admitted in the presence of Coach J, "I admire Coach Holly. If she has something to say she take us to the side and talk to us, we ask questions when we do wrong.' But this had no effect on Coach J. I asked the vice-captain of Zatti why he was like that. 'He is an ex-commander. It's hard for the man to talk soft, we are used to it now but some of us can still feel bad.' He continued, 'African discipline works even in school; the teachers flog us to get us to do well. Some players need it or the Coach will suspend them. We are African players.'

Being 'African' was a strong part of the players' identity that adults were able to manipulate. This reality was used as an excuse to set low expectations of them and to mete out harsh punishments. Whilst Coach J as an adult continued to use the youths' 'African' status to establish his violent hold over them, the players continued to live up to their expected behaviour as 'Africans'. It became a way for adults to exploit, enforce and encourage youth behaviour. By threatening and punishing players in such a way their junior status was emphasised and reiterated through floggings and the hierarchical forms of lecture and scolding.

Pa K

Other adults established hierarchical relationships with the players in a different way. Hierarchy and the relationship between adult and youth were, however, recurrent themes. Pa K is a senior staff member and manager of the youth centre. He regularly engages with the players, especially when dealing with player suspension and punishment. At times he would join the post-training meetings and reiterate the need for players to improve their discipline, particularly the way they communicated with each other, the coach and the referee. He would begin his address with a 'Hello' and all the players would respond with a 'Hi'. Sometimes this was repeated until all the players were fully attentive. This was the same greeting heard before each class began at school as a way of drawing the children's attention. The way he would converse with the players was in contrast to that of the coach. He spoke softly but using basic language. He would ask them questions and they would all respond together with a 'yes' or 'no' when prompted. He referred to them as a collective but at times changed their title. For example, on occasion he would refer to them as 'youth-adults'. This was usually when they were required to take responsibility for something: 'The youth centre has no money for travel to the game, as youth-adults you need to take yourselves there.' Once he was lecturing on discipline and advised them: 'As children of the youth centre you need to behave according to our rules, do you understand?' They obediently responded 'yes'. Social worth and acknowledgement for these players was then determined by the theme of the lecture. They were not challenged for their opinions or asked to express their views; they were required merely to give the expected response. This was all done with the players sitting on the floor in front of the seated elder. It was hard to believe some of these players were over the age of twenty-five.

Coach J was not the only adult to have regular contact with the players. The managers at the youth centre also took interest in the game and the players. They conversed in a calmer manner with the players but continued to infantilise them and manipulate situations for their own convenience. Through football a multitude of adult–youth relationships conditioned youths into childlike behaviours and states. Players lost their tempers in response to Coach J's provocation. The squad would be reduced to reciting responses collectively to an overseeing adult when accepting conditions set by the management team. Despite the players' lack of enthusiasm for much of the adult-conducted formalities of listening to post-training lectures and squad prayer, they accepted this as part of the game and a necessity to maintain the adult–youth relationships within football. They acquiesced in their infantilisation.

Zatti Players Outside the Fence

Rather than promoting self-worth and personal development, football trapped Zatti players in the position of youth. In this way, it reinforced social processes off the field which had a similar effect. While we have seen some of these processes in the previous chapter, it is important to show how the Youthhood of Zatti footballers is specifically linked to their lives away from the game—regardless of their actual chronological age.

For many players the routine throughout the week followed similar patterns: chores, school, football training, chores and socialising (in that order). This is not to paint a picture of a particularly regimented highly organised routine. These activities were completed—or in some cases attempted—usually behind schedule, whilst attempting to find any variety of distraction or source of amusement. Players had many recreational pursuits, generally involving women, drinking alcohol, playing games, going to video clubs and gambling. When none of these were accessible due to financial restraints, boys would loiter or walk the streets in small groups talking and socialising with others as they moved. The quest for money making, women and having fun was a constant game for these players and just like in the fence their behaviour and choice making was directly linked to their youth status.

Adults Go to Church, Youths Rest

Religion and believing in spiritual powers like *JuJu* are a central aspect of Liberian youth culture which continues into adulthood. Waking up on a Sunday always felt strange; the streets were quiet except for the occasional motorbike. The usual sound of children noisily walking to school, students singing the national anthem or reciting lines, against a backdrop of car traffic, horns beeping, brakes squealing, palava and hustle and bustle all disappeared on Sunday morning. It was replaced with stillness, calm and deserted roads. Families were up early washing, dressing in their best clothes and walking to their chosen churches. It was initially confusing where all the people disappeared, but once the church music systems started and the crackling of the Ministers' microphones powered by noisy generators and shouting voices began, it became clearer. Music, clapping, singing and preaching were the noises that filled the air. In my naivety I presumed everybody went to church, as the noise that filled the varied structures and the emptiness of the streets implied. Yet many Zatti players stayed within the family home during this time to 'rest' so they were not publicly seen missing church. They would appear in the afternoon to enjoy the more relaxed atmosphere a non-working day brought. Increasingly it seemed that going to church had stronger associations with adulthood than Youthhood. Yet, this act of rebellion was puzzling: surely by attending they would be sharing in an adult pursuit?

Not going to church proved to be a stigma; it raised questions about a person's moral fibre. Morality is associated with adulthood in Liberia. However, going to church required money; a donation was expected and in some churches was compulsory; formal dress was also expected. This was a deterrent to many youths who lacked fine threads and therefore did not want to be embarrassed in front of community residents. Church attendance offered the opportunity to showcase one's ability to commit to a faith and participate in an adult-led environment. In many cases financial constraints prevented them from attending and—in truth— some youths were genuinely preoccupied or resting from their pursuits on Saturday night. Attending church was an important aspect of an adult's weekly routine within a community; however, this had little to offer youths and adults had nothing to gain from youths' attending. This is an example of an off-the-field activity in which adults and youths could not benefit from each other so the divide in attendance caused little upset. Attending church is an instance of entrenched divide between adults and youths. Players in the team were, however, keen to pursue other interests no matter what the social consequences would be.

A Necessary Evil: Youths and Girls

A trip into central Monrovia with two young Zatti players sparked some interesting debates. It was not often that I was able to engage players individually outside of Matadi but I had met them at the junction waiting for a taxi and they volunteered to escort me. It was rare for players to ask too many personal questions but on this occasional they must have felt bold. Their questions began thus: 'Do you have a husband? Have you born yet (given birth)?' I was slightly surprised at their bluntness but answered willingly. I explained that I was too young to have children and be a parent and as yet I had not found love. Their response was, 'Wow.'

Young people having children in Liberia is common; most of the Zatti players have children, one of the players accompanying me had a 3-year-old son and he was only 18 years old. In the Liberian context I was of the age where I would have had multiple children and be married, although it is rare to meet married couples; getting married requires money. I asked them if they had girlfriends. Frank replied with a nod but as I understood it, Frank liked 'women business' and had a number of girls he would liaise with; different girls would arrive at training to walk home with him. Sam shook his head: 'Women are a necessary evil. If a man don't have money he don't have love. I don't like too much women business.' He described how he wanted a relationship to be: 'I want to be married with children, my wife will be strong and cook me food and work hard.' I challenged his views a little: 'So your wife would have to cook, clean the house and look after the children? What if she asked for your help like sweeping while she cooks?' He grinned, looked at Frank and began to laugh: 'You see what I mean about white women,' he said. 'It would be an insult for me if my wife asked me to sweep. The only time I help is when she is sick. I would do all, but the moment she is better she start to work. The only thing that would change that is IF my wife has job and she make more money than me then I have to do more.' The notion of a monogamous relationship was an ideal to the players. They had clear ideas of how they wanted a woman to behave in relationships and the role they would assume within monogamy. However, for the Zatti players this was unlikely to be achieved as—without the status of being a financially independent and stable adult—this was not the sort of relationship available to them.

The relationship between males and females has implications for youths. The lack of ability to establish committed relationships due to financial shortfall questions a male's masculinity and maturity. Questionable maturity is a consequence of Youthhood regardless of sexual relationships, but amongst the male youth's peer status aligns with masculine supremacy and is well negotiated. The football field and the game are the perfect environment to showcase physicality and dominance, but off the field they have little control over their perceived masculinity and this is especially true in relationships with the opposite sex. Adults and females have the ability to emasculate youth footballers as they can be manipulated and exploited for others' personal gain.

Liberia is a sexualised environment to be in, especially for an outsider. Young people enjoy dancing and day-to-day activity involves music, usually Nigerian, Ghanaian or American, and the dances performed are provocative to a Western eye. Young girls wear extremely small clothes, exposing cleavages and with hips concealed in tight jean shorts often sizes too small. The movies broadcast in video clubs were graphic in nature and as long as one had the entrance fee the age of the viewer did not matter. Such places turned into seedy venues after football matches had finished. A large part of young people's free time was occupied by attracting and communicating with potential partners. Players from the team would call to passing girls: 'Fine girl; what your name?' The response was generally a shy, albeit encouraging smile. Part of the attraction of playing fixtures in other areas was the possibility of finding new girls; mobile numbers were regularly exchanged after a short introduction and the players would compare how many interactions they had had. Any social, religious, political or sporting event was seen as a way to attract and interact with the opposite sex. In fact, pursuing women was a constant distraction, especially when Zatti and the girls' kickball team travelled to games together. The boys would discuss the girls and the girls would discuss the boys.

It was not uncommon for players to have shared the same girlfriends or be pursuing the same girl. It was accepted almost as an informal right that unmarried men would stray from one girl to another. In return, girls had sexual relations with boys for money as a survival tactic, which they called 'Money Love'. Although the young boys found it hard to seek employment, girls found it harder; most were uneducated and understood that children and domestic work were inevitably going to be their principal duties in the future. As one girl explained: 'When a man is married he still loving to girls but he can take care of them and give money to the girl.' Another girl added: 'We don't make money, so if I need money I find a man, when I want clothes I have another man, when I need food I know another man.' Girls know that men are expected to provide for their women even as a casual arrangement. It was not uncommon to hear the players complaining: 'She has a man when she want her nail painted, another to get her hair fix, another for clothes, another for food, another for money, there is no true love in L.I.B.' The players were more than aware of what women expect from a lover and this earned many young girls the title of *Hobo Jo*, meaning prostitute or promiscuous woman. Men, however, accepted this situation and in turn enjoyed having 'plenty women' and getting reputations for 'women business'. It was a constant cycle of casual sexual relationships; inevitably this led to youth footballers becoming parents at very young ages. Adults also engaged in promiscuous relationships, even when married, but as long as the marital family was well provided for and acts of adultery were not too public, such extramarital affairs were generally accepted.

Love was not really accessible to youths as their lack of financial security deterred faithful partners. Love was a pursuit for adults, and courtship was a game they resented. Trust, love and faithfulness were concepts they were accustomed to in principle; yet, their status deprived them of such luxuries. Instead they pursued random sexual encounters. Adult males enjoyed both committed relationships and promiscuity. This adult model caused much resentment and admiration amongst the youth footballers: woman gave themselves to adults but they stated their terms with youths. Masculinity provided status amongst youths; football enabled the players to showcase and assert their physical credentials on the field, but out of the game, females and adults reduced the players to boys.

Zatti Fathers

Most players were without fathers. Some had been killed during the war, and others were displaced and were living in the interior with their new family and siblings. Some just did not know where their parents were. The role of a 'father' was anyhow ambiguous. The notion of being a 'father' was parallel with that of any male elder, a figure of power, a superior who should not be questioned or challenged. In a broad sense this characterised the relationship between the Zatti players and Coach J, although challenges were witnessed and public palava between them did happen. The absence of a father figure was common and repeated by many of the Zatti players who had themselves become fathers but had little involvement in their children's lives. Most Zatti offspring were in the care of their grandparents. This was a fairly common living arrangement in Liberia as young parents were unable to provide for or parent their children. As I walked with players, some would point out to their children and most of these children would acknowledge their father by calling them by their first name or nickname, none however were referred to as 'Pa'. This reinforced their youth status as not mature enough or financially able to support their child or wife and that is why the child was not taught to refer to them with an appropriate title.

Having children was a consequence of youths only having random sexual experiences. In most cases adults took the responsibility of parenting and supporting the child confirming the fathers' immaturity and lack of financial independence. The lack of acknowledgement given to these youths by their children was emasculating and a reminder that they could not provide as a father should. Adults and youths had little relationship when it came to raising children; adults dominated the process and prevented the youths from forming a relationship and taking responsibility. The youths accepted this and were arguably relieved when they were removed from the situation and able to continue their carefree promiscuous ways. The disconnect between youths and fatherhood was another component of youth identity that had become prominent in the post-conflict era.

The Things that Liberian Men and Women Do Wrong

Practices such as hustling, corruption and the pursuit of women are shared by adults and youths. However, conducted from a position of seniority with resources, they create success and status, whereas when these are practised by youths, they have the opposite effect. An article in the Liberian daily newspaper *Exclusive* examined the wrongs Liberian men and women do in relationships and towards the opposite sex.

I have met hundreds of Liberian women, ate with them, slept in the same bed with them; cook together, help with their children, I have even had many in my home when times were bad on them, but the question still stand, why am I not very close to any beside family?[10]

The football players that presented the article to me did so to prove their point about the untrustworthy Liberian women. For them this story provided the evidence of their promiscuous ways. The article was read with the boys behind muttering 'you see' and pointing to one of the fifteen points in the article. Fifteen reasons were described of the failings of Liberian women including, 'A Liberian woman will quickly pick up a married man than a single man because in the old days, they were the ones that could help the most financially'; another stated: 'A Liberian woman will not leave a man because he is sleeping around, but will leave him if he cannot afford to impress her friends.' The article finished with a scolding conclusion: 'Ladies, ladies, ladies, you need to change your mindset; this is not good, not good at all. … The average Nigerian woman gets married and starts school, whereas a Liberian woman gets married and forget herself completely.'

In the same issue, the same style of article focused on Liberian men with twenty-seven points of failings. The beginning was slightly different:

It's me on top of the world, it is wonderful to have you all informed about what is happening in our society, please focus on this issue and deal with it. This is too good to be true. Let us learn to change, God will do the rest. Together we can make a better Liberia. If anyone is in these shoes, please hang-up and resist from such things. With kind regard and respect… God bless U.

I began to read out a few of the points to gauge the reaction from the players. 'A Liberian man will have five women that he is dating and will still be out there trying to pick up another one'—the players laughed, resigned to try and deny this. 'A Liberian man will use these words or phrases to describe their women: "Play thing"; my "little thing"; my man, I am trying to eat that thing; my side thing.' These phrases I had heard before. The players regularly used them when talking about women but until now I

---

[10] 'Things Liberian Men Do That Are Wrong!!!' and 'Things Liberian Women Do That Are Wrong!!!' In *Exclusive*, April 2010.

was not sure of their actual meaning; 'eating' something literally meant having sex. The article also highlighted Liberian men's lack of paternal instincts or sense of responsibility towards children. The majority of the players in Zatti had children but most did not live with their children, and sending babies to live with grandparents was the norm; some who lived in the same community as their children did not even visit them. The article claimed: 'A Liberian man cannot tell you honestly how many children he has, they simply don't know.' Another observation of young couples in Matadi was their lack of public affection towards each other and their lack of commitment to publicly acknowledge an exclusive relationship. The article explained: 'I have yet to see a Liberian man hug and kiss or even hold his wife's hands in public, they are so scared that another woman will see and not want them.' The article concludes with a warning: 'A Liberian man cannot tell you he has not slept with another woman since he got married to you; ladies ask your spouse. Remember men, we already know the "who, where, when and why", so lying is not an option.'

None of the boys argued with the sentiments but stressed that women cause men to embark on such behaviours. One argued: 'Why put all of yourself into one person when they are always looking for someone better that can provide more?' With the majority of the Zatti players unemployed and struggling to gain an education they realised that as individuals they were not high on women's dating pecking order. Adults and youths partake in many similar money-making pursuits, leisure activities and share a similar appetite for pursuing women and casual relationships. Yet, despite their similarity, the effect and consequence is quite different; youths become entrenched and further infantilised, adults get bigger and sustain their 'big man' status. Cause and effect is dependent upon social worth and status in Liberia.

Going Round in Circles

Whilst ageing in Liberia is a path with no end the desired destination is 'eldership'. But becoming an adult is virtually impossible for so many, so they walk a path that goes round in circles. Becoming somebody with status is a dream for Liberian youth footballers. The Zatti football team became the perfect micro study of Liberian youth and brought with it the principles of SDP through the beliefs and mission of the Salesians of the DBYC. My role as an observer became more involved than planned but in retrospect this was a fortuitous turn of events that enabled a much richer, personal, detailed and valid experience.

Adults believed Liberian youth were too quick to be satisfied, seeking instant gratification; this led to mistrust. The relationship between youths and adults changed depending on the circumstance and so did the behaviour and expectations amongst them. Youth footballers were a group that could be manipulated to suit the situation.

Father M used football as a means to engage and access youth and expose them to muscular Christian principles. He struggled with their characters and youth culture as his initiation into the youth centre saw acts of theft and levels of immorality he was not expecting. This left him constantly second-guessing their intentions and balancing the desire to develop their moral characters with mistrust and scepticism. Pa K followed the intentions of Father M, but as a local man, he displayed the behaviour they were more accustomed to. As mentioned previously he would infantilise them, ensuring they were seated on the floor whilst reciting expected responses.

Coach J was the principal adult who interacted with the players. An ex-commander in the civil conflict he still led with the voice of a man about to go into battle. He represented the authoritarian villain in the game and was the principle source of palava, corruption, conflict and resentment. He had the power to promote them or expel them from the game, usually depending on how much money could be exchanged in the process. This highlighted the youth adult relationship again. Their youth category was one that relied on the support of adults to either provide opportunities or continue to lock them into this low status. On the football field it was a constant power struggle between the coach and the rebellious youths who were perceptive of his immoral ways. Yet my contrasting style was met with conflicting responses. They enjoyed the open and supportive environment created and the isolation and novelty of different fitness and skills training but within the youth centre their behaviour in competitive matches deteriorated. The need for authority was genuine but Coach J took this element to the extreme with his open adoption of 'African discipline'—which further infantilised the players.

Off the field players were not recognised by their children as fathers. This title was reserved for those who could provide and were acknowledged as such by the wider community. Religion is the corner stone of Liberian culture but this is also an adult pursuit and one that youths more or less voluntarily dismissed. The relationship between men and women was also insightful as their low status made them hustle for love and compete for girls. Those who could provide in the short term gained instant gratification and automatic masculine status. This was not exclusively a feature of youths; however, when an adult pursued the same interests and ventures it was good for prestige and valuable for sustaining status although it had the opposite effect for youths. This further caused tension and conflict between youths and adults, as the adults were again at the top of the pecking order. The consequence was tension as competition between them was rife.

NGOs and SDP projects view youths in global terms and too often give little consideration to the local meanings associated with such labelling. SDP projects and in particular the youth centre in Matadi promoted football to fit the requirements of a post-conflict environment. Yet observations highlighted themes that question the rhetoric behind such support. Football inside the fence was an effective tool to bring together youth and unite them physically in a shared passion. Football also became the activity that encouraged corruption and money making for personal gain and team promotion. Football for peace and development has to be questioned: arguably football creates youths and as a concept adds to and sustains their low status and identity in this post-conflict society.

References

Adams, M. (2009). Playful places, serious times: Young women migrants from a peri-urban settlement, Zimbabwe. *Journal of the Royal Anthropological Institute, 15*(4), 797–814.

Amit, V. (2001). Youth culture, anthropology. *International Encyclopedia of the Social & Behavioral Sciences, 24*, 16657–16660.

Bellman, B. L. (1984). *The language of secrecy: Symbols and metaphors in Poro Ritual.* New Brunswick: Rutgers University Press.

Bucholtz, M. (2002). Youth and cultural practice. *Annual Review of Anthropology, 31*, 525–52.

Cote, J. (2000). *Arrested adulthood: The changing nature of maturity and identity.* New York/London: New York University Press.

De Waal, A., & Argenti, N. (Eds.). (2002). *Young Africa: Realising the rights of children and youth.* Trenton/Eritrea: Africa World Pr.

Durham, D. (2000). Youth and the social imagination in Africa: Introduction to parts 1 & 2. *Anthropological Quarterly, 73*(3), 113–120.

Durham, D. (2004). Disappearing youth: Youth as a social shifter in Botswana. *American Ethologist, 31*(4), 589–605.

Evans-Pritchard, E. E. (1969). *The Nuer: A description of the modes of livelihood and political institutions of a Nilotic people.* New York/Oxford: Oxford University Press.

Gable, E. (2000). The culture development club: Neo-tradition and the construction of society in Guinea-Bissau. *Anthropological Quarterly, 73*(4), 195–203.

Harley, G. W. (1941). *Notes on the Poro in Liberia.* Cambridge, MA: The Museum.

Honwana, A., & De Boeck, F. (2005). *Makers and breakers: Children & youth in postcolonial Africa.* Oxford: James Currey.

Jones, G. (1988). Integrating process and structure in the concept of youth: A case of secondary analysis. *The Sociological Review, 36*(4), 706–732.

Jones, G. (2009). *Youth: Key concepts.* Cambridge/Malden: Polity Press.

Maclay, C., & Özerdem, A. (2010). 'Use' them or 'Lose' them: Engaging Liberia's disconnected youth through socio-political integration. *International Peacekeeping, 17*(3), 343–360.

Malinowski, B. (1929). *The sexual life of savages in north-western Melanesia.* London: Routledge.

Mead, M. (1928). *Coming of age in Samoa: A psychological study of primitive youth for Western civilisation.* New York: Harper Collins.

Reynolds, P. (1995). Not known because not looked for: Ethnographers listening to the young in Southern Africa. *Ethnos, 60*, 193–221.

Richards, P. (1995). Rebellion in Liberia and Sierra Leone: A crisis of youth? In O. Furley (Ed.), *Conflict in Africa.* London: Taurus Academic Press.

Shaw, R. (2005). *Rethinking truth and reconciliation commissions: Lessons from Sierra Leone.* Washington, DC: United States Institute of Peace.

Sommers, M. (2012). *Stuck: Rwandan youth and the struggle for adulthood*. Athens/London: The University of Georgia Press.

UNICEF. (2007). Sport for development: FIFA. www.unicef.org/sports/index_40936.html.

US AID. (2009). Liberian youth fragility assessment. Report produced for the USAID/Liberia under task order 9 of the global evaluation and monitoring. Prepared by the Aguirre Division of JBS International Inc & Associates for Global Change. http://pdf.usaid.gov/pdf_docs/PNADQ258.pdf.

Utas, M. (2003). Sweet battlefields: Youth and the Liberian Civil Wars. Uppsala University Dissertations in Cultural Anthropology, 1, 288pp, Uppsala.

Utas, M. (2005). Building a future? The reintegration and re-marginalisation of youth in Liberia. In P. Richards (Ed.), *No peace, no war: An anthropology of contemporary armed conflicts* (pp. 137–154). Athens: Ohio University Press.

Utas, M. (2008). Abject heroes: Marginalised youth, modernity and violent pathways of the Liberian Civil War. In J. Hart (Ed.), *Years of conflict: Adolescence, political violence and displacement* (pp. 111–138). Oxford: Berghahn Books.

Utas, M. (2012). *African conflicts and informal power: Big men and networks*. London/New York: Zed Books.

Vigh, H. (2006). Social death and violent life chances. In C. Christiansen, M. Utas, & H. E. Vigh (Eds.), *Navigating youth, generating adulthood: Social becoming in an African context* (pp. 31–60). Uppsala: Nordiska Afrikainstitutet.

Weiss, B. (2002). Thug realism: Inhabiting fantasy in urban Tanzania. *Cultural Anthropology, 17*(1), 93–124.

Wyn, J., & White, R. (1997). *Rethinking youth*. London/Thousand Oaks/New Delhi: Sage.

Zakaria, Y. (2006). Youth, conflict, security, and development. *The Reality of Aid*.

7

Creating a New Community

In August 2013 the UN General Assembly approved by consensus a proclamation establishing an International Day of SDP. This confirmed the UN's continued support and intention to promote sport within the development agenda. The International Olympic Committee (IOC) President Jacques Rogge claimed:

> The true worth of sport is determined not by words on paper, but by how sport is practised. Stripped of its values, sport is combat by another name. Sport with values is a gateway to cultural understanding, education, health and economic and social development. We have seen the true worth of sport and physical activity many times. It helps young people learn the value of self-discipline and goal-setting. It builds self-confidence. It defies gender stereotypes. It provides an alternative to conflict and delinquency. It can bring hope and a sense of purpose to refugees, impoverished communities and other people in need. It helps keep young people in school, it brings health. (IOC 2013, n.p)

SDP assumes a number of potential outcomes from the use of sport within the development agenda. Firstly, sport helps to build a civil society; secondly, sport constructs and instils values; and thirdly, sport creates

© The Editor(s) (if applicable) and The Author(s) 2016
H. Collison, *Youth and Sport for Development*,
DOI 10.1057/978-1-137-52470-6_7

opportunities for engagement, education and intervention. These combined outcomes are thought to support society and local communities to develop youth towards future citizenship. In 2005 the UN Inter-Agency Task Force on SDP claimed that sport is about

> inclusion and citizenship. Sport brings individuals and communities together, highlighting commonalities and bridging cultural and ethnic divides. Sport provides a forum to learn skills such as discipline, confidence and leadership and it teaches core principles such as tolerance, co-operation and respect. Sport teaches the value of effort and how to manage victory, as well as defeat. When these positive aspects of sport are emphasized, sport becomes a powerful vehicle through which the United Nations can work towards achieving its goals. (United Nations 2005, pi)

The UN remains the primary global development and security organisation whilst assuming leadership and the role of policy director to those tasked with CSR and development agendas. SDP has therefore become a primary initiative for many who link the concept of social change with the use of sport—predominantly football.

This universal enthusiasm for football has shaped the modern era of global development and built partnerships based on assumptions of its value and its functions for local populations and society in general. Yet, in Liberia I was unable to observe any projects directed by the UN as they were no longer operating. DBH remained an SDP supporter but was not actively implementing any projects. The LFA had no youth programmes other than their competitive league competitions and school leagues. The concept of SDP was, however, fully endorsed by the DBYC in Matadi. It shared the UN rhetoric and placed them in line with their own ethos of muscular Christianity and the needs of their community.

Although there are many opportunities for youths to participate in football it is at the community level where players choose to train, compete and perform on a regular basis. Community football is sustainable through the cooperation of adult community residents, accessible free space and an abundance of players seeking regular team practice and competition—unlike many SDP projects in Liberia which were short-term, donor-led, one-off gestures and not sustained. Despite the need for adult sponsorship to enter and participate in local leagues and coaching it is the players themselves who tended to organise, structure, focus, direct, discipline and maintain the team's training and playing format and schedule. Football provided a rare platform for these youths to manage themselves and each other, and to perform and showcase their skill, character and identity. The game therefore provided an opportunity for the players to create their own football culture and community that adopt and reflect their attitudes, values and personalities. Football in Liberia serves to draw many different groups of people together and this becomes particularly important and relevant to community football teams in Liberia as it provides a stage to be seen and heard by all generations and sectors of residents. Football may be the most powerful, representative, reflective and sustained activity for a Liberian youth but as is the case with many elements of community, the issues of status, social worth, ageing, identity and generational relationships are ever prominent and relevant.

The Structure of Zatti FC

The youth centre has two football pitches: the large pitch is for Zatti and the 'bigger boys' and the small pitch at the back of the youth centre is for the 'children' and the fourth division team. The fourth division team is coached by Richie (a voluntary position) after Father M asked him if he would take on the responsibility and support them throughout the season. The players in this team are young teenagers. They are looked upon as an academy within the youth centre; if a player develops and becomes strong enough, he will be given opportunities to train with Zatti on the big field. There is a distinct hierarchy within the youth centre's football programme and within Zatti. Within this structure there are unofficial criteria for progress. Zatti's 'small players'—in status, not size—are high school students; above them are high school graduates without formal employment; players further in education or vocational training assume positions above them; those with regular informal work become the elders of the group. By advancing in education and accumulating informal financial gain players can develop from a 'pekin' or 'small player' to a 'big player' and senior member of the team, independent of footballing skills. Coach J and a volunteer referee from the crowd have ultimate seniority throughout training sessions and matches. Father M, Pa K and the youth centre staff have authority over Coach J and the players. Arguably, the players' parents or guardians and community residents have the ultimate power and status within the overall structure as they can stop a player from attending training and can influence participation by asserting their opinions to the youth centre personnel. Within the Zatti team players' status affects the roles they assume; small players will be expected and told to fetch water and carry equipment, and senior players will lead prayers, lecture to control palava and supervise training.

Hierarchy

Football directed, endorsed and resourced by adults constructs a youth-focused structure within an adult-led and centred framework. There were a number of factors that could influence relative status among and between the players in the team. The adult levels of hierarchy were stable positions. Personality, identity, character traits, behaviour, willingness to conform, ability to play by the rules, individual skill and performance influenced notions of status and power amongst the players. Within the team, leadership roles are assumed by players; this drives the hierarchical management and organisation of the squad. However, whilst the overall SDP framework is managed by adults, the youth-centred structure is vulnerable. A more detailed account of the Zatti team, its player organisation and use of the game will provide an insight into football's functions and outcomes from a player's perspective. Within the analysis of the SDP theory and the Zatti FC reality a combination of factors needs to be considered. Firstly, the function of football to the players; secondly, the social effects of football; thirdly, the impact and effect football has on youth identity; and finally, the role and perspective of the audience and involved adults.

Creating a Football Community

Football is a repetitive structure for Liberian youths; it is highly performance-based and as will be discussed later has significant social outcomes. It is important to note that football in Matadi incorporates a number of ritual-like elements. As Baumann suggests: 'Rituals are symbolic performances which unite the members of a category of people in a shared pursuit that speaks of, and to, their basic values or that creates or confirms a world of meanings shared by all of them alike' (cited in De Coppet 2002, p. 98). Football in Matadi can be well understood in this frame. Ritual theory has been applied to sporting events and games to understand sports' social value and functions (Stevenson and Alaug 2000, Cheska 1979). Whilst football itself is not a ritual—largely due to the competitive aspect as opposed to the unifying function of ritual (Blanchard 1988; Gluckman and Gluckman 1977; Guttman 1978; Harris 1983; Levi Strauss 1966), seen from the perspective of a single team of young people (in opposition to adults) the activity of playing football serves many of the same functions commonly attributed to ritual.

That said, the consequences for status and ageing, when playing football, become socially relevant both on and off the field for youths. Victor W Turner applied Gluckman's approach[1] alongside the ritual theory of Arnold Van Gennep, who considered transitional rites of passage. These rites of transition contained three phases: separation, marginality and aggregation (Van Gennep 1960). Focusing on the second phase Turner (1969) considered the 'liminality' implicit in rituals. According to Turner the liminal period is ambiguous and represents marginality. This social limbo precedes social statuses and cultural states: 'Liminal entities are neither here nor there; they are betwixt and between the positions assigned and arrayed by law, custom, convention, and ceremonial' (1969, p. 94). The principle of liminality is clearly applicable to Liberian youth. As Utas (2005) notes for Liberian youth this could be an indefinitely prolonged phase as the process of completing the rites of passage to adulthood is so fragile and reliant on adult-controlled factors.

---

[1] Gluckman's theory considered rituals as an expression of complex social tensions and an enactment of social relations within the context of a specific group (Bell 1997, p. 38–39).

A link between stagnant ageing, ritual theory and participation in sporting activity was considered when Turner extended his theory of 'liminality' and ritual to modern leisure pursuits like sports. To characterise this phenomenon he used the term 'liminoid'. Turner also used the term 'communitas' instead of the word community to distinguish the modality of social relationships. In such 'areas of common living', a form of social control—used by adults and youths—was separation via the game of football (1969, p. 96). Communitas is a characteristic of people experiencing liminality together. SDP advocates presume football will develop unity and citizenship to build a civil unified community. This is potentially true; in the case of Matadi, Communitas united a group of marginal youths in their shared passion for football but all the while distinguished and separated them from adult citizens.

In response, Matadi youth footballers constructed a community within a community as a defence. This was recognised by Turner (1974), who considered 'normative communitas as a subculture or group who feel themselves initially to be utterly vulnerable to the institutionalized groups surrounding them and therefore they develop protective institutional armour' (in Harris and Park 1983, p. 152). Football, being the global and national phenomenon that it is, acts as the ideal framework and forum to unite youths. This in turn draws adult interest—consequently adopting a somewhat protective space for youth expression. Indeed, this is the value of football for SDP; football is seen as a bridging mechanism for adults and youths in a step towards building a peaceful civil society. A consequence of this is that football can provoke negative youth behaviour and enforce youth stereotypes, which will expose and infantilise them further. Here I consider Zatti as an alternative structure within the community and within the framework of Liberian generational categories.

Turner (1974) claimed: 'Communitas exists more in contrast than in active opposition to social structure, as an alternative and more "liberated" way of being socially human, away both from being detached from social structure and also of a "distanced" or "marginal" person' (in Harris and Park 1983, p. 154). Here it needs to be acknowledged that although up to this point Turner's theoretical principles of liminality, communitas, ritual and sport are appropriately applied to this research area, I make an important distinction. The notion of communitas suggests that marginal individuals create a generic bond and protective group, yet within Zatti this leads players to establish platforms of seniority between members of the communitas. This reality reflects the culture of establishing status and power in the wider society beyond the Zatti communitas. Community football has then constructed a new structure both within and mirroring the community framework. Owing to the youth status of football players, we can argue that this represents a liminal space. The youths who, in the eyes of adults and elders, represent chaos in their community have created structural order in an organised space.

Meta-Society

Harold Olofson's (1977) interpretation of a Hausa youth festival in Zaria, Nigeria, provides alternative and supporting ways of thinking about the reworking of social relationships by youths. This particular youth festival takes place at night during the dry season and is named *wasan misisi* or 'the play of the misses'. Young people play leading roles imitating elite hierarchical social structures. Olofson describes the complex role play that illustrates the Hausa elite characters that have been replaced by post-colonial political characters; positions include the governor and his orderly, the queen, the prison warden, policemen, a treasurer, the judge, a secretary and medical staff (1977, p. 169). The point of the performance is not to educate the audience about the colonial government or the original emirate but to set the stage for flirtation and interaction for young boys and girls. Yet Olofson argues: 'The possibility arises that the play-kingdom is a meta-society, "a society about society" and the elements in it so combined as to provide subtle teaching on the wider context' (p. 172). Within the festival a 'play frame' is created in which rivalry and competition manifest themselves. This is a structurally identical metaphor to that witnessed in 'ordinary life' in the frame created by the nation-state. Yet the festival provides a stage and a distinctive perspective on social life—it is a 'society *about* society'—a metaphor (Wagner 1986). Mimicking the roles of elites gives these young actors a chance to play the part of important or 'big men', something which for many will remain a part in a play far from reality, and as a result affords both the youths and the audience a perspective on those roles: 'At the crux is a meta-society which leads people to awareness at some level of ascribed status which prefigures life chances' (p. 173). SDP assumes that one of the functions of community football is social integration and unity; yet if the outcome is the exposure and mimicking of the hierarchical nature of the community outside the fence, then this *exacerbates* the divide between the generational categories and *confirms* status.

Within the Zatti football team, players create their own play frame in which competition and at times rivalry and tension are displayed. I would strongly argue that they have created their own meta-society, playing leading roles on the community football field every day in front of an audience. Even their organisation mimics that of 'real life': their coach has ultimate power but considering his involvement in the war as a rebel commander, is he playing a character in a position of authority to recreate his status during the war or to show the audience that he has a responsible position leading the community youth? The captain and vice-captain although still classed as 'youth' have completed high school and are pursuing higher education, so in their play-society they act as elders leading the players, giving advice and policing them when needed. They organise themselves internally by unwritten rules, and are aware of who has been in the team longest and who is older and younger, which dictates how much respect each player receives from the team. Football is a game and as Caillois claims:

> Games reflect forms which, while doubtless remaining in the domain of play, evolve a bureaucracy, a complex apparatus and a specialized hierarchical personality. … They sustain permanent and refined structures, institutions of an official, private, marginal, and sometimes clandestine character whose status is nonetheless remarkably assured and durable. (1961, pp. 40–41)

This system is almost an exact reproduction of the ordinary life of the society in which the Zatti players live, where in their own play society they can act in the leading roles and progress with time, unlike their journey and quest for adulthood, which too frequently seems unachievable and stagnant. The meta-society protects and provides opportunities to be seen by adults. Moreover, in its relationship to everyday social life, the creation of a subculture affords a perspective on the role of youth and football within the community. Through football much can be learnt about youth culture, social practices and identity; this consequently constructs ideas and images of the relationship between youths and adults. Yet the experience of play is by no means empowering. Football provides a rare opportunity for inter-generational contact outside of family structures but this has little impact once the game is finished. Acquiring formal employment is the most significant barrier to gaining the status of adulthood but being a football player only reaffirms the status of youth.

Performance, Characterisation and Identity in the Fence

Having established the structure of the Zatti team it is pertinent to examine the players' attitudes, behaviour and interactions within the fence. Little consideration has been given by SDP advocates, policymakers and implementers to youths as individuals or the varying personalities and characters within a youth group. The complexity of youth and their identity has been largely ignored by SDP practitioners.

The Field of Play and the Characters on It

Players had multiple potential identities, especially within the fence. Footballing credentials, personality, ethnic identity and character all influenced nicknames and how players were acknowledged in a host of different situations. Many players would not openly introduce themselves until prompted and then a range of responses would be given by the same player depending on the day.

All the Zatti players were given nicknames. Most copied their favourite professional football players. Zatti had a global squad list drawn from TV broadcasting of the game: 'Pele', 'Tevez', and 'Gerrard', to name but a few. Some had acquired their own personal nicknames like 'J Cool' and

'Nation'. These nicknames were used on and off the field. Identity for the players was thus more than just a name; they had their names given to them at birth which highlighted their ethnic heritage, their playing nicknames which reflected their football identity, their personal nicknames that expressed their personalities and the labels that they gave to each other to reflect their character, attitude and behaviour. The youth identity was a complex structure constructed of multiple layers.

Players pigeon-holed each other as 'troublesome', 'good', 'bad', 'joker', 'rude', 'stupid', 'smart' or 'fisci', (fisci is a Liberian English term meaning untalented or not very skilful). Describing a youth as 'good' or 'bad' provided an insight into their morals and ethics as well as their usual behaviours; a good person does not hustle but pursues legitimate money-making activities, for example. Those considered 'jokers' were playful and juvenile in nature; they mocked players mischievously and would play-fight on the field during breaks in training. Senior players tended to monitor such players and in many ways mentored them and provided guidance; jokers were embraced on the team but were quick to be silenced by senior players when inappropriate. The brand 'rude' was given to players who openly challenged adult authority or senior players' instruction and were thought to cause embarrassment to teammates and the youth centre. To be called 'stupid' was a common insult to a player for making poor playing decisions on the field or pursuing pointless palava. Players who challenged others without a cause or chance of victory were thought of as 'stupid', 'stupido' and, ultimately, juvenile. Being 'smart' was associated with wisdom and maturity; someone good at lecturing and showing signs of adult-like behaviour. Such labels had many connotations of child-like or adult-like behaviour. This influenced status within the team and affected the amount of respect given by adults. The 'good' and 'smart' players were given responsibility and opportunities by the youth centre staff. Hence Richie, regarded by the youth centre staff as both 'good' and 'smart', was asked by Father M to help coach the young boys on the small pitch in the youth centre—not a recognised position outside the fence but an acknowledgement no less.

Titles were also in the mix when it came to naming: the Fathers based at the youth centre were known by their religious positions and also as 'brother', 'uncle' and 'pa'. Coach J was known by his position and title as Coach as well as by the names given to him during the conflict as a rebel commander. Descriptions of people were also used to greet or gain attention; pekin, boy, small or small-small were all used as ways to refer to someone and establish hierarchy. The acknowledgement and awareness of youth, adult and elder hierarchical divides was obvious. Adults were acknowledged by titles and this acknowledgement gave respect, insinuated commendable moral behaviour and character traits associated with wisdom and adulthood to the recipient. Something that was far more complex and diverse was the identity, perception and internal hierarchy within the youth category. Having nicknames, football names and character labels all contributed to youth footballers' capacity to have multiple identities and demonstrated the unstable nature of being without a high formal status. This dynamic feature of football contributed to the performance and characterisation that occurred within the fence.

He Is Rude

Identity within the team was complicated and usually required numerous observations. From these observations, I spent many hours mapping patterns of social interactions and relationships that influenced an individuals' identity. Interpreting identity required me to consider numerous actors inside and outside the fence. Identity outside the fence had consequences for identity within the team and an established football identity impacted upon identity outside the fence. Furthermore, the labelling and characterisation of players could be used by adults to punish and exploit youths whilst justifying their own behaviour.

Jackson was never seen without a football. He was 21 years of age and enjoyed showing off his kick ups and tricks to the other players. He was an ideal player to coach; physically very fit and usually beating the others in sprint drills, he went about training in a quiet non-oppositional way. Yet the tension between him and Coach J could not be hidden or ignored. Constantly challenging each other, Coach J would claim he was 'rude' and he would be the focus of many of Coach J's rants. Jackson thought he was being picked on and always blamed and punished for incidents whilst others would do worse and not be reprimanded. Jackson rarely started games in training or in league fixtures although he was very talented. He would support his team every second they were playing, occasionally shouting, 'You can make it, Zatti, press.'[2] Even when he was suspended for refusing to leave the playing field on the coach's order he still supported Zatti for matches and observed training sessions. Jackson's biggest fault was his mouth; he could not hold his tongue. When challenged or criticised by the coach, he would shout back to explain what had happened or try to justify his actions. This was seen by spectating adults as a direct challenge to the coach's authority and a show of disrespect. The coach would make him run round the pitch as punishment whilst shouting at him and, in severe cases, suspending him. Jackson would also make palava with the referees during training. Being a skilful player, he would try to hold onto the ball for too long but the sand slowed him down and he could not escape the inevitable tackles. If he did not receive a free kick, he would challenge the referee, complaining, 'He play foul this is a cheating game.' Sometimes the referee would sit him to the side for a few minutes as punishment. Anytime Jackson misbehaved the Coach branded him as 'rude'.

During the rainy season the team moved to a pitch near the junction which had soft sand that better absorbed the rain. This exposed the Zatti team to members of the community who would not usually spectate at the youth centre. Any display of football in Liberia attracted a crowd so the players were expected to be on their best behaviour in front of a new audience. Zatti already had a reputation for having 'rude players' so it was important not to live up to such a reputation. A training game began against another local team. As always it was competitively played and this was heightened by the presence of more spectators. Zatti scored an early goal and were playing with confidence but Jackson lost possession of the ball, which resulted in the opposition equalising. The angry coach shouted at Jackson. I tried to call him to one side to give him the technical version of what Coach J was saying but he had already lost his temper. He was substituted and in defiance threw his bib to the ground and sat alone on the other side of the field. The coach turned to me and said: 'You see Rudeness.' At the end of the training session the coach

---

[2] Press meant surge forward to create a goal-scoring opportunity.

approached me once more: 'Jackson's behaviour was not correct, he made the team shame.' He wanted to permanently suspend Jackson.

The next training session was back at the youth centre. As Jackson arrived I sat next to him to see what had happened. He looked sorrowful at the prospect of being permanently removed from the team. He spoke openly: 'He (the coach) always want me to be suspended, he try to make me angry and have palava, I wanted to say sorry yesterday after training to the team but I didn't get chance.' He described an incident when a player named Seki had palava with the coach and cursed him, even insulting the coach's mother. Seki and Jackson are close friends in the team and although Jackson was present during the incident he never joined in with the cursing or insults. When Coach J reported the incident to Pa K and Father M he blamed both Seki and Jackson and wanted them both suspended for 3 months. Richie was called in to give his account and confirmed that Jackson did not curse or insult anybody and that he should not be punished. Seki was suspended but Jackson remained an irritant for Coach J. I asked why he thought it was so. 'The coach were loving to my girl but I did not say anything but he knew cos I finished it with the girl ... when I suspended the last time my pa came and begged the team for me to play. They accept his words but the coach no satisfied for that but the team want me to play so now he always try and make me angry so I lose my mind and get disturb.' The rumours and whispers of Coach J 'loving' the players' girlfriends was a regular topic of conversation along with him 'eating money', 'liking too much women business' and generally being corrupt although none of these indiscretions challenged his position of coach or his role within the team. When Jackson's father came to the youth centre to beg the team to let him come back they respectfully accepted the elder's wishes. Unfortunately for Jackson, this was his only bargaining tool. His father was a respected elder but his family was poor. Other players on the team who had access to adult networks or financial assets were rarely punished in the same way or spoken to in the same manner. A handful of players had relatives in America who helped finance their education. Two senior members of the team had regular informal work, one as a money-changing operator and the other had learned how to fix generators. These players could be beneficial to the coach off the field and could pay for opportunities to play. Such players were not branded as 'rude'.

Jackson is a student. Delayed in his studies, he is self-supported and from a poor family. Any money he generates is from ad hoc manual work or hustling. He is firmly placed in the youth category. The Zatti players respect him for his talents on the field but Coach J saw little benefit from him. The Zatti players tend to be very protective of their own and never encourage suspensions. It seemed Jackson was an easy target and acted as the black sheep of the team; he had no power away from football and no higher status within the team. Unfortunately his inability to control his temper fed into his label of being 'rude'; yet away from Coach J, Jackson was always well behaved, appreciated by his teammates and, from my experience, very coachable. The tension between Coach J and Jackson was personal. Coach J took advantage of his limited social resources for his own purposes. Because of this Jackson's reputation and label of being rude continued on and off the field. In this case, Jackson's identity as a youth was established in relation to the coach, his social position and the class and status of his family. A number of actors, including the youth centre staff, contributed to the construction of his individual identity and his status as a youth footballer.

The Krahn Brothers

Characteristics and manner could also be explained through indigenous ethnic identity or upbringing. Ethnic heritage was quite irrelevant in terms of access and acceptance into a community football team but this feature of identity was regularly discussed and used by players as an element of characterisation. The players explained to me that Kpelle were thought of as 'soft people' to the point of being naive, Krahn, Gio and Mano were aggressive by nature, and Bassa people had the stereotype of having 'plenty borning', being 'playful' and liking 'women business'. The majority of players on the Zatti team were Krahn. Most were born in Grand Gedeh County and had migrated during the conflict. There was closeness between these players not seen with the others; they referred to each other as my 'brother'. They were quick to defend each other when palava occurred during matches and if one of them was reprimanded by the referee, they would defend his actions no matter how bad the act was. If one of them received a bad tackle and fell to the floor one of the Krahn brothers would get him water and rush to his aid whilst the others sought retribution. Belonging to this Krahn brotherhood meant defending and protecting each other but it also gave them a reputation to uphold. Having an aggressive nature and being quick-tempered was always associated with this group and if an outsider was looking on, these players made sure they did not deviate from their stereotype. This was explained by other players who would claim that Krahns are a 'rebellious tribe', 'it's in their blood they can't help it.'

Weekends with league games were always a highlight for the Zatti boys. Preparation for the game was always executed in their casual manner with laughing, joking, playful palava and a little jogging and stretching followed by some passing with the ball. On this particular weekend, games were running behind schedule, as is usually the case, and the boys became restless. This usually meant they became mischievous. They gathered in a circle and decided to play a game called 'pass to your brother'. The Krahn brothers led the game passing to each other and enjoying their superior numbers. Then Ben intercepted the ball. Bernardo looked at him and said, 'You're Gio; we don't like each other.' Bernardo smiled and allowed him the ball. Richie was given the ball but he did not have any Grebo brothers on the team, so they laughed at him and he had to sacrifice the ball. It was all done in good humour.

Ethnic identity was important to this group of players; it formed part of their characters and shaped the expectation others had of them. Although it brought players from the same indigenous group closer, this bond was more apparent outside the fence with matters away from football. It was seen more as a sense of responsibility towards each other or an obligation to defend and protect. On the football field players only referred to ethnicity when describing character or explaining behaviour. Yet it also had negative connotations when defining the character of youths. For example, adult Krahns were thought of as power-hungry and aggressive but this made them strong and, once considered adult, they were not to be challenged. This stereotype has strong links to the civil conflict. Samuel K Doe was a proud Krahn man who ran a Krahn regime. Many famous and feared rebel commanders such as 'General Butt Naked' were Krahn. A number of indigenous ethnic stereotypes emerged through the conflict and remained post-conflict. Although this was not a cause for tension or discrimination it was used to explain behaviour and create images of character. Youth Krahns were thought of with the same stereotype but without power and status and this made them potentially volatile, violent and rude. Ethnic identity was a stable character trait that caused no prejudice on the football field between players but this feature of characterisation did contribute to explaining the behaviour and the bonding of players outside the fence. In many ways defining identity by ethnicity provided adults with cues to adopt stereotypes and create prejudice.

I Can Make It: The Need for Characters and Unity

One element of performance and characterisation was the uniting effect it had on the players and the team. Ben was the team's 'joker'. At the age of 24 years he liked to think of himself as a 'bigger boy' but he was always the centre of joking amongst the boys and everyone smiled when they saw him arrive for training. Not a natural athlete, he worked hard and enjoyed the physical nature of training. In the usual manner he would arrive late to training and run through the gates shouting, 'I can make it!' The players would shout, 'Ben ... You can make it!' It soon became the team's catchphrase. Every fitness drill would begin with 'I can make it!' This phrase also worked well as encouragement for players struggling during training or when a striker missed a shot. The players enjoyed the camaraderie this brought. Ben did not often play the National League games but he was a supportive sub and his catchphrase could regularly be heard from the Zatti bench during the games, encouraging teammates— a welcome sound that broke the noise of Coach J's chastising.

Another common phrase among the players was, 'You gotta improvise.' Players would turn up for training with a range of footwear. Some were lucky enough to own their own footwear, while others would borrow boots, and some wore shoes or plastic sandals. A common complaint was that 'Zatti player need boots' to which the coach would respond, 'Gentlemen, you gotta improvise' and generally they did, wearing any footwear available to them, no matter how unorthodox. In order 'to make it' you had to 'improvise'.

Invitations were received to play against teams in other subregions of Monrovia and, if accepted, travel and food money was needed to facilitate the trip. This usually cost 125LD (£1.25) per player. For some, finding this amount of money was achievable, but for others, it was beyond what they could afford. When money was collected the players unable to contribute were advised 'You gotta improvise.' Any complaints of hardship were usually followed with the same advice, usually in good humour. At times the Krahn brothers would help to finance each other or small players would seek help from the senior members of the team.

The characterisation of players was a constant feature that enhanced the performance of football in Matadi. Identifying and acknowledging players according to their skill, personality, character, behaviour and indigenous group reflected their dynamic function as a group. This form of labelling also created and enforced roles and hierarchical structures within the team—senior players were confirmed as such through character labels and so were small players. As a result adult staff involved with the team and adult spectators used such labels to cast judgements about individual players and this in turn had consequences for the players outside the fence.

Bernardo: The Uncontrollable Individual

The element of characterisation and adopting numerous identities within the team had various outcomes. As well as attributing to the performance aspect of the game it had consequences that affected the youth–adult relationship. Negative labelling and identities enforced youth stereotypes held by adults. This in turn could have consequences for the players outside the fence. As one commentator of Liberia, Stephen Ellis, claims:

> Younger Liberians, especially those who came of age during the war, often have views and attitudes significantly different from those of their elders.

One obvious difference is that young Liberians today are generally far less respectful of their elders than would have been thought proper in the past. (1999, p. 285)

He further argues that young Liberians are more individualistic in nature and this has 'brought in a lot of sophisticated crimes that seek to place materialistic urge at the podium, emphasising individual glory over community well-being' (ibid). Bernardo was arguably Zatti's most controversial and complex character. His behaviour in and out of the fence resulted in multiple labels and descriptions of his personality and character which influenced a number of his relationships with fellow players and adults.

'Bah' or Bernardo (Bah was his Liberian name but Bernardo was the European version as he particularly admired the player Ronaldo) as I was to call him was one of the biggest characters on the team and caused much of the theatrics within the fence. Tall and muscular, the central defender on the team, he was aggressive whilst playing, never backing out of a challenge and at times 'playing foul'. He was a natural leader—although lacking in responsibility; he had a big presence, was popular amongst his teammates, was always joking and was the one to air his opinion to Coach J about other players and about the coach himself whilst others were too scared. He had a reputation for being troublesome, unpredictable and at times a 'bad boy' but his humour and carefree attitude made him very likeable.

He worked at a gas station at Matadi Junction lifting and carrying barrels of fuel and lived with his mother, grandparents, girlfriend and newborn daughter nearby. If there was no work for him some day, he would walk up and down the main road of Matadi 'hustling', approaching girls and joking with friends. He was the same off the field as he was on it, known in Matadi as having a quick temper but unlike the others on the team he was also quick to fight, never making empty threats. He was a proud 'Krahn man', a key aspect of his identity the players of Zatti would use to justify and defend his behaviour: 'He can't help it, it's in his blood', or, 'it's not his fault, he was born in the bush.' They identified him as an uncontrollable member of the team and accepted his temperament as a consequence of his tribal upbringing.

The day his daughter was born he walked through the youth centre gates, late as always, with the same troublesome grin. He worked extra hard that session, showing the others what he could do when he tried. He played the part of an 'individual' with a cocky persona not showing the same level of respect to his coach as the others by purposely provoking him, not singing and praying with the others at the beginning and warming up in a casual manner, participating in his own style. He had little interest in the training side of playing football; he enjoyed the contest of a match more, enforcing his superiority over opposing players. During the training match he scored a goal; he ran to the Zatti players waiting to be substituted and celebrated by mimicking cradling a baby in his arms. As the players gathered after training, sitting on the ground removing their boots and wiping the sand from their feet, Bernardo declared he had something to say. 'Coach, I'm a changed man.' The other players laughed and clapped, all with scepticism that the man was not for changing.

Bernardo was no stranger to the police and described to me his experiences of being in prison. Petty criminals are kept in small neighbouring police stations, usually for a night or until a relative could pay money for their release. Bernardo found himself in trouble after he and his brother sold a mobile phone that did not belong to them. When the owner discovered what had happened he contacted the police and Bernardo was arrested. He was released in the early hours the next morning and his day continued in its usual way.

On the 8 April 2012 Arsenal played Manchester City in the Premiership League, a match that saw Arsenal win 1–0. I was in the video club that day watching the game with a number of Zatti players. That day the score was irrelevant; the focus was on Mario Balotelli, an unpredictable Italian player who was sent off during the game for his second bookable offence. Balotelli's challenges were deemed dangerous and the actions of the player and referee on the day caused chaos in the video club. Palava could be heard from every corner of the wooden structure, each person's comment inciting a further debate. The next afternoon Bernardo strolled onto the playing field and declared: 'Gentlemen, today you can call me Balotelli.' From then on anytime he played foul, chants of 'Balotelli' or 'Mario' emerged from the crowd and Bernardo was happy to play up to this.

In the same week the Zatti players were to practice against the 'outsiders'. The game was competitive and at some points overly competitive with the sand encouraging rash slide tackles, and arms and upper body strength being used to overpower opponents. This at times caused argument between players of opposing teams, which in turn led to Coach J scolding the Zatti players involved, and this resulted in palava between coach and player. Players usually touched hands after such altercations as a sign that there was no bad feeling between them. A lot of pride was at stake in these games even though they occurred daily. Discussions of the game, players' performances and incidents would continue well into the night. Bernardo was unhappy that Zatti were losing 1–0 because of a mistake made in the midfield. He cursed the players at fault but took offence at an opposing player who was heckling the Zatti team. He called to him, 'You!' with a clenched right fist, the index finger pointing towards the air. This gesture is known to be a challenge in a scolding manner, a person who accepts this challenge will approach the person and force the finger down indicating 'you are not bigger than me' and this will usually initiate a physical fight. If the person does not want to enter into such a challenge they can walk away in defeat at the threat. The player turned and at the sight of Bernardo's gesture withdrew. That would usually be enough to satisfy a player's dominance and distaste for certain behaviour but not Bernardo. When the opposing player in question made a run with the ball towards the goal he jumped into a tackle leaving marks on the player's ankle. Players ran from all sides to remove Bernardo from the field. Some were aggressively having palava between themselves while others were trying to calm down the situation. The referee was helplessly blowing his whistle in the middle of the field whist Coach J was scolding Bernardo and telling him to sit alongside the suspended players. Calm was eventually restored by the senior players and youth centre staff and the game continued without further participation by Bernardo.

At 6 pm the referee blew the final whistle. Players were discussing the game, mostly Bernardo's sending off. Some were defending his behaviour as they thought that the opposing player was being rude; others believed that Bernardo was rude and that what he did 'was not correct'. Either way it was accepted that such behaviour was possible from him as he was known to be troublesome and seemed to enjoy the reputation it brought. He would not face suspension but the senior players lectured him at length until Coach J arrived and all fell silent. Coach J began shouting at them in his aggressive tone, claiming that their discipline was not correct and that they would bring embarrassment to the youth centre when they began their league games if their behaviour did not improve. Bernardo sat at the back in silence looking smug, uninterested and proud, waiting for the coach to challenge him directly—but he did not.

Bernardo represented the dynamic, changeable and varied multiple identities of the players in the team. Bernardo was bold in his interactions, regardless of environment, circumstances and status of those he conversed with or expressed to. He was known by his birth name and football nickname, labelled with character descriptions; troublesome and rude—elders would refer to him as a 'bad pekin'. He was also known to be a hustler and—to some—a likeable rogue. He was also a father. His ethnic identity of being Krahn enforced the stereotypes of him being aggressive and unpredictable. He was the individual in the team, disrespectful to authority and elders and the only player not to follow protocol when praying and training. Yet he was admired by the players for his honesty, perception, humour, strength and skill—although they would regularly complain about his behaviour and the embarrassment he caused. Bernardo's uncontrollable and multiple personalities created much tension and conflict between him and the adults inside the fence. Despite this his charisma and physical superiority identified him as an invaluable member of the team. Bernardo acted as the vocal and most obvious character in protest against adult control, injustices within the game's framework and indeed the realities of community around him. The status of youth is dual. Firstly, the relative status of youths amongst themselves on the team is constructed by establishing hierarchies based on levels of education, financial resources, years in the team, physical skill and strength and the ability for individuals to assert and claim authority. Secondly, their status as youths as opposed to adults and elders is established and confirmed by their struggles on the pitch.

Meta-Societies and Play Communities

If football is stripped back to its basic format as a game then 'play' becomes a relevant factor in its analysis as a youth pursuit. Zatti players refer to football as 'play' as they do with other recreational activities where one can win or lose; youths refer to gambling as 'playing', and the pursuit of women and sex is 'play'. Here, I use the work of Huizinga (1950) to analyse the concept and relevance of play in culture. Although his work may have been completed some 60 years ago he is still considered a pioneer in his field and continues to be referred to extensively when discussing play. Huizinga claimed: 'In play there is something "at play" which transcends the immediate needs of life and imparts meaning to the action. All play means something' (1950, p. 1). One meaning football brings to Matadi youths is the creation of a structure and space separated from life outside the fence, like Turner's communitas, whilst constructing solidarity and mimicking hierarchies and authority structures seen in the community. SDP agencies use the term 'play' to seduce donors and potential partner agencies by constantly evoking images in their publicity of young people having fun and gaining from the experience of playing as a group. But this image is in many ways counterproductive to the cause.

Social Value of Play: Creating a Play Culture

The social context of play and its capacity to remove one from 'ordinary life' is what places play within a social context and links the youth practice of football with the notion and practice of ritual. Football provides a form of social construction and this makes such play significant to cultural environments and more specifically Matadi youth. Generally speaking, play

> adorns life, amplifies it and is to that extent a necessity both for the individual—as a life function—and for society by reason of the meaning it contains, its significance, its expressive value, its spiritual and social associations, in short, as a cultural function. (Huizinga 1950, p. 9)

Huizinga argues that 'play and culture are interwoven' and that genuine, pure play is one of the main bases of civilisation (p. 5). Caillois (1961) argues that play is a reflection of society and mirrors its nature, environment and culture. Caillois supports Huizinga's theory of play but develops the analysis with the classification of diversified forms of play (Caillois 1961, p. ix). Formulating his own definition of play, Caillois categorised play thus: 'One plays football (*agon*), roulette (*alea*), pirates (*mimicry*), dizziness and disorder (*ilinx*). Each form of play takes into consideration the role of competition, chance, simulation or vertigo' (ibid., p. 12). The classification of *agon* is obviously crucial to this analysis albeit some crossovers are relevant. Caillois defined agon as 'competitive like a combat in which equality of chances is artificially created … (it) is a cultural phenomenon among homo sapiens as the spirit of the game is centred on equality of rules and environment' (ibid., pp. 14–15). The artificial creation of equality of chances is what is significant here—this is a space where relationships take place out of the context of ordinary life but are structurally distinct from Olofson's relation to off the field.

Huizinga believes that the act of play, stepping out of 'ordinary life' and entering a temporary sphere of activity with a disposition of its own is important when studying a culture. This is a key element to my overall argument. Many Zatti players like Richie are unemployed, still being schooled at an older age, and are living with parents. Their playing provides a platform for them to take the lead in a daily event and step away from their lack of social worth and dependency within the community. In the youth centre they become the most important and acknowledged members, all the while displaying their characters, having fun and playing by the rules of the game from the structure they establish amongst themselves. It is thus that football constitutes a meta-society; playing football reflects the society around them and informs the structure of the team and the manner in which they play the game. That said, Zatti play in a protective space and within their own determined structure; they have created a 'bubble' with children, adults and elders watching from its boundaries. SDP is promoted with the assumption that football promotes youths' social integration and community development. Yet, in Matadi, football produced a 'civil society' somewhat insulated from life away from the pitch in which youths live as a visible and separate group.

The game thus highlights generational hierarchies in the community and in Matadi this prevents youths from entering into adulthood.

Tension in the Community: Conflict in the Game

Tension and conflict are prominently featured throughout Matadi, in multiple environments and situations. Power struggles, asserting status and survival combine to form a potentially toxic environment. The quest to age to gain authority is a constant battle at the community level and ironically this is transferred to the football field. The attempt to gain status within the team dominates and dictates much of the players' efforts. The outcome of this is tension and conflict within the team.

The theme of tension plays an important role in both Huizinga's and Erving Goffman's (1961) work. Tension is part of the appeal of all games and play; it creates drama, performance and atmosphere. For Goffman, the tension experienced during games identifies a player's perception of discrepancy between the world that one embraces spontaneously and the 'world one is obliged to dwell in' (Goffman 1961, pp. 41–45); quite simply the tension reflects social alienation. For Matadi football players the discrepancy between social status on and off the field is the key factor in constructing a meta-society. The fact that the Zatti players have to create a world away from their community to feel valued, express their identity and perform further highlights their low status outside the fence. Although football for them is an escape it is also the activity in their lives that further reinforces their position as youth. As we have already seen in the case of Richie, opportunities are limited for achieving status and social worth, so the options are to play in the community team and be further associated with the label of youth or leave and face the realities of being a youth alone trying to achieve the impossible.

The options posed here are by no means rhetorical; it is suggested here that football has become the answer to the problem of failed—or delayed—adulthood for many of these young men. Marginalised in one community, with no opportunities to escape, they create their own football community. The game has taken on a whole new meaning, function and purpose for youths at the community and grassroots level. No longer is it 'just a game' but it has become an outlet that provides social worth and status. Along with recognition from adults who come to spectate, it creates a society that they are not alienated from but manage themselves in, which fosters cohesion amongst its members. Players take on roles to organise, support and perform whilst gaining acknowledgement from outsiders and community members. Football then provides the stage for young males to be heard and seen; even their nicknaming of players creates characters.

Erving Goffman's sociological perspectives on human expression consider the social situation that surrounds the game. Branding games as a fundamentally relevant form of human encounter and an apt metaphor for social life he describes the act of play and games as

> a matrix of possible events and a cast of roles through whose enactment the events occur constitute together a field for fateful dramatic action, a plane of being, an engine of meaning, a world in itself, different from all other worlds except the ones generated when the same game is played at other times. (Goffman 1961, pp. 19–20)

This notion of games as a metaphor of social life is a valuable tool when considering Matadi footballers and their construction of a meta-society. Goffman postulates a series of rules governing the field of play in general terms beyond the legal scientific rules of any given game. What he terms the 'Rule of Irrelevance' argues that the social status of players is of no pertinence once the game has begun. In Liberia, social recognition is a major barrier to gaining adult status; if this aspect of human interaction is eradicated through play then surely this can be identified as a significant aspect towards participation in the game and making the game an attractive pursuit for the players. Goffman suggests that 'gaming encounters provide us with fine examples of how mutual activity can utterly engross its participants, transforming them into worthy antagonists in spite of the triviality of the game, great differences in social status, and the patent claims of their realities' (ibid., p. 39).

The Zatti football community provided players with status and importance. Adopting roles and individual identities the players mimicked the hierarchical nature of the community outside the fence. They followed adult patterns of asserting supremacy and demanding acknowledgement. In football this was conducted through the displays of physicality, power and masculinity. Notions of character and identity contributed to recognition within the team, but the environment demanded physical performances and drama to claim seniority and hold the attention of the adult spectators. The Zatti team have found an activity that most immediately they enjoy and are skilled at, but in broader social terms, which also breaks down the barriers associated with status in their community.

Adults Affecting Play: Football as a Form of Social Control

Although play is deep-rooted in spontaneity and removal from 'ordinary life' it also requires participants to play by the rules. Any deviation from the unwritten or written rules of play spoils the game or performance and devalues its worth. Following such rules is paramount to the game's sustainability and is the fundamental principle holding this temporary state together. The notion of play and tension is important and apt in the case of youth football in Matadi. The uncertainty of play and the reliance on players' cooperation provoke a constant tension amongst these unpredictable and dynamic youths.

The game was driven by drama. The indiscipline observed by many of the Zatti players constantly led to the game being disrupted or ending early. Adult authority figures would have to intervene, lecture and punish the deviant youths, thus propelling the players from a state of escapism in the world of play back into ordinary—non-playing—life. Not playing by the rules openly transferred the power back to the adults and confirmed the players' subordinate youth status. Their indiscipline, freedom of expression and the modes of asserting authority within the team tested the rules and the manner in which they were expected to play. Zatti players became the most significant determinant of how long their play community could engage; breaking adult-determined rules caused the game to end and allowed elders to assert their authority. The level of freedom players found in football often led to other forms of mirroring social norms outside of play but corruptive pursuits to ensure victory threatened the support of the Fathers who funded the team. The players' inability to manage behaviour and follow rules was the principal indicator of low social status and adults used this to assert their higher position from outside the fence.

Although play, and specifically football in Matadi, is a temporary world away from the marginalisation and the harshness of 'ordinary life' certain realities disrupted the course of play. In many cases players were called for by family members to help with chores, and some were forbidden to play as a form of punishment. Goffman applied another set of norms to that of Huizinga's analysis of play called 'transformation rules'; in this argument, games, whilst not a metaphorical image of the everyday, are also not separate from other portions of life. For the youth of Matadi playing football is something that rids them of their low social status, but only temporarily, because their escape from ordinary life is fragile. The demands placed by hierarchical structures outside the youth centre are a constant threat to their play. However much football acts as an activity away from ordinary life it must be acknowledged that without the support of the fathers of Don Bosco, and the acceptance of parents or guardians allowing them to take the time to participate the community's football players would not be able to establish a strong play ethic or have a regular outlet. The elders dictate the success and timing of the play world and are the most significant potential barrier to participation. Football acts as a form of social control for adults to assert and affirm their status within the community.

Spectators

Performance is key to the football experience. The uneven sand of the playing surface sets the stage for a multitude of unrehearsed scenes that promise unpredictable outcomes. This is what attracts the audience; the drama, theatrics, skill and the unscripted contest. The spectators of daily football games in Liberia play a key role in all of this. Their participation and gesturing enter their own phase of play: laughing, mocking, having fun and observing a youth-led game. Observers voluntarily place themselves at the edge of the performance and have their own rules. This act away from home forms another play community; their reaction to the performance can influence the stages of play and its course over a period of time. Play without willing spectators creates a whole new, less dramatic environment. Football thus provides a rare opportunity for adult–youth interaction outside the family unit. However, this is a double-edged sword; adults can witness and acknowledge strong performances and credit the youths who behave well and manifest adult-like traits of taking responsibility and leadership, but, they also observe youths behaving badly and displaying characteristics associated with youthhood. Football can be used by adults to reinforce low status, as a proof of immaturity. Inside the fence being a spectator represents a position of power and status

Adults Own the Game, Youths Play

In the absence of impact and sustained structured SDP football projects, Liberian communities have been the primary site for resourced and locally managed football programmes. The result of this is that players have adopted ownership within their teams through commitment to daily training, performance, structure and management. Due to this, football in Matadi follows ritual-like forms through its practical elements, function and outcomes. As a social convention football facilitates expression and the opportunity for its players to adopt characters and multiple identities. This reflects identity both as a group and as individuals, thus reinforcing the notion that players have multiple potential personalities, are an unstable group—in terms of personal representation—and are highly complex individually and collectively. Arguably, the lack of predictability within the fence on the football field further represents Liberian youth; potentially, football structures and simplifies the chaos outside the fence whilst replicating social processes (Olofson 1977; Gluckman 1965; Frazer 1922). The social effect for players is therefore highly dependent upon adult-determined factors and restricted to a very specific time and space. Football constructs its own cultural context (Rollason 2011) rather than contributing to a wider civil society or developing youth programmes towards adulthood.

The meta-society of football reflects the processes of acquiring status and the tension, conflict and competition this provokes for the players. Adults endorse and accept youth football in the local community context in part because it enforces the generational category of youth in its present format. It is a compromise to keep the unpredictable youths satisfied whilst confirming their status. This highly unpredictable, fragile, creative and energetic football team is reflective of the world in which they live outside of the compound. It is constructed as a consequence of youth being marginalised and frustrated. In football the youths seek an activity that provides acknowledgement from adults within and outside and also provides opportunities to experience status. It would seem that football is the ideal mechanism for youths to unite and experience being part of a community where they play a role. Yet, with time they understand that their role in the team can progress and develop unlike their position off the field.

Only with the permission of adults can youths attend daily. Adults from within the fence or outside can stop the game with immediate effect. Whilst youths are playing football they can never be considered adult but without football they are not only alienated from adult conventions but isolated from the security and unity of the team. The control and power remain with the adults and elders and this may account for the frequency of palava, conflict and frustration on the pitch. Although this meta-society is occupied primarily by youths for youths, it is controlled, financed, managed and facilitated by adults. As with most aspects of Liberian community it is the adults who dominate and dictate the processes; football is engulfed in social politics as the marginalised continue to be controlled in order to sustain and reinforce the low status of youths.

SDP advocates consider youths as a mass of people without consideration of their internal dynamics. Football attracts global partnerships, it does target and engage youths, it can provide values of unity but it also establishes a platform for asserting status amongst youths. The game produces tension as youths compete for social recognition, and thus it acts as a tool for adults to assert social control. Whilst aiding the construction of youth identity, football enforces the stagnation of the players' social position. The football community can act as a means for adults to deny youths the position of recognised citizens in the community. Arguably youth development can only occur if the effects of football are transferred to the wider adult community but football in Matadi acts as a barrier to adulthood. If the building of an inclusive civil society via football programmes is the aim of SDP then it fails in this case. The football community in Matadi highlights the hierarchical nature of the wider community by confirming players as socially marginal youths.

References

Bell, C. (1997). *Ritual: Perspectives and dimensions*. Oxford/New York: Oxford University Press.

Blanchard, K. (1988). Sport and ritual: A conceptual dilemma. *Journal of Physical Education, Recreation and Dance, 59*(9), 48–52.

Caillois, R. (1961). *Man, play and games*. Urbana/Chicago: University of Illinois Press.

Cheska, A. T. (1979). Sports spectacular: A ritual model of power. *International Review for the Sociology of Sport, 14*(2), 51–72.

De Coppet, D. (Ed.). (2002). *Understanding rituals*. London/New York: Routledge.

Ellis, S. (1999). *The mask of anarchy: The destruction of Liberia and the religious dimension of an African civil war*. New York: New York University Press.

Frazer, J. G. (1922). *A golden bough: A study in magic and religion*. New York: Macmillan.

Gluckman, M. (1965). *Politics, law and ritual in tribal society*. Chicago: Aldine Publishing Company.

Gluckman, M., Gluckman, M. (1977). Chapter XII on drama, and games and athletic contests. In *Secular ritual: A working definition of ritual* (p. 227).

Goffman, E. (1961). *Encounters: Two studies in the sociology of interaction*. Indianapolis: Bobbs-Merrill.

Guttman, A. (1978). *From ritual to record: The nature of modern sports*. New York: Columbia University Press.

Harris, J. (1983). Sport and ritual: A macroscopic comparison of form. In Janet C. Harris & Robert J. Park (Eds.), *Play, games & sports in cultural contexts* (pp. 177–189). Champaign: Human Kinetics Publishers.

Harris, J. C., & Park, R. J. (1983). *Play, games and sports in cultural contexts.* Champaign: Human Kinetics Publishers.

Huizinga, J. (1950). *Homo Ludens: A study of the play element in culture.* Boston: Beacon.

IOC. (2013). Olympic Charter. http://www.olympic.org/Documents/olympic_charter_en.pdf.

Levi-Strauss, C. (1966). *The savage mind.* London: Weidenfeld and Nicolson.

Olofson, H (1977). Playing a kingdom: A Hausa meta-society in the walled city of Zaria, Nigeria. In D. F. Lancy, & B. A. Tindall (Eds.), *The study of play: Problems and perspectives* (pp. 172–173). West Point: Leisure Press.

Rollason, W. (2011). *We are playing football: Sport and postcolonial subjectivity, Panapompom, Papua New Guinea.* Newcastle upon Tyne: Cambridge Scholars.

Stevenson, T. B., & Alaug, A. K. (2000). Football in newly united Yemen: Rituals of equity, identity, and state formation. *Journal of Anthropological Research, 56*(4), 453–475.

Turner, V. (1969). *The ritual process: Structure and anti-structure.* New Brunswick/London: Transaction Publishers.

Turner, V. (1974). Liminality, play, flow, and ritual: An essay in comparative symbology. *The Anthropological Study of Human Play, 60*(3), 53–92. Houston, Texas: Rice University Studies.

United Nations. (2005). Sport as a tool for development and peace: Towards achieving the United Nations Millennium Development Goals. http://www.un.org/sport2005/resources/task_force.pdf.

Utas, M. (2005). Building a future? The reintegration and re-marginalisation of youth in Liberia. In P. Richards (Ed.), *No peace, no war: An anthropology of contemporary armed conflicts* (pp. 137–154). Athens: Ohio University Press.

Van Gennep, A. (1960). *The rites of passage.* London: Routledge and Kegan Paul Ltd.

Wagner, R. (1986). *Symbols that stand for themselves.* Chicago: University of Chicago Press.

8

The Seduction of Football

Seduction, Persuasion and Cooperation

As a collective, 'youth' are an integral demographic of any civil society. Many Heads of State and International Development Organisations appreciate the connection between youth investment and engagement and building a peaceful society for the future. The UN declared 2010 as the International Year of Youth and informed its member states thus: 'Failing to invest in children and youth triggers substantial economic, social, and political costs resulting from negative outcomes such as early school drop-out, poor labour market entry, risky sexual behaviours, substance abuse, and crime and violence' (n.p). As previous discussion has illustrated, there is a disconnect between adults and youths in Liberia which has created what is termed the stagnation of ageing, alongside hierarchically determined relationships and ultimately tension between the generational categories. Due to these factors adults, state institutions and organisations have sought strategies to engage and access youth for numerical supremacy and personal promotion.

© The Editor(s) (if applicable) and The Author(s) 2016
H. Collison, *Youth and Sport for Development*,
DOI 10.1057/978-1-137-52470-6_8

The connection between football, seduction and youth participation can be made with the way that football is included into post-conflict peacekeeping strategies, SDP programmes, community projects, political environments and any other events in Liberia that desire the access, engagement and attention of youth. In so many instances football is used by local adults to seduce youths as a form of distraction to provide a platform for selling ideas and concepts to them without their considered consent (Althusser 2008). The ability for football to seduce youth and draw them into contact with international and local organisations as well as individuals has confirmed footballers as youths and has influenced their post-conflict identity.

Dropping the Ball but Keeping the Image?

> In a world which seems so divided and torn by suspicion and doubt it is becoming more and more important to find ways of bringing peace and reconciliation without the aid of 'experts'. And believe it or not football for some people can do just that. Through its high profile, its world-wide appeal and the demands of the game itself can make it an instrument of reconciliation. (Fr Joe 1997)

Father Joe was based in Liberia for many years endorsing the function of football in this Don Bosco (DB) religious organisation's strategy, especially during the civil conflict that was depriving so many of a childhood. He came late to football; he had no interest in the game prior to the 1990s. It was he who persuaded DB's primary supporters, Catholic Agency for Overseas Development (CAFOD) based in London, to support a team of Liberian boys involved in or affected by the war to undertake a football tour of England. Father Joe documented their trip for CAFOD and his account was published on their web site. Their individual case studies[1] highlight the players' experiences of conflict and the value DB placed on football.

---

[1] These case studies were written by Father Joe and published on the Salesian web site.

Rehabilitation and Reunification: Michael

Michael, 14 years old, joined a local faction during the war after his father was killed and he was separated from his mother. At the end of the war he returned to find his mother still alive, he was welcomed back into the family home, however, he had brought with him behaviours learnt from his time as a soldier. He smoked and drank heavily and was unwilling to follow instruction from his mother, eventually despite counselling from his mother, social workers, priests and elders in the community he was written off as a 'bad boy'. Michael remained isolated until young boys in the community encouraged him to play football, he was good, but his new teammates refused to let him on their Don Bosco team until he stopped drinking and smoking and became good again. It is noted that his conversion was neither instant nor painless but he gradually settled back into the community and with his family. He was one of the lucky ones selected to travel to England.

Reconciliation and Winning: Frank

Frank had been a fighter in the army throughout the war and when he was 15 he came back home to his community, the same one as Michael. He was not known as an aggressive soldier and had little experience of actual fighting but he was all too aware of where he had been and what he had seen and, most importantly, what that made him. He fought for a different faction to Michael. He too found himself being invited to play on the football field which he did but was worried others would realise his past. By the end of the game he was made aware that the boys were from five different fighting factions and that the only thing that mattered was winning their next game.

Father Joe proclaimed:

> It would be foolish to claim that the universal application of football would heal the world's division. No one would claim that playing football is the perfect therapy for people exposed to violence. However in areas of the world where professional resources are scarce and often inappropriate, where whole populations have been torn apart by violence and atrocities, it

is one way forward. (Information provided by Father Joe from his diary entries on the Salesians web site)

Father Joe recognised the need for a low-cost, community-based activity that could engage groups of young ex-combatants and those affected by the trauma of conflict. DB's rehabilitation, reconciliation and reconstruction aims and objectives found a new strategy centred on the game of football.

The above account of a football project targeting former child combatants provides an example of the perceived functions of football to post-conflict youths. It is a seductive genre; SDP is considered innocent and a strategy that can provide hope, an intervention that can facilitate the rehabilitation of a broken society and dysfunctional group of people. History would suggest otherwise. Global sporting events like the Olympics—a major partner with the UN SDP initiative—function with the following message: 'The goal of Olympism is to place sport at the service of a harmonious development of men, with a view to promoting a peaceful society' (IOC 2013, p. 11). Yet the history of the global games would demonstrate sport's connection to politics, social control, discrimination, violence and the role of 'big men' removed from the actual arena of competition.

It was the former IOC President, Avery Brundage, who incredulously proclaimed: 'Sport is completely free of politics' (Cashmore 1990, p. 485). Ironically this concerned the 1936 Berlin Olympiad, which became synonymous with Adolf Hitler and his promotion of the Nazi regime. The Berlin Olympics was used as a political tool to promote the Aryan concept of a master race whilst isolating those who did not fit Hitler's ideals around eugenics. In contrast to Brundage's claim it is argued here that sport has been used throughout history to promote and protest against political ideals and ideologies. Olympic boycotts of 1936, 1956, 1964, 1976, 1980, 1984 and 1988 placed political protest on the global sporting stage. Other political demonstrations include the murder of eleven members of the Israeli Olympic team by the Palestinian 'Black September' organisation during the 1972 Munich Olympics, Cuba and the Soviets used the Olympics and sporting events to promote communism, while a sporting ban was given to South Africa to show the international communities' disapproval of their Apartheid politics. The acknowledgement of sport by development organisations grew from the expansion and power of global sporting events like the Olympic Games. The appeal of competition, performance and worldwide viewing and the ability of those involved to convey consciously and unconsciously non-sporting messages are seducing.

Whether sport is used as an expression of diplomatic recognition or non-recognition, or as a vehicle of protest or propaganda, or as a means of gaining prestige for international and internal cooperation and unity building, sport is inherently political (Nafziger and Strenk 1978). It is also too good an opportunity to miss. The 2014 World Cup Final was watched by over one billion people worldwide. The game is enchanting and a proven method for seduction. This is realised by national governments, sport-governing bodies, the UN and merchandising and advertising companies and, crucially for this study, NGOs.

The Seduction of the Theory

An important part of the DBH rhetoric—specifically within peace-building—was the use of football. The fathers, NGO managers and youth workers all supported and engaged a number of community teams in and around Monrovia by providing kits and footballs, which in turn meant young players were obliged to spend time with SDB youth workers. As well as instruction in football the players received informal counselling and vocational training opportunities; football was the means for accessing these youths, operating *seductively* as an attractive cover for other projects, completely unrelated to the game. The use of football by SDB youth workers was evident intermittently throughout the civil conflict but mostly during the immediate DDRR phase in 2003 whilst many former combatants were in UN-managed camps. Football was a way of bringing together groups of young boys affected by conflict not only for peace-building but for attempts at reintegration and rehabilitation. This coincided with the DB organisation creating its own NGO based in Monrovia. It organically emerged and formed as a result of their work with young people throughout and after the conflict. This now formal organisation sought international support from partners or sponsors. Football was seductive in this strategy: its images were ideally suited to selling the DBH brand. Crucially, however, between 2009 and 2012 football was no longer an active strategy of SDB; that said, it remained part of their rhetoric and imagery. The seduction remained even if there was no consummation ever evident; Paul Robson's visit highlighted the use of images without the implementation of the project.

The DBH project was not alone in this strategy. The UN endorsed sport for peace programmes during the immediate phase of peace[2] but, similarly, these were not active during my time in Liberia. Yet the rhetoric and images of SDP remained part of the UN mission in Liberia. A plethora of independent agencies and national embassies also set up football tournaments in the name of unity and peace. The French embassy organised an annual football tournament in Monrovia aimed at 'fostering peace and unity among all citizens of Monrovia'. The Finance and Administrative Manager of the embassy claimed: 'Sports is a common language that everybody understands across the world, as such peace building cannot be achieved in the absence of sport' (insight 2005–2013). The impact of this project was evaluated primarily through how many turned up. Some thirty-two teams competed. The day was a success in the eyes of the organisers.

However, that participation is highly ambiguous. Youth footballers are invited to play in tournaments and their acceptance confirms them as 'youth' via such competitions; however, they feel recognised and significantly engage with adults. Once the event is over they return to ordinary life and wait for the next opportunity to be singled out and acknowledged. It is thus seductive. In this case seduction—and therefore football—is part of a wider social strategy. I have already shown how an important function of play, and football specifically, is the removal of youths from everyday life, much as Baudillard claimed that part of the draw of seduction is the 'nullification of the real' (Baudrillard 1990, p. 154). The theme of seduction supports the theory of youths using football as an alternative

---

[2] Right to play: Liberia promoted its work with Liberian refugees in camps across West Africa during the conflict and established an office in Monrovia in 2006. I made several attempts to observe projects but was told by an office employee that no projects were active in Monrovia. A UNMIL SDP project took place across Liberia for 5 weeks in 2007.

to the realities of their lives. Football pulls youths in and gives them hope, yet football places them under the control of adults without benefitting from it.

Liberia v Cape Verde

I realised the degree to which football can seduce on 5 June 2011, when Liberia played Cape Verde in an African Cup of Nations qualifier at the Samuel Kanyon Doe (SKD) stadium. I asked Richie if he wanted to go with me to watch the game a few weeks previously and he told me that he had not seen Liberia play before and that he would be excited to go. I also told another team member, Dorbor, that I wanted to go and he warned me: 'Those games as risky. You shouldn't go; people have died before in the stadium. Make sure your friends at the LFA look after you and protect you.' I assured him I would be fine. I purchased the tickets from the LFA office whilst Coach Tamba lectured me about being safe, getting their early and insisting I take Richie and another team member with me for safety.

Although the game was scheduled to start at 3 pm Richie insisted we leave Matadi at 9 am to ensure we got there 'before the crowds'. Another Zatti team member, Sam, joined us. We got a taxi from Matadi junction to the notorious Red Light district. Red Light was known to be a risky area notorious for crime, armed robbery and open drug use but the main junction acted as a transition point for commuters travelling to the interior. It took 25 minutes to reach Red Light junction and it was noisier and busier than usual. Police patrolled the junction controlling traffic and arbitrarily charged taxis a 'fee' to enable them to turn around and seek another fare.

It was a 15-minute walk from the junction to the stadium along the roadside. Despite arriving 5 hours before the scheduled start, the queue from the stadium entrance gates was five-people wide and trailed the circumference of the grounds and back towards the junction. The calm and controlled queue was secured by a dozen young boys aged between nine and fifteen, wearing karate suits and carrying long wooden sticks. Two large adult karate instructors stood at the main gate with even larger sticks. An LFA official stood behind them; he would be validating entrance tickets. A group of ten UN military peacekeepers sat behind them under the shelter of a tree.

Reluctantly and somewhat sheepishly we stood opposite at a distance from the line of supporters, observing the growing excitement whilst debating our strategy for entering the stadium. Coach Tamba phoned and told me to get seated as soon as possible. Soon after a small boy selling water came over to us and told us to look in the direction of the line close to the entrance gate. As we looked up a group of boys were beckoning us to join them. Richie thought this was a good idea so, with me wedged between Richie and Sam, we cut into the line. Through a few mumbles from behind us we began to move closer to the entrance. Sam assured me these guys wanted to help us and were keen to talk to me. However, Richie went into my bag and paid the group 100LD[3]: their intentions were now clear. As I walked through the gate I was met by a UN peacekeeper who singled me out. He asked for my phone number so he could protect me but I thanked him and declined.

The stadium steadily filled up. Staggered concrete steps, which made for the seating, prevented any order to the admittance. Alcohol-fuelled boys and men ran laps around the stand clapping, singing and dancing but as more spectators entered, people became more territorial, claiming a space as their own. The boys in karate suits—the only form of security—attempted to prevent people from randomly moving around. The scene presented a range of contradictory images of youths: heroes on the field, villains off it and vigilantes policing it. There was no police presence or UN peacekeepers evident inside the stadium.

At 3 pm news travelled through the ground that the game would be starting at 5 pm. The stands became more and more crowded, the supporters outside had broken down the metal entrance gates and rushed through all security measures and entered the stadium. Boys and men were the vast majority inside the stadium but some male spectators brought a female companion. As time went on the alcohol had a greater effect on the boys and men who became louder and more confrontational. Any fights, however, were quickly broken up by the surrounding

---

[3] Equivalent of £1.00.

spectators. A young male seated near us became boisterous and loud towards those sitting around him whilst holding a liquor bottle. An older man stood up, took the bottle, hit him on the back and forced him to sit back down with a clear warning: 'You stay frisky[4] I will remove you.' A few minutes later he was removed by two karate instructors as the nearby spectators waved him out of the ground, laughing. Mimicking adult-like behaviour by getting into the stadium and drinking liquor demonstrated bragging rights, known locally as *bluffing*, which was essential for establishing pecking orders amongst peers. Newell (2012) considered the act of imitation and the bluff in Cote d'Ivoire and described bluffing as a performance and the 'act of artifice through which young men and women project the appearance of success' (p. 1). The negative effect of this was the confirmation of low status by fellow spectators and adult observers.

As the crowds swelled so did the energy running through the stadium. Chants of 'Evil spirits … AWAY' echoed in the hopes of bringing the team good luck. As the players ran onto the field the sound of clapping and cheering was deafening; as they warmed up a *juju* man walked around the pitch, which encouraged the chanting, sending evil spirits out of the stadium. Richie told me that the team would pray inside with a Christian pastor but would also look to juju for good luck. As the game began people who were waiting outside the stands surged forward to get a view. The heat was overpowering and the cramped conditions became uncomfortable but there was no escape as all the entrance tunnels were full of people jostling to enter.

The game was competitive and Liberia scored early, lifting the crowd into a frenzy of celebrations that continued to echo from a distance minutes later as news spread outside the stadium. Liberia maintained their 1–0 lead to half-time. The heat continued to increase as the stadium was filled beyond capacity. Spectators were threatened with water cannons to cool them off, which seemed to excite them further. A handful of spectators, overcome by the heat and the crush, were lifted over the 10-foot metal fencing separating the crowd from the pitch onto stretchers.

---

[4] 'Frisky' is a slang term meaning confrontational or someone who pushes boundaries.

This made me anxious. People were still pushing and climbing the railings to get into the stands without any resistance. I decided I needed to leave and I told Richie but he said: 'There's no way. The place too pack.' This was true, although I also thought that he wanted to stay to watch the rest of the game. I started to panic and told Sam I wanted to go. Fortunately, a man in front of me overheard. He called a man standing at the back of our section dressed in an army uniform. Climbing over the people he grabbed my hand and forced his way through the crowd. He led me to the tunnel surrounded by supporters still competing for space. Two girls seated near the tunnel tugged at my trouser leg and offered reassurance: 'Don't be scared. This is Africa.' Meanwhile the man shouted and pushed those filling the entrance and told them to make space for my exit. They did so without protest and he escorted me outside with Richie and Sam following. I thanked him and he entered without challenge back to his place. Even amongst apparent chaos, euphoria and frenzy the power of being uniformed—the incontestable mark of a recognised adult[5]—could control hyped-up and determined youths.

By the time we arrived back at Matadi, news had spread that the game had finished 1–0. Sam enquired if I was feeling better, and when I responded that I was, he took me for a walk to the main road that took traffic in and out of central Monrovia. The streets and roads were filled with people celebrating, running around, dancing, eating and drinking. Children copied and joined in. The roads were jammed with cars and motorbikes that duetted with a chorus of beeps and loud music from their stereos. Youths and children ran in the roads, weaving in and out of the cars, arms raised, forcing their way into the euphoric scenes. The football-related celebrations continued well into the night. Never before had I witnessed such scenes in and around football. The hype before the game was intoxicating and drew thousands of Liberians together.

---

[5] Wearing a uniform in Liberia was the most obvious sign of adulthood. Those in uniforms proved their status with recognisable formal income. Due to this many employees insisted on wearing uniforms and identification badges.

Although football draws people together it is still highly controlled and creates tension. Tickets for the game ranged from US$10 to US$100. Coach Tamba told me that previously tickets started at US$5 but there was too much trouble at the stadium, so they increased the price. US$5 was affordable to youths but US$10 was out of reach to many. Even at a football match it seemed that adults were the desired market and youths were blamed for overcrowding and violence. The LFA was trying to price youth out of the international game. However, their plan failed as many of the people at the stadium did not purchase tickets and it was groups of young males who were particularly committed to entering the stadium by force and trickery. When the gates were forced open the majority of those who rushed through were young men, whilst others climbed the high parameter fences around the stadium. Buying tickets was associated with adulthood; determined but marginalised youths had to improvise to be part of this occasion. The football stadium was a metaphor of Liberian society.

Alcohol was also a big feature on that day. Youths openly drank Cane juice from small liquor bottles, a luxury that was normally associated with those who had money or the 'big men'. The problem in this case was the effect of the alcohol as it exposed behaviours and traits associated with youth: palava, violence, recklessness and a lack of composure and control. Although Liberian adults drink alcohol and indeed use it as a status symbol, getting drunk and losing control is looked down upon by other adults and bring the drunk's status and stature into question. Sustaining status for adults is just as important as acquiring it in Liberian society. Drunken behaviour would only give others an opportunity to claim moral superiority and overtake the drunken person's position. Significantly, in this society marginalised youths have little to lose, so taking risks and losing control is of little consequence. And on such a day as a Liberian International fixture, playing the 'big man' could potentially provide status amongst peers. The ability for football to seduce so many people in so many ways was overwhelming, hypnotising and exhausting, and youths were central to the scenes witnessed that day. Seduction facilitated opportunities for hustling both for adults and youths, it provided a platform for youths to adopt adult-like behaviour—by attending the game and drinking alcohol—which for many resulted in displaying child-like behaviour. Seduction pulled youths and adults together but instead of uniting and integrating them in a shared passion it gave adults the opportunity to assert their authority and control the environment.

Grassroots: The Art of Seduction

This same game provided insight into the broader cultural seduction of the game. Yet football at grassroots level provided greater detail of how the game is inseparable from adult interests. The lower division national league games in Liberia were played on community playing fields and organised by subcommittees financed by the LFA. The third division league games were open to all to spectate free of charge. These weekend fixtures could attract a large crowd, which would encourage people selling food and drink to attend, as well as adults who could use the opportunity for self-promotion and networking with spectators—in effect *bluffing* while the youths played. The presence of the adults increased the pressure on the youth footballers to perform and showcase both their talent and implicitly their characters. This level of football was at its most basic level an organised community football league. But all was not as it seemed. The power that football gave the adults managing the league as well as the inherent ability for the game to bring so many community members and adults to the pitches facilitated attempts at money-making and opportunities to manipulate and use the youth players for personal gain.

As mentioned previously funds were provided by the LFA to each subcommittee[6] at the beginning of each season. Such funding purchased footballs, hired the playing pitch and employed match officials. Zone four was the subcommittee Zatti participated in and was for many an inadequately managed committee. The pitch Zatti played on had unorthodox features with concrete slopes on either side of the pitch that were

---

[6] There are eight districts that participate in the third division in Monrovia and each has its own subcommittee that takes responsibility for match organisation, officials and equipment. Each district's leagues have between five and eight teams; once these have played the top two qualify for the second phase. Once these have played the top teams qualify for the knock-out stage nationwide, and the eventual winners are promoted to the second division.

used during the game to play the ball up and over a defender. Rarely did the games begin on time, teams would have to bring their own footballs to play the game—despite the subcommittee charging the LFA for such equipment—and although a referee was always present, rarely was there a linesman to assist as per procedure. An easy way for the league organisers to make money was to fine teams for late arrival; each team was expected to arrive for inspection 30 minutes before the scheduled start time. If this did not happen the team would be fined. Fines were also given for yellow and red cards and when a money-making game was being arranged the chair of the subcommittee would take his cut to allow the transaction to take place between team manager and referee. On one occasion a rival team from Matadi arrived so late that their opposition were called for inspection and eventually awarded the points. The team captain admitted he had confused the playing schedule. This caused palava between both the players and their captain and the captain and the subcommittee, as the captain claimed the schedule he was given by the subcommittee had the wrong timings. Much discussion followed between the different parties as the players knew that by sacrificing the points they would not qualify for the next stage of the tournament. As I sat with the Zatti players, observing the show of disgruntled and gesticulating players, their captain emerged from the subcommittee office and summoned his players. Moments later they began to clap. Ben came to me and told me the captain had paid the subcommittee US$30 to have the game rescheduled. It seemed only with the exchange of money was the youth and elder relationship harmonious and somewhat balanced.

The presence of adult community members placed additional pressure on the youth players to behave respectfully towards each other and the officials, and to play in accordance with the rules. One player admitted to me: 'During league games we have discipline. Outsiders watch us and if we do well, they could promote us.' 'Promote' in this context means to be given opportunities to be scouted into higher division teams. A well-behaved, talented player could potentially gain the attention of an adult with the hope of being given access to a higher division team or be singled out as a 'good' person. A 'good' person stood a better chance of entering the small informal world of work in his community—if an adult considered him worthy of patronage—as he was more likely to be considered trustworthy. With that in mind the subcommittee understood that they could penalise players and endorse money-making schemes safely in the knowledge that the players would not complain or publicly protest because of their belief that football could bring them life-changing opportunities.

These acts of exploiting players and indeed corruption within the game are done discretely away from public viewing. The adults involved benefitted financially, usually by a collection from the team members to cover the fine or match-fixing fee; in return the youth players are allowed continued access to the game. The presence of adult spectators in the youths' minds potentially provides football opportunities and personal promotion, yet during my observations no player ever gained from adults through football in this manner. What football did provide was the opportunity for youth players to be *recognised* by adults, which usually came in the form of a handshake or applause during play. However, this recognition could also be negative; heckles and mocking were regularly heard from the sidelines for poor play and inappropriate behaviour. This was the risk that football presented for youth players.

Football seduced youth and adult males in a number of ways; adults could gain financially and socially through association with the game and youths recognised this as part of the game and the route they had to tolerate and take to gain access. They also believed that being seen on the pitch by adults created opportunities for acknowledgement and potential promotion and employment. Yet this was chasing a dream and part of the seduction of football.

Politics and Football: Seduction in Political Life

Once Liberian 'youth' reach an advanced chronological age (i.e. 18 years plus) they become political agents and in some ways more recognisable by the state. For youth this recognition is focused towards presidential elections and times of disrepute and collective dysfunction. Bayart (1992) considers 'youth' as political agents and in doing so reflects on the 'the politics of the powerless'. Continuous themes occur within political arenas that focus on youth; these are narratives of crime, violence, rioting and looting—all activities engaged in by Liberian youth during the civil conflict. As Bayart observes in what he terms the daily deconstruction of the state, 'the explicitly political, in parties and associations, is controlled by the dominant elders, the implicit politics of those without power must proceed by mobility, by ambivalence, by what isn't said' (Bayart 1992, p. 40). Youths in this context in Liberia are used for strength in numbers by adults for political and state power and yet are branded villains by the same adults in times of crisis and disorder. A youth's body becomes valuable to adults in the quest for political power.

Philosopher Giorgio Agamben (1998) studied the relationship of human life with political power. He termed this 'Homo Sacer' and claimed that people either have a bare life or have a politically recognised life which is not bare because it has political recognition and representation. The transition from a bare life to a politically recognised life turns a bare life into a valuable or 'good' life. Those who have 'bare lives' only have their bodies and in many cases will have only 'powerless agency'. At a basic level Liberian youths are not considered adults or 'citizens'. Those with political value—locally defined as adults—are considered 'citizens'. Liberian youths could be seen as having 'bare lives', living outside the terrain of adults who are politically powerful. Their bodies are their most valuable asset and the only token of their presence within society. It is through the (non-rational) process of seduction that these *bodies* are generally recruited for political purposes in Liberia.

A Political Meeting

On 17 April 2011 I was invited to a political meeting in Matadi. Local residents formed a committee to arrange such gatherings to allow the community to make informed choices about the political candidates standing for elections to represent their district. Liberia operates according to the American congressional system in which citizens vote for representatives, senators and the president. This has proved to be an overly complicated process with over thirty candidates running for the presidential seat and many others trying to get elected as district representatives and senators. Many standing for elections are unknown to the people they are representing. This can cause great confusion on polling day, especially as illiteracy rates are so high in Liberia.

I arrived promptly at 5 pm as instructed by a community football player who was part of the organising committee. White plastic chairs were placed in rows between houses. I was the first to arrive and was greeted by the committee who were trying to get a sound system working to play music and a microphone for the speeches. Loud American and African music was played meanwhile to entice the community to join them and entertain those waiting; in true Liberian fashion the event did not begin until 7 pm, 2 hours later than scheduled.

The organising committee sat opposite the community members, distinguishing themselves as part of the organisation. I was invited to sit with them but preferred to be disassociated from the political group as a neutral observer. Upon formal introductions to the community they made it clear saying, 'We are here to support the re-election of Ellen Johnson Sirleaf.' I learned that all the invited speakers were candidates for the position of senator and representatives supporting current President Ellen Johnson Sirleaf's Unity Party. Amongst the crowd were a few elders, mainly females, but the majority were young males and females aged between sixteen and twenty-five. When the introductions were completed, a large black Hummer vehicle with flashing blue lights and playing loud music arrived. The black tinted windows did not allow observers to see inside the vehicle but the excitement of the crowd at such a scene was evident. The young people jumped to their feet and began clapping at the display of wealth.

A young man approximately 30 years of age jumped out from the car. A younger male assistant followed. They were wearing jeans with polished shoes and large items of gold jewellery around their necks and wrists. Both were wearing sunglasses, although the sun had been replaced by the moon. The candidate for representative greeted the crowd, encouraging their excitement and shaking hands. As he took his place before the crowd he apologised for his lateness, claiming he had had four other appointments that day and had 700 requests on his desk for appearances. Continuing the narrative of his own importance, to the point of getting his assistant to hold the microphone for him in front of his mouth, he proudly declared: 'I have my own business. I make US$10,000 a month so I not running for election for money. The US$2000–3000 I will earn as representative will go to the Zone 4 district of Matadi.' The crowd approved of such a statement and continued to cheer as he talked and gestured. He claimed to be training as a lawyer at the Liberian University, and that the organising committee had asked for a generator and canopy so they could continue to operate during the upcoming rainy season. He told them he would deliver this request soon. He spoke for 15 minutes and then abruptly left, thanking the crowd and the organising commit- tee, and shaking hands hurriedly as he moved towards his car.

Food and drink provided by the committee was handed out, the music played once more and a social gathering began. Many discussed what they had just witnessed. Most were impressed, although the football play- ers in attendance were sceptical. They had experience of this man and his promises. Those who liked him were quick to assure me, against my scepticism: 'He is a local man, very humble. I am his friend and he is a good person.' I could not help but test this further: 'Do you think it is correct to speak of personal money, arrive in such a way in front of such a poor community and still not mention his intentions?' They thought for a while somewhat surprised at my response. They agreed that he had not discussed political ideas but still stood by their candidate and believed quite simply that 'he is good'. But he was not as good as his word: the canopy and generator never arrived.

Actual political experience beyond the hyperbole of intentions and strategy if elected was never discussed by the candidate or the electorate. The extravagant entrance, showmanship and talk of money were enough to impress, especially the young boys who would initiate the cheering and proclaim their support. I asked a young man what he thought of the can- didate. He replied: 'He's good, he can make it; his money will help our district.' But many in the community regularly preached: 'The problem with our youth is that they are quick to be satisfied.' Youths were drawn by the image and rhetoric of the candidate. The seductive stage and props set by the aspiring politician turned seduction into non-rational persua- sion and recruitment. This is typical of the political process in Liberia— seduction created meaning in the absence of truth.

How to Gain the Youth Vote the Liberian Way

In the quest to gain community support, candidates sought the environment and activity that could engage a large group and seduce a crowd. The choice was obvious: football. The same representative candidate recognised that and a football tournament was arranged for the community that was his potential electorate. Teams were approached by his young followers in the Matadi district and invited to a 1-day event with the promise of a day's football, team transport and new jerseys for each participating team.

On the day of the tournament an old open-backed truck arrived to take the team on the 10-minute journey to the field just outside of Matadi. The teams played their games and as always enjoyed this sporting stage, being with their peers and playing the game that meant so much to them. Yet, this was a slightly different environment; it was beyond the relative protection and comfort of the youth centre compound and saw the teams exposed to communities that covered the electoral district targeted by the aspiring politician.

Spectators gathered to watch the event. T-shirts were handed out bearing the candidate's name and his allegiance to the Unity Party and President Ellen Johnson Sirleaf. The candidate himself enjoyed the attention, shaking hands with the players and making jokes. He played up to the 'big man' who was the prospering politician; he proudly held his mobile phone which rang continuously and interrupted conversations. The young boys and men just wanted to play, and the majority were not particularly political-minded; debating football was more relevant to them than state affairs. The players were attentive when he spoke to them but as soon as he moved on they continued their conversations about football and girls that had caught their attention. Their focus was on the game. They enjoyed competing and being engaged in an activity they were not only passionate about but which also gave them an identity and purpose. For them these were football's integral seductive qualities. The invitation to the tournament gave them a sense of importance as they waved to community members from the back of the truck on the journey and sang Zatti football songs. The promise of jerseys only added to the prestige of the event and raised the young players' satisfaction. Some players spoke with the candidate about things they needed, namely more hand pumps. Whilst the candidate listened he would nod; he would then shake their hands and move to the next team. To the boys this was good adult behaviour: they had engaged with a 'big man' who had given them a personal invitation and supplied the stage for their athletic process.

At the end of the tournament players waited for their transport to take them home, it never came. The candidate had left with his support team before the final game. The boys walked home both disappointed and embarrassed: 'That man just bluffing,' they said angrily. The players were advised that their jerseys would be delivered in the coming weeks. They never arrived and the candidate was not to be seen until his speech the following month. They had been lied to and most recognised this, but football was a proven strategy to access, engage and seduce a large number of people in a non-political environment in the campaigning phase of an election. Football created a large crowd and facilitated the candidates' message, carried as it was by the statements on the T-shirts players proudly wore; it was like having a VIP pass at a concert, a status symbol for the day. Yet when they returned home, walking through the main street of Matadi, dirty, sweaty, hungry and thirsty, the sense of higher status they had briefly glimpsed had disappeared. They faced the reality of the situation. They had been used by an adult for a campaign with the promises made unfulfilled.

The President's Son

Local politicians were not the only political figures to use football for self-promotion. The most recognised and well-known candidates were also involved in the game. Football was central to the political process and style of campaigning in Liberia from the bottom to the top. In this sense, seduction—football—was a form of entrapment. The Liberian President Ellen Johnson Sirleaf, who came to power in 2006, always acknowledges the importance of football in her country. In 2007 she was photographed kicking a football to begin a match for a 5-week UN-backed 'Sport for Peace' project and always sends good luck messages to the national team before a match. Football would play a part in her strategy for promotion and re-election through her own support and public appearances and by her family and political partners.

> Barrack Young Controllers FC (BYC) was founded on May 3, 1992 at the Barclay Training Centre as a community entertainer during the heat of the senseless Liberian civil war. The team came into existence to help provide and secure a virginal place for hope, love, and respect among our teenagers who were being incessantly lured to violence by war lords. It was also founded to promote tolerance and peaceful co-existence among our youth whose families and relatives were being slaughtered daily by other teenagers. The team was intended to help create a peaceful environment for the growth of soccer artistry at the then World Cup Field that existed at the corner of Broad and Lynch Streets. (Massalay 2011)

President Ellen Johnson Sirleaf's son, Robert Sirleaf, is the benefactor of Liberian Premiership team BYC. He has sponsored the team since 2010. In recent years BYC has become one of the most successful clubs in Monrovia. Sirleaf has associated himself with the club since its success. Formed with humble beginnings the club has built itself into a national favourite through investment and victory. In 2011 BYC were top of the Premiership league with three games to play and were selected by the LFA to play against the National Liberian team at the ATS in a warm-up match before an African Nations Cup Qualifier. The game ended 1–0 to BYC and the stadium was filled beyond capacity. His status gave his team opportunities and those opportunities were rewarded with personal recognition towards a non-footballing cause.

In June 2011 I was invited by the LFA to attend the opening of a football ground in central Monrovia. As I walked into the ground through large iron gates the noise of a music sound system sent vibrations through the sand floor. Young people filled the ground wearing the same white T-shirt with a green picture of Ellen Johnson Sirleaf with 'Unity Party' clearly written on it. The football pitch was mainly sand; an attempt had been made to plant grass but this was patchy and uneven. The lines of the pitch had been hand-drawn on the ground and the seating area or 'stadium' as it was marked consisted of cement blocks. It was not a full-sized pitch but it was adequate for training. An attempt had also been made at including an 'academy pitch', a half-size pitch, alongside the main one. This had overgrown grass in between sandy mounds. However, the lack of finish and prestige was not important, nor was the emphasis on the opening of the stadium; the main focus of the day was the 'Re-election of President Ellen Johnson Sirleaf' campaign as written on T-shirts and banners. Hundreds of people filled the ground to the sound of African and American music. Young people danced on the pitch, a queue formed to receive their free T-shirts and children and young boys enjoyed penalty shoot-out competitions whilst older youths gambled 'small money' between themselves regarding who was going to score.

The seduction of football was evident; hundreds, possibly thousands, walked through the stadium gates that day, all receiving a T-shirt which they were told to wear. Robert Sirleaf began to sponsor the team a year before the 2012 elections just as his mother declared her intentions to run for a second term. Upon her successful re-election, teams across the country celebrated with parties and football games in her honour. Adults with finance controlled football in Liberia. Money brought recognition, access to youths, adult supporters and status through the seductive powers of football, which drew these people in, obscuring the real interests and plans of politicians and, it needs to be said, stifling rational debate. It was the perfect strategy to engage youths who collectively formed the majority voting population.[7]

Football and the Church

The world of politics is not the only institution to use football to access and seduce youth. The youth centre in Matadi is a religious place that seeks to encompass play within religion guidance, although, increasingly, play takes preference over prayer for the players. As Father L, head of

---

[7] However, there has been evidence that youths have rejected their voting rights elsewhere in Africa (e.g. Durham's 2004 research in Botswana). Liberian youth are extremely political-minded and actively discuss and monitor political activity. The youth centre in Matadi is also a voting station for the community and provides safety and support during voting and this encourages a high turnout.

the centre proclaimed, 'In most environments our challenge is to introduce religion and get people coming to church but here that is not our problem, everyone here goes to church and believes in God.' This is an accurate observation. On Sundays the streets of Monrovia are empty and all that can be heard is preaching and singing. There is a church to suit everyone; traditional indigenous churches that communicate in specific ethnic dialects, all denominations of the Christian faith, Mosques and Jehovah Witness halls exist amongst various idiosyncratic churches of various strands of Christianity.

One Zatti football player called Sam, aged twenty-two, invited me to meet his family and have food before going to church. I arrived by 9.30 am. He explained that he lived with his mother, stepfather and 'plenty' of children from both of their previous relationships. His biological father was a minister now based in the USA, preaching in his own church. During the war Sam's family travelled across most of West Africa, escaping the conflict and basing themselves in different churches where his father preached. Religion was thus an important part of his upbringing and he and his brothers would play the organ during services and sing hymns in front of various congregations. Currently, however, he goes to church occasionally and mostly stays at home on Sundays. As his mother sat with me inside the house discussing her job as head of a women's rights organisation, Sam went about his duties. He ironed his mother's dress and wrapped, fetched water for the children to bathe in, heated water over the coal fire for his mother to wash with and brought the food and drink to the table from the kitchen. We sat and continued to talk whilst trying to enjoy hot pepper soup with fish and rice. His mother wanted her son to attend church more frequently but did not pressure him as long as he completed his chores to help her get there with the small children.

Sam's Sunday routine was not unlike that of many of the youth of Matadi. Many would help prepare food, iron clothes and fetch water but would rest once the home was quiet. Church attendance was not forced by peers or family members. This possibly strengthened the cycle of youths having little expectation placed upon them by adults. Some churches began to recognise this pattern and began hosting football matches after services and going on marches through Monrovia to promote the church and concluded with sports activities upon return. One church leader explained that 'the key to getting youth into church and receiving spiritual guidance is through exciting them with an activity they enjoy and plenty love football and kickball.' This is also a form of seduction: indeed the youth centre's Catholic Fathers cannot force religion onto the youth of Matadi but can try to engage them in between football training sessions. By supplying the space and resources to play football they form a relationship with the players that allows interaction and provides an open door for players to use in times of hardship.

The church will always be a significant part of the Liberian culture, openly spoken about in everyday conversations and cited in most situations, but many of Matadi's youth do not practice what they preach—unless there is football involved. Just like the politicians, the church had sought in football a positive solution to their problem of accessing youth. But whilst they were engaging with the church through football they were showcasing their youthhood amongst the mainly adult congregation.

The Seduction of the Ball

Arguably it is the Global North and its development practitioners that have been seduced by football. As Bruadillard claimed: 'Being seduced is still the best way of seducing. No one can seduce another if they have not been seduced themselves' (1988, p. 160). Football's global appeal, its sporting celebrities and huge money-making opportunities combine to make for a seductive package. This has been utilised in the past decade by those seeking answers to complex and unfamiliar development problems. The image, hype, sponsorship opportunities and selling capacity that football brings for potential partners draw policymakers and project planners to the game. The *seduced* becomes the *seducer*. The Paul Robson case supports this theory. DB's UK-based support understands the benefits of the football image for their own promotion. The distribution of T-shirts and the story seduced DBH and its sponsors despite their lack of active football interventions. This CAFOD campaign seduced youth due to the football theme of the visit and the distribution of free T-shirts.

Both parties were seduced by the image, concept and value but for opposing reasons.

The seduction of football was a useful strategy for Westerners to gain access to Liberia. Arguably, I myself was guilty of using football to engage youth, although my entry into this specific theme was quite organic and unintentional. Whilst staying in central Monrovia I met a student from the UK, who was also interested in post-conflict youth and rehabilitation. His placement was with a large NGO that operated throughout Liberia. He explained to me that his way of making Liberians relax and accept him was to carry a football wherever he went. His ability to do tricks with the football facilitated conversations and opportunities for access. It was used as a way to break the boundaries between Liberian youth and a white European male, a relationship generally bound by status that was not expected to be deepened. On his final day in Liberia he organised his belongings: things he would take home, things he would give away. The hardest decision that day was to whom he would gift his football, in his mind the most valuable of all his possessions. The point being made here is that the majority of NGOs, embassies, political organisations and aspiring individuals use football to seduce, engage and access personal gain, imagery and to fulfil the fashionable SDP theory and rhetoric. But this also occurs at a micro level, where individual outsiders use the game as part of a strategy for self-acceptance.

A Seductive Cycle

The global phenomenon of football is used and recycled as a strategy by many for fund-raising, raising awareness, access to targeted groups, engagement with potential charity partners and in some cases personal gain and development. Football in Liberia provides an identity platform for youths, yet it also has the ability to seduce youths, adults and elders, males and females in rare events that engage collective populations upon common ground. The power and popularity of football thus makes it susceptible to manipulation for various forms of self-promotion, both individual and institutional. The ability for adults and SDP organisations to *seduce* youth with football inadvertently enforces generational hierarchies and confirms youth status; they are used in that moment and then left and forgotten. Votes are won, attendance records increase, messages are delivered, the event—game—deemed a success or a win by its providers, but as the final whistle blows, the players are sent back home from where they started. The themes of impact and sustainability so crucial to SDP rhetoric are largely absent. Some may question why this is such a problem: after all youth get to play the game and enjoy it. Surely all are winners? But the problem lies deeper than the game. Using youth and football for personal gain and organisational success makes those youths pawns in an adult game which bolsters adult position and status whilst continuously proving to those involved that they are youths and useful and valuable only in a game of numbers. Potentially then football has more of an impact for the individual sponsors and SDP associations who facilitate and organise the games than on those they claim to be targeting and helping.

Football has the ability to seduce youths in Liberia and various institutions, organisations and individuals are fully aware of the game's appeal. This is primarily used for support and access. Their tragic histories as victims of conflict and the images circulated globally of children as innocent suffers or forced soldiers seduce NGOs and development agencies into joining the post-conflict rehabilitation process. Subsequently, the images and reports of young males playing football within SDP and community projects seduce the UN and encourage its partners and the media to resource and fund such projects—occasionally this is achieved with a high-profile fund-raising football match.

The continued support of SDP is arguably due to football's continued global popularity and the game's continued ability to engage and provide access. Seduction works as a strategy because it disguises alternative agendas and meanwhile does not require explanation. Minogue (2006) claims that the ones being seduced could also be considered victims but such victims might also have an upper hand over the seducer (pp. 18–19). If Liberian youth understood the power they had in number, then they could take the advice of Novellino and refuse to take part in a project designed to confirm their status of youth for the benefit of international organisations and Liberian adults. However, in this cycle of youth–adult relationships, NGOs and post-conflict SDP projects, football is the most powerful actor and its lure and appeal to youths and adults in Liberia will fuel its continuous inclusion at every level of social life and civil society.

These young boys and men are continuously playing the role of pawns for people and organisations to achieve their aims and for some the overall outcome is not to these players' advantages. One should not underestimate or devalue the importance of play in the context of these boys' lives; it provides friendship, protection, confidence and social skills. Throughout it has been argued that the problem faced by contemporary youth in Liberia is not conflict or tension between indigenous groups—as the causes of civil conflict would suggest—but internal hierarchy, generational relationships and the lack of opportunities provided for them to mature and age into adulthood. SDP organisations proclaim that sport unites and aids the processes of reconstruction, reconciliation and rehabilitation in post-conflict societies, yet the issues facing Liberian youth have little to do with these areas. The limited access to adulthood is what deprives Liberian youth of independence, status, power and acknowledgement. Gaining opportunities for employment, meaningful recognised education and reducing barriers between the generational categories would better address the youth problem in Liberia than football programmes. It may be the case that current SDP projects and the adoption of such practices by internal agencies and individuals encourages and affirms youths as youths: playing football is the most visible indicator of youth identity.

References

Agamben, G. (1998). *Homo sacer: Sovereign power and bare life.* Stanford: Stanford University Press.

Althusser, L. (2008). *On ideology.* London/New York: Verso.

Baudrillard, J. (1990). *Seduction.* New York: St Martin's Press.

Baudrillard, J., & In Poster, M. (1988). *Selected writings.* Cambridge: Polity Press.

Bayart, J. F. (1992). Le politique par le bas en Afrique Noire. *Le politique par le bas en Afrique noire: contributions' aa une prőblaematique de la d̋aemocratie.*

Bayart, J.-F., Mbembe, A., & Toulabor, C. (1992). *Le politique par le bas en Afrique noire: Contributions à une problématique de la démocratie.* Paris: Karthala.

Cashmore, E. (1990). *Making sense of sport*. London: Routledge.

Durham, D. (2004). Disappearing youth: Youth as a social shifter in Botswana. *American Ethologist, 31*(4), 589–605.

Father Joe Glackin. (1997). More than just a game. http://www.salesians.org. uk/Table/Salesians-Articles/Page-5.html.

Insight. (2005–2013). Insight News Online: French Embassy tourney makes impact.

IOC. (2013). Olympic Charter. http://www.olympic.org/Documents/ olympic_charter_en.pdf.

Massalay, M. S. (2011). Squabble over Liberian Soccer Club BYC: The real story. http://theliberianjournal.com/index.php?st=news&sbst=details& rid=2154.

Minogue, K. (2006). Seduction and politics. *The New Criterion, 25*(3), 17–23.

Nafziger, J. A. R., & Strenk, A. (1978). The political uses and abuses of sport. *Connecticut Law Review, 10*, 259–289.

Newell, S. (2012). *The modernity bluff: Crime, consumption, and citizenship in Cote d'Ivoire*. Chicago/London: The University of Chicago Press.

Epilogue

The Final Whistle

Just sitting on the run way waiting for take-off, its 2 am and very humid. I like watching the Liberians, Americans and Lebanese in the one-roomed airport. The Lebanese embrace the Liberian airport staff appreciating the benefits of good business relations. The Americans are loud yet seemed relieved and underwhelmed; one American man is unhappy about being searched by security and makes sure everyone knows his displeasure. The Liberian travellers are quiet, most are reading bibles, most are flying solo. I am writing my final diary entry before home. I'm excited to go home, my mind and body can have a rest but I feel guilty.

The Zatti boys had a game in my honour today against a collection of premiership players who live or used to live in Matadi. Coach Tamba and Coach Cooper came too, Father M, Pa K and Father L said a few words which was nice, my ability for public speaking has definitely improved! We went to a bar in Matadi afterwards and had some drinks. I was sad to say goodbye to the boys, staff and my coaching friends—I have just left Richie and Dorbour outside the terminal; I could not say 'I'll see you next year' like I had said previously and I know they will wait outside until the plane takes off. I feel guilty,

© The Editor(s) (if applicable) and The Author(s) 2016
H. Collison, *Youth and Sport for Development*,
DOI 10.1057/978-1-137-52470-6

Richie has lived well this last 4 months away from the swamp; he has eaten well too. I have left him with my last $20 although he did not want to take it. He will move back to his mum's today and train as usual this afternoon.

I first came to Liberia wanting to observe, learn and ultimately analyse and interpret. The plan failed! I became a coach for my community team, I adopted twenty footballer players. I was so absorbed in the team and Matadi. The agreement made was so simple; I would coach them and they would play. I miss them already; I have never laughed and enjoyed my time with such an unorthodox group in the most dysfunctional of surroundings. They frustrated me, angered me on several occasions—especially Bernardo—I lost count how many times I had to save him from suspension, but it became the most rewarding and valuable experience. Life's going to be boring now. I still feel guilty; tomorrow's training will be back to the old regime, Coach J will shout at them and palava will happen on every corner of the field—I wonder how many will be suspended. I know my role in the team will have no lasting legacy other than the mention of my name during lectures or when they shout at coach J and use me as a comparison—it was embarrassing the first time that happened! I hate take-off!

I thought by writing this book I would construct potential answers, unearth new ideas or directions for development but if anything the disconnect between football and the building of a peaceful civil society seems wider and more complex. The final piece of this work reaffirms my findings, acknowledges the need for further similar research and suggests that a better understanding of local populations and specific cultures is key to designing any SDP intervention. In the case of SDP one design does not suit all and never will.

The division of Liberian society by civil conflict has caused a real concern for conventional aid and NGO intervention in the last 20 years. Consequently SDP has been mainstreamed in discourse concerning international development. Central to this method of development are the linked notions of youth development, community and the promotion of the game. As we have seen, the underlying structure of SDP projects supposes that through the promotion of football, youth can be engaged and integrated into a wider community. In 2011 Coakley claimed that SDP was the culmination of 'unquestioned beliefs grounded in wishful thinking' (p. 307). In essence this has been the overall problem concerning the lack of sustainable, active SDP projects and the absence of post-project monitoring and evaluation. When considering projects based on assumption and belief, how do you recognise a project's social effect or impact? What are the criteria for success? Thus, whilst trying to interpret my experiences and construct answers, the challenge has been centred on understanding discussions and considerations based on belief, generalised ideal terms and untested methods of intervention.

For me, the initial challenge was to contextualise the key terms of SDP in order to better understand their operation in the field as opposed to in international rhetoric and incentive. This can be difficult because the terms used by SDP practitioners often correspond to those in use by people on the ground. The notion of 'community', for example, was central to the development claims of SDP as well as local ideas of communal habitation arrangements. People in Matadi believe community to be an important part of safety, livelihoods and supported living within Liberia's fragile society—yet it fails to function for its largest residential group as SDP discourse would suggest: youth are systematically marginalised by the structures of community in Matadi. For international practitioners, community was a seductive notion to justify interventions as 'local' and appropriate, and to contribute to the images of development being sold. In Matadi, however, it acted as a platform to assert status and confirm identity; this created tension, competition, prejudice, discrimination and ultimately youth stagnation. Communities were structured and operated by adults for adults.

We have seen that youth are the largest generational category in Liberia but socially marginal, powerless and invisible to meaningful cornerstones and conventions of society (Utas, 2003, 2005, 2008). Traditional rites of passage have been eliminated for urban youth due to displacement during the conflict. Their education had also been delayed preventing them from gaining formal employment or respect and restricting pathways to becoming recognised as contributing *adult* citizens in Liberia. Post-conflict youth presented a very real problem to Liberia's nation building and faced very specific challenges and barriers to development. Youth had become a convenient identity for those in higher status positions; the sheer mass of youth contributed to their negative identity as youth and helped to present this group as a problem in Liberia. To keep youths locked into that identity benefited those trying to sustain and maintain adult and elder social positions, and this must have relevance—to questionable impact and effect—to any form of development intervention aiming to build civil society in Liberia. Yet SDP narratives fail consistently to grasp the marginalising effect of the label 'youth'. SDP needed vulnerable and powerless youths to operate; despite the large numbers of adults interested in the game they were not targeted for reconciliation or rehabilitation interventions—yet was not it adults that started the conflict and controlled the divisions in Liberian society? Yes, but NGOs tend not to target adults for their SDP interventions; they need a population without options to ensure successful participation numbers. Another presumption of SDP is that it is only children and youths that will be interested in playing sport—this also makes for more compelling imagery. Crucially, SDP depend on youths, therefore reproducing youth identity, thus, unwittingly, reproducing a marginalised social category. Youths have become the easy answer in what has become a thriving industry. SDP is therefore arguably designed by adults for continued adult control in challenging post-conflict environments.

Footballers were considered youths, no matter of their ability; the most successful footballer would gain respect on the pitch and off the pitch by his peers but still be dominated and dictated to by the adults around him; footballers were not reliable, resourceful husbands or contributing community members. Potentially they were *super youths*, popular and physically desirable, but still poor, unemployed and with dim prospects for advancement—setting an example of the limited tangible rewards football could offer.

Football did, however, offer an alternative social structure that drew lines between the generations and placed youth at the centre. Players could perform and express their skills, character and identity to adults; creating a rare platform for interaction outside of family networks. In essence, they formed a football community or meta-society that gave them control of the practice of football and structure of the team. I am suggesting that SDP can create 'community' but in isolation. At the same time, football confirmed the unequal relations between the youths and adults as adults facilitated the game, intervened, disrupted and used participation as a form of reward and punishment. In this way, football replicates community social patterns and broader Liberian hierarchical frameworks but was dissociated from normal and recognised adult patterns of living. Adults' capacity to find in football a form of social control to confirm youth identity and infantilise players questions the very nature of football interventions for development and unity. Football was controlled by Liberian adults for Liberian adults at the grassroots level.

SDP Reconsidered

Something struck me whilst working with DBH and within the DBYC; what were their overall development goals? Surely before any form of development or intervention takes place the problem and ideal outcome need to be identified. DBH advocated the rights of the child and spoke often about the problem of street children and dysfunctional youth; their overall intention was to return displaced young people to their parents and provide palava management to school children. The youth centre Fathers spoke of respect, taking responsibility and an array of moral and behavioural attributes they wished to instil in the youth who walked through their gates. But these aims are vague, broad and impossible to quantify or even to identify the rubrics of success. It is very difficult to meet a target that has not been set and, more importantly in this case, adopt a strategy when lacking overall strategic goals and frameworks. So, why football? The answer is simple: image, access to a community, engagement with youth, self-promotion and funding; or to sum up— *seduction* on a number of levels.

In Coalter's critique of SDP he claims there is an 'over-inflated and imprecise claims, lack of systematic monitoring and evaluation, lack of robust evidence of poorly defined (but always ambitious) outcomes' (2013, p. 34). The beliefs and assumptions that provide the basis for SDP theory contribute to poorly placed and broad forms of intervention. SDP's lack of theoretical academic support makes the whole concept vulnerable to conflicting interpretations and potentially a damaging intervention.

Image

Throughout the process of this project, I have continued to read and engage with the vast range of SDP literature from UN agencies, aid partners, donors, NGOs and their critics. One thing remains consistent: the image. I have stared at endless images of young African boys holding footballs, playing in the sand, swinging off goal posts and celebrating on the field with friends. The image distracts from the overall lack of evidence-based theory as well as evoking an emotional reaction to the unproven assumption that sport is an appropriate tool for youth development. The typical image of the joyful youth player is a snapshot, a single moment in time; it does not show those around him or where he goes after the game. It does not show him the next day or the day after; an image has no intention of proving impact, effect or sustainability; rather, it provides an emotional justification. I could easily have filled this book with snapshots but it would not have done the team justice; the image would be patronising by reducing their complex identities and social positions to a decontextualised illustration. The image silences the participants and reduces them to a universal group without individual identity.

The image lures donors and supporters to the cause which in turn directs policy writers and project managers. The image is what drives the theory and continues to distract the monitoring and evaluation process. Quite literally the image portrays a game with no opposition; there is a clear absence of contest, competition or a loser. In SDP everyone is a winner. Until someone like myself learns about the local context in which the game is played and spends a significant amount of time with the players. Would Richie describe himself as a winner? I doubt it. Would I now describe the field of play and the practice of the game as innocent? Development driven? Progressive? Appropriate and valuable to building a civil society in Liberia? No. I have argued in this book that football actually—despite its image and support in the country—forms a platform for adult social control and contributes to the identity of youths as youths. When DBH staged a football image it was not organised with the intention of youth development; it was planned for self-promotion of the staff, donor and the NGO. It was a 1-week funding strategy implemented for adults by adults.

Seduction

The process of SDP can be broken down into a simple formula: those tasked with international security and peacekeeping—the UN—found in SDP the method that raised their profile, provided images and emotional reactions could be implemented at low cost and could be sold to its members and partners without theory-based evidence. The UN was seduced by sport,—especially football. Sport came with an unquestioned global interest, a heritage of a lasting history and legacy of the sporting ethic. For them this was the answer to creating peaceful civil societies after conflict. The notion was packaged by its advocates and promoted to its partners—they were seduced and recognised SDP's potential for their development, humanitarian and philanthropic agencies. But it still needed momentum to secure its place. SDP and its advocates needed a high-profile backing to raise the strategy's profile. Sporting celebrities were the obvious desired ambassadors to the various SDP causes and they were seduced by the plight of those SDP targeted and understood their responsibility to the initiative and their obligation to raise not only awareness but also funds. SDP became immersed in and integral to development, with a broad theory assuming connection to social development and peacekeeping which was backed by partner support and high-profile athletes. Once the projects began, the images flowed and filtered in all directions to justify SDP interventions and continue the seductive cycle. Implementing SDP in divided and troubled societies was not a challenge; sport seduced the young and its adult facilitators. Yet, the seduction is limited: football does permit access and engagement; and it does bring youth together; but as I have suggested throughout, few other positive effects can be attributed to the SDP projects and events I witnessed in Liberia. The positive impact of the seduction of SDP is the resources and donor opportunities it offers to local NGOs (c.f. Mosse, 2005).

Sustainability, impact, effect and development are not essential to continue the donor-development agency partnership. A broad-based strategic framework, vague development goals and photographically recorded, token SDP gestures are all that have been required to secure funding for youth-focused development agencies with an SDP image. The cycle of seduction crosses oceans and comes back to one simple belief that sport can break the boundaries of conflict and construct social unity. Meanwhile thousands of young Liberians are playing a game that sustains their identity as youth—which is the main barrier to their development. So we might ask, who is SDP saving? SDP has been brought into the development sector by adults largely as a consequence of the failure of other initiatives, in Liberia, namely peacekeeping and DDR programmes. In the context of this failure, the game is a seductive mask. SDP makes organisations like the UN relevant and benefits adults, who fund, direct, manage and implement development strategy. A strategy devised by adults for adults.

Over the last 4 years, many people have shown great interest in my project and have been intrigued by my decision to spend such a long time in Liberia. As my answers to their questions have developed with more clarity and confidence, the primary question has remained, 'But, what's wrong with being a youth? It sounds great! You don't go to work, you get to play football and be with as many women as you want without consequence.' It's a fair point and I would not be so naive to summarise with an unbalanced argument. The Zatti players had fun, they loved playing football every day and they enjoyed the pursuit of women. Their characters and mannerisms brought so much laughter and that is the image I chose to take away from the team. But, over 4 years the image has not changed: I saw the same players, the same pursuits and the same game in the same place. Despite some players' advancement in education, their social position and membership to the team remain unchanged. To survive every day is a challenge and another form of a game; the winners will find food and shelter from adults. The losers will take any necessary risks to achieve the same but with the knowledge that their actions could have adult-controlled consequences. The efforts that the players will go to assert authority over one another demonstrate how important feeling powerful and valuable is to them. Survival is not living with satisfaction; relative happiness is fragile in Liberia and the risks of further social exclusion and adult-enforced punishment never fades. Youths are incredibly vulnerable in Liberia. Football provided an escape, a space where young men joined in the relative security of the youth centre fence under the watchful eye of authority figures. Football gave them controlled control—an adult-dictated opportunity for performance-based play and expression. But whilst at the youth centre playing, their identity is unchangeable in relation to the adults: youth remain youth; they do not become adults by playing football.

Could SDP be effective? Yes, and I recognise that Liberia represented a particularly challenging and volatile environment for effective SDP programming. But, any SDP project would have to recognise the social effects that sport has within Liberian communities, specifically the way in which it contributes to reinforcing the marginalised status of youth. Adult control would need to be eliminated through possible youth-apprenticeship schemes, and clear development pathways would need to construct a framework from a sports-based strategy to effect impact out-side of the game. The gulf between on-the-field and off-the-field would need to be bridged, as would the disconnect between youths and adults because of the game. Essentially, what is needed is an in-depth knowledge of the cultural complexities on the ground and the primary obstacles that restrict development and social progress. In the case of Liberia this was employment, gaining independence and skills. SDP has to cease to be an alluringly simple and apparently functional development tool and needs to be redesigned using football as the initial step to offer wider and more appropriate interventions. Without doubt more monitoring and evaluation is needed and more realistic and locally relevant models of youth intervention are required. Alternatively, we might simply consider football as no more than a game, an opportunity to bring players together and provide respite from the realities of young lives in Liberia. Local knowledge is the key to the development of the development sector is dependent upon local knowledge. This in turn is an essential component of the effectiveness of the social development of youth populations within the practice of SDP. The Zatti players, I hope, have provided insight past the image, past the seduction and past the adult.

Bibliography

Basedau, M., Mehler, A., & Smith-Höhn, J. (2007). Public perceptions of security in post-conflict urban Liberia and Sierra Leone part I–Liberia: Caught between international, state and non-state actors. *Journal of Peacebuilding & Development, 3*(2), 84–96.

Baumann, G. (1992). Ritual implicates 'others': Rereading Durkheim in a plural society. In D. de Coppet (Ed.), *Understanding rituals* (pp. 97–116). London: Routledge.

Bicker, A., Sillitoe, P., & Pottier, J. (2003). *Negotiating local knowledge: Power and identity in development.* London: Pluto Press.

CAFOD. (2003–2013). Our standards and commitment. http://www.cafod.org.uk/About-Us/Open-information-resources/Standards-Commitments.

Coakley, J. (2011). Youth sports: What counts as "positive development"? *Journal of sport And Social Issues, 35*(3), 306–324.

International Labour Organization. (2009). A rapid impact assessment of the global economic crisis on Liberia. http://www.ilo.org/wcmsp5/groups/public/---ed_emp/---emp_policy/---cepol/documents/publication/wcms_116721.pdf.

IOC. (2013a). Peace through sport: UN creates International Day of Sport for Development and Peace. http://www.olympic.org/news/un-creates-international-day-of-sport-for-development-and-peace/207997.

© The Editor(s) (if applicable) and The Author(s) 2016
H. Collison, *Youth and Sport for Development,*
DOI 10.1057/978-1-137-52470-6

IYSPE. (2005). 2005 International year for sport and physical education. www.un.org/sport2005/a_year/facts.pdf.

Kidd, B. (2008). A new social movement: Sport for development and peace. *Sport in society, 11*(4), 370–380.

Lancy & Tindall (1977) A. B. (Eds). *The study of play: Problems and perspectives.* West Point: Leisure Press.

Monibah, J. (n.d). Empowering Liberia's youth: Don Bosco Programmes-Media Unit. http://www.salesians.org.uk/Saesians-Articles/empowering-liberia-s-youth.html.

Novellino, D. (2003). From seduction to miscommunication: The confession and presentation of local knowledge in 'participatory development'. In J. Pottier, A. Bicker, & P. Sillitoe (Eds.), *Negotiating local knowledge: Power and identity in development* (pp. 273–297). London: Pluto Press.

Robben, A. C. (1995). The politics of truth and emotion among victims and perpetrators of violence. In C. Nordstrom, & A. C. G. M. Robben (Eds.), *Fieldwork under fire: Contemporary studies of violence and survival.* Berkeley: University of California Press.

Rousseau, J. J. (1974). *Emile* (Trans. B. Foxley). London: J. M. Dent.

Young, K., & Atkinson, M. (2012). *Qualitative research on sport and physical culture.* Bingley: Emerald.

Index

A

Amit, Vered, 100, 128
Anthropology & Sport, 1–4
Armstrong, Gary, 40, 50, 59, 79

B

Baudrillard, Jean, ix, 204

C

Caillois, Roger, 174, 189
Community
 Development, 99–102,
  121–123
 Theory of, 95–98
Community, Local Context
 Crime and Security, 118–121
 Employment, 113–116 (see also;
  Hustling)

Free time, 116–117
Hierarchy, 106–108
Housing, 111–113
Modes of Speech, 103–106
 (see also; palava and lecture)
Neighbourliness, 102–103
Spaces, 108–111
Corruption, 11, 85, 115–116,
 146–147, 159, 162–163, 212

D

DDRR, 6, 37–39, 52, 85, 203
Development
 Anthropological theory,
  56–58
 Definition of, 55–56, 70
 And Football, x, vii, 65–66,
  77–80, 101, 138–139,
  168–169

© The Editor(s) (if applicable) and The Author(s) 2016
H. Collison, *Youth and Sport for Development*,
DOI 10.1057/978-1-137-52470-6

In Liberia (see also; Don Bosco
  Homes), 78–79
And Sport, 58–60
Don Bosco Homes, 79–89
Don Bosco Youth Centre, 49, 51,
  81, 129, 135–143, 149, 154,
  162, 169–170
Durham, Deborah, 133, 219

E
ECOMOG, 33–35, 64
Ethnography, 4, 10–11, 15, 19, 21–22

F
Football
  Communities, 171–175,
    188–192, 194–196
  Identity, 175–182
  And Local Politics, 212–219
  Money Making, 146–150,
    210–212
  As Performance, 182–187, 190,
    193–194
  As Social Control, 192–193,
    210–212
  Team Hierarchy, 168–170

G
Goffman, Erving, 190–191, 193
Green, Maia, 56, 57, 79, 86

H
Huizinga, Johan, 3, 188–190
Hustling, 113–116, 121, 139,
  141–142, 144, 209

I
Indigenous Groups, 27–30, 103,
  180–183, 224

J
Johnson-Sirleaf, Ellen, 12, 40, 69,
  217–218

L
LFA, 5, 12, 15, 18, 101, 146, 148,
  168, 210, 217
Liberia
  Civil Conflict, 25, 32–36
  History of, 26–32
Local Speech
  Lecture, 103–106, 142, 144,
    152–153, 170, 192
  Palava, 103–107, 136, 138–139,
    209

M
Marginality, 21, 130–132, 171,
  172–174, 190, 193–196,
  229–230, 235

O
Olofson, Harold, 173, 189, 194

R
Researcher Identity
  Gender, 10–14, 16–17
  Race, 10, 12–17
Ritual Theory, 171
Rollason, Will, 4, 195

S

Seduction, ix–x, 100, 200–224, 231, 233–235
Social Control, 129, 172, 192–193, 196, 202, 231–232
Social Mobility, 16, 131–133
Sport for Development and Peace
  Adoption by the UN, 64–69, 70–74, 167–168
  Imagery, 78–89, 232
  Monitoring and Evaluation, 74–77, 87
  Staging and Performing, 17–18, 83–89, 203–204
  Theoretical Critique, 58–60, 69, 73–78, 88, 231

T

Taylor, Charles, 33, 35–36, 50–51
Turner, Victor, 104, 171–172, 188

U

United Nations History of Peacekeeping, 60–65
UNMIL, 36–39, 64, 76–77
Utas, Matts, 129–131, 171, 229

Y

Youth
  Case study, 45–53
  Footballers, 154, 161–163, 203–204, 230
  Local Definition, 128–131, 133–135, 139, 229–230
  Relationships with Women, 116, 154–158, 159–161
  Relationship with Adults, 106–108, 137–138, 139–143, 153–153 (see also; Community, Local Context)
  Theory of, 13, 20–21, 127–128, 131–133